It is my distinct pleasure to join with others in honouring our colleague and mentor, Gabriel Daly. *The Critical Spirit* evidences the remarkable range of his work, while at the same time reflecting its clear focus on the important issues of faith and culture

Darrell Jodock
Drell and Adeline Bernhardson Distinguished Professor of Religion
Gustavus Adolphus College, St Peter, Minnesota

Trenchant springs to mind when I think of the writings of Gabriel Daly. No theologian of the post-Vatican II era has contributed a clearer, more incisive, and more effectual comment on the issues of faith and culture in a wide variety of venues. The essays gathered here are a splendid tribute to one who has served the church most faithfully by 'doing theology "on the boundaries"' and in so doing has held up to the church a faithful mirror. *Ad multos annos!*

David G Schultenover, SJ
Professor of Historical Theology
Marquette University, Milwaukee, Wisconsin

This rich collection of essays in honour of Gabriel Daly OSA is an invitation to participate in a dialogue between faith and culture. From different perspectives the authors encourage the reader to draw on memory and imagination in order to understand the past and the present. *The Critical Spirit* is a valuable resource for all who struggle to make sense of the relationship between faith and culture.

Ellen M Leonard
Emerita Professor of Theology, University of St Michaels's College, Toronto

A superb team of theologians from Ireland and elsewhere wrestle here with some of the most gripping and fruitful issues of our time. The range and depth are impressive, and a fine tribute to Gabriel Daly, who for decades has been one of Ireland's wisest theologians. His fascination with the interplay of faith and culture is here developed in ways that are both instructive and stimulating, and again and again distil from Irish history and experience something of wide relevance.

David F Ford
Regius Professor of Divinity, University of Cambridge

Edited by Andrew Pierce
and Geraldine Smyth OP

The Critical Spirit:
Theology at the Crossroads of Faith and Culture

ESSAYS IN HONOUR OF
GABRIEL DALY OSA

First published in 2003 by
the columba press
55A Spruce Avenue, Stillorgan Industrial Park,
Blackrock, Co Dublin

Cover by Bill Bolger
Origination by The Columba Press
Printed in Ireland by ColourBooks Ltd, Dublin

ISBN 1 85607 418 8

Contents

Tragedy must always be a drowning and breaking of the dykes that separate man from man, and … it is upon these dykes that comedy keeps house.

W B Yeats

… let us sing Alleluia, not in the enjoyment of heavenly rest, but to sweeten our toil. Sing as travellers sing along the road: but keep on walking.
Solace your toil by singing – do not yield to idleness … Sing up – and keep on walking.

St Augustine

Editors' Introduction

This overdue tribute to Gabriel Daly OSA was first mooted a number of years ago by the editors, in conspiracy with Seán Freyne, then Professor of Theology at Trinity College, Dublin. The result was a series of public lectures in Trinity College, focused on the theme of faith and culture. Not surprisingly, the inaugural lecture was given by Gabriel Daly, on whom this theme has exercised a profound fascination for many years – a fascination that he has shared with generations of theology students at the Irish School of Ecumenics, Milltown Institute of Philosophy and Theology, Trinity College Dublin, and further afield.

This collection of essays includes papers from that lecture series, as well as contributions from a number of Gabriel's colleagues, friends and former – if 'former' is the correct term –students. From the outset, this *festschrift* was constructed with both senses of *telos* in mind. Not only is its purpose that of celebrating Gabriel's theological career to date, but also the celebration is directed to the end of providing a resource to the growing number of study programmes in faith and culture. The issues presented here – dialogue, history, hermeneutics, Ireland, ecumenism, authority, imagination, the exercise of power in the churches – have been contested, and remain contested in contemporary theology. This collection continues that theological contesting of vital issues.

The opening chapter, by Denis Carroll, situates Gabriel Daly's contribution to contemporary theology against the backdrop of the increasingly conscious politicisation of the theology of creation. With customary courtesy, Denis Carroll highlights a number of the key concerns evidenced by Daly's writings: theology's critical function in relation to religion, the ambiguities exhibited in human personhood, the value of theory to practice. Modernity, along with its post-modern moment of critique, requires theological engagement beyond the traditional comfort zones of the churches of the post-industrial West (and North). The doctrine of creation, by definition, is not limited in its scope to selected bits of the world. This leads us into the territory of the prophet, but the prophecy has been chastened by its encounter with the pluralities and ambiguities inherent in the experience of modernity.

The next four chapters, by Andrew Mayes, Seán Freyne, Terence McCaughey and John D'Arcy May, may be read as case studies of certain classic episodes, or paradigms, in the history of the interpretation of faith's relationship with culture. Taking as his starting point an essay by P. D. Miller on 'Faith and Ideology in the Old Testament', Andrew Mayes probes beneath the opposition posited by Miller between 'faith' on the one hand, and 'ideology' on the other. Recent work on ideology has often operated with a distinction between the three levels at which ideology functions – social integration, structural legitimation and distortion. Yet the priority of ideological integration is open to question, and – in the context of representations of Israel's early history – Mayes underlines the importance of acknowledging that ideology arises in situations of conflict. The faith-ideology dichotomy is thus found to be misleading, since faith – necessarily located in a social context – is in fact ideological through and through, offering a contested utopian critique of alternative powers that could – and should – be.

Remaining *ad fontes*, Seán Freyne examines the emergence of Christian and Jewish self-understandings in a context shaped by interpretative conflict over shared symbol systems. These conflicts helped to generate the classic literature of both Judaism and Christianity, within whose histories of reception, mutual recriminations have been institutionalised and perpetuated. Despite the dispositions of misunderstanding enshrined in each tradition, this chapter argues that a shared re-examination of this time of origins may permit dialogue to commence, a dialogue with a real other, as opposed to an ideologically projected other.

The current vogue for spirituality, and especially for allegedly 'Celtic' spirituality, tells us a good deal about our cultural attachment to colonising the past and domesticating its otherness. In striking contrast to this pervasive attitude, Terence McCaughey introduces us to the otherness of the Ireland to which Patrick came, to the Christianity he brought with him and to the kind of Christianity he found there. The mission to which Patrick believed himself called – although seriously out of step with contemporary episcopal practice – relied upon a sense of how the

Christian faith could be inculturated among the *Hiberionaces*, gained during his years of slavery, combined with a widely-felt cultural unease occasioned by the collapse of Rome.

'Dionysus always strikes back' is Gabriel Daly's repeated warning to theologians who overestimate the capacity of Apollonian reason to hold religion's primal elements in check. A further case study in the relationship of faith and culture is provided by John D'Arcy May, whose chapter examines the impact of – predominantly British and Irish -- Christians on the world of Australian Aborigines. Nineteenth-century European notions of civilisation and progress, like all undue sweetness and light, were haunted by a repressed shadow. In encountering Australia, Europeans' denial of their own otherness, projected onto the Aborigines, led to catastrophe. Christian incomprehension of its own otherness, and consequently the otherness of others, provokes a reassessment of contemporary European theology – adjudged a failure by May – possibly more far-reaching than the more frequently noted criticisms of Karl Barth. The past cannot be undone, but it can be reinterpreted, and this chapter explores a number of theological and aesthetic attempts to listen, both to the land and to the Aboriginal people of Australia.

Two chapters follow, by Geraldine Smyth OP and Enda McDonagh, in which the focus is on the current cultural context in Ireland. Geraldine Smyth explores the ways in which ecumenical praxis calls into question Ireland's tribal religious identities that have been forged into mutual opposition. Teasing out the inherent complexity of identity, this chapter probes both defensive notions of identity in which otherness is defined as threat, rather than fruitful challenge or enrichment; and the euphoric celebration of otherness as pure enrichment, with no element of threat whatsoever. These reflections on identity are given concrete expression in a discussion of eucharist and eucharistic discipline.

John McIntyre once remarked that a well-nourished religious imagination may help us to negotiate the dark places of our experience. Similarly, Enda McDonagh raises the question of whether the crisis facing the Roman Catholic Church in Ireland requires the imaginative assistance of the poet, in order to be understood, let alone resolved. The poetic capacity to attend to embodied experience – to imagine it as it is, and as it might become – is explored with reference to a number of contemporary Irish writers. The imaginative and poetic 'cure' advocated in this chapter is an indictment of a style of theologising that – in Maurice Blondel's nice phrase – sees too clearly to see well.

Imagination is also crucial to the argument advanced by Dermot A. Lane, who commences his chapter with an appraisal of the current dark night of the ecumenical soul. Turning to the classic text of Roman Catholic ecumenism, the 1964 *Decree on Ecumenism* of Vatican II, he notes the council's ecumenical imperative, the lasting impact of which needs to be borne in mind when interpreting recent texts, notably *Dominus Iesus*. To break out of the current impasse, Lane proposes that christology be treated with greater ecumenical seriousness than it has received heretofore. Hence, the importance of the categories of both memory and imagination, in focusing attention on the ecumenical centrality of Jesus the Christ.

The ethical significance of the ambiguous – and sometimes ambivalent – relationship between Christian faith and modern European culture is explored in Maureen Junker-Kenny's chapter. Contrasting Friedrich Schleiermacher's positive appraisal of contemporary European culture with Søren Kierkegaard's angst in the face of an allegedly christianised European culture, Junker-Kenny highlights the inherently dialectical nature of the faith-culture relationship, past and present. How then should religion – as for instance in Christian ethics – contribute to contemporary culture? Should Christianity receive legal protection as the inspiration behind modern European culture, as Wolfgang Pannenberg suggests, or is there another way for this contribution to be made?

In his 'Theological Reflections on the Future of Faith and Culture', Johann Baptist Metz anchors all talk of the future in a *memoria passionis*, an actively recalled memory of the suffering of others – the others whose suffering has made possible this present and its future. To acknowledge the suffering of others as authoritative is, as Metz observes, all too easily interpreted as a sign of weakness, yet it has enough strength to challenge the post-modern desire to keep our moral responsibilities constrained by ever-shrinking particular contexts. The future of faith and culture is thus dependent on the past – not a triumphalist account of the past based on amnesia in the face of so much suffering – but an acknowledgement of, or better, an empathy with, history's victims.

Ireland has been slow to claim George Tyrrell, whether as a prose stylist of genius or as a theologian of enduring importance. Andrew Pierce's chapter suggests that Tyrrell's complex notion of 'experience' repays close examination, despite obvious discontinuities between his context and ours. In certain ways, the late nineteenth and early twentieth centuries were as fascinated by religious experience as the post-modern, twenty-first century – yet the concept of experience has undergone considerable modification in the course of a century. Not every late nineteenth/early twentieth century thinker can, however, be dismissed as an experiential positivist. According to Pierce, a theologian like Tyrrell may have something to tell us – not just about the modernist crisis – but about theological responsibility to acknowledge the complex, disorientating, socially embedded, physically embodied notion of experience to which theology makes its appeal.

As the epigraph to Michael Paul Gallagher's chapter – from Schleiermacher's *Speeches* – makes clear, there have been theologians with an awareness of the theological significance of imagination. St Thomas Aquinas was one such author, but his insight was lost to neo-Thomism, especially in the aftermath of the modernist crisis. The theological recovery of imagination, detected by Gallagher in the work of Rahner, Lonergan and von Balthasar, has often operated with a culturally elitist sense of what qualifies as imaginative. To counter this tendency, Gallagher introduces the work of William Lynch, a writer sensitive to the imaginative input required in the less exotic fields of mundane existence. Yet it is those who imagine the mundane with care and attention – for example, the novelist Niall Williams – from whom theologians have much to learn.

H. Richard Niebuhr's five ideal types of faith-culture relationships are helpless in the face of the 'impossible' Simone Weil, whose life and thought incarnated modernity's inherent tensions. In his chapter, David Tracy explores the complexity of this Christian Platonist, whose fierce desire to attend – in a way that was both physical and intellectual – made her curious in both her Christianity and her Platonism. As Tracy observes, hers was a radical relating of faith with culture in which the activist's activist was one with the intellectual's intellectual, or to refer back to Niebuhr, the Christ against Culture was identified with the Christ of Culture. Weil's concern with form appropriate to content leads to comparisons with Pascal – an equally impossible character. 'Impossibility' emerges as a vital term for understanding not only Weil, but also the relationship of faith and culture, as well as key developments in post-modern approaches to the God question.

Can we love God? That is the remarkably Augustinian question posed by Werner G Jeanrond's chapter. No matter how much the rhetoric of 'love' is abused or reduced to utter banality, Christianity has to deal with the obligation to love God, neighbour, enemy and self. Love, moreover, does not occur in a cultural vacuum. It is understood theologically as both cultural construction and divine gift. Significantly, love must be directed both to the other, and to the lover's otherness, and this presupposes an acknowledgement of the otherness of the other and the otherness of the self. To affirm our ability to love God obliges us to hold together a hermeneutics of retrieval with a hermeneutics of suspicion: Jeanrond's closing remarks emphasise the apophatic modesty, as well as the necessity, of 'love' in theological discourse.

Paul Tillich – one of Gabriel Daly's desert-island choice of authors – liked to insist on the importance of doing theology 'on the boundaries'. The distinction drawn by David Tracy between the various publics addressed by theology – academy, church, society – reminds us that not only has Gabriel contributed to each one of these 'publics,' he has also dwelt – theologically – on their shared boundaries, and has played a pivotal role in interpreting their respective rights and responsibilities to one another. For those who know Gabriel only through his work in the publics of academy and society, Desmond Foley OSA, concludes this *festschrift* with an Afterword highlighting Gabriel's unique contribution to the public of the church, and specifically to the Augustinian Order.

It remains for us to thank the contributors for their enthusiasm and commitment to *The Critical Spirit*. We have received a great deal of assistance from Seán Freyne, Suzanne McEneaney, Deirdre O'Dwyer, John O'Grady, Hyo-Jung Kim and Sláine O'Hogain in preparing these essays for publication. Seán O Boyle, Ciara Doorley and Brian Lynch at Columba Press guided us with gentle insistence, for which we are grateful. Most of all, however, with these essays, we express to Gabriel Daly our lasting appreciation for his friendship: our indebtedness to him is not easily quantified, but – to adjust Baron von Hügel's acknowledgement of John Henry Newman's influence on him – we talk Daly even oftener than we know.

Andrew Pierce
Geraldine Smyth OP

CHAPTER 1

An Essay in the Theology of Creation: Gabriel Daly and the Challenge of Modernity

Denis Carroll

Religious people have found it easy to bemoan secularisation. Was this simply an excuse for their failure creatively to rethink their tradition in the light of new knowledge? I believe both that there was such a failure and that the unease of religious people about secularisation has deeper causes.[1]

— *Brendan Lovett*

I CREATION AND CRITICISM

Even until recently, creation theology seemed a poor relation within the theological family. Certainly, it was included among the other members. Yet it was rarely mentioned and infrequently consulted. At a pinch, it was a collation of philosophical definitions unconnected to more important questions like christology, trinity or grace. Worthy as were the efforts to explain *creatio ex nihilo*, they conveyed a somewhat diminished view of God, humankind and creation generally. They conveyed little of the vitality which Christianity affirms about our relationship with the living God. An architectonic model of creation presented God as the great artificer and the world as an inert theatre of human operation. Nor did these views reflect the historical dimensions in the Christian story of creation-redemption. On ethical questions posed by modernity, such an ontological concentration had little to offer. It is no exaggeration to say that 'creation theology' dragged out an anaemic existence on the theological periphery. As a vibrant provider of spiritual sustenance its potential lay fallow and unharvested.

Fortunately, there were exceptions to the shortcoming. Great systematicians from Aquinas to Barth saw creation/eschatology as an essential part of Judaeo-Christian insight. Valuably, M. J.

1. Brendan Lovett, 'Marginalisation, Secularisation and the Third World,' in *Diagacht: Theology Bulletin of the Western Theology Research Association* 1 (1996) 6.

Scheeben, Michael Schmaus and Leo Scheffczyk reminded us that creation was inseparable from redemption. They placed creation / eschatology within an intelligible framework comprising scriptural theology and spirituality. Nevertheless, catechisms, official documents, even those which emanated from the Second Vatican Council, seem impoverished when it comes to the question of creation.

Meanwhile, the achievements of modernity proceeded apace. For centuries, the role of critical reason had been asserted. A differentiation of morals, art and science enabled further developments in these areas. The dogmatic principles associated with religion came under strain. New modes of argument emphasised freedom of enquiry and research. Personal rights *vis-à-vis* the political community were formulated and sometimes vindicated. Genuine advances at the social, political and artistic levels formed an apparently unquestionable heritage. All this was part of the 'first' Enlightenment commencing with René Descartes, Isaac Newton, John Toland and Immanuel Kant.[2]

Unfortunately, the enlightened gait was uneven. Its regard was not always benevolent. That is to say, alongside unquestionable achievement the Enlightenment had troublesome limits. While scientific and technological revolutions brought much good, they also exacted a cost on the environment and on peoples unable to accept 'modernisation'. Nor did they distribute their favours in consistent proportion to need. Thus, questions ranging from environmental protection to social justice remained (and still remain) unsolved. While science-based technology is essential to solving these problems, the answers will not come from rigid 'scientism'. The practitioners of science and science-based technology have their own prejudices which can result in an unfair distribution of technology's benefits. When Langdon Gilkey wrote of the mythic 'man in the white coat,' he argued that dimensions of reality elude even the scientist and technologist. Where the mysteriousness of being is reduced to the quantifiable, a certain 'Flatland' is installed, a 'monological gaze' is made the universal measure.[3] Thus arises the necessity for a 'second' Enlightenment which takes account of factors

2. See the helpful account of Roy Porter, *The Enlightenment: Britain and the Creation of the Modern World*, London: Allen Lane, 2000.
3. The terminology is that of Ken Wilber. See his *Sex, Ecology, Spirituality: The Spirit of Evolution*, London: Shambhala, 1995.

ignored by the earlier progression. It must be emphasised, however, that denigration of hard-won freedoms is both unwise and self-defeating. In social studies, in psychological and hermeneutical sciences, in all branches of physics, undreamt-of advances have been made. Indeed, one of the great fruits of the Enlightenment is such democracy as we now enjoy.

In the main, a grudging suspicion ensured that churches and theological disciplines lagged behind these advances. Since the competencies of religion and science differ, this is hardly surprising. Territorial wars are never pleasant and it is indisputable that exorbitant claims were made both by scientists and theologians. The idea of epistemological pluralism was not born easily. Today, it would be a tragedy if religion were to perpetuate 'battles long ago' (just as it is a problem when proponents of the scientific worldview dismiss any view other than their own). We need to address issues which affect our basic presuppositions on the shape and direction of our world. Unfortunately, defensiveness seems to prevail within Roman Catholicism even on the implications of pluralist democracy. The modernist crisis of the early twentieth century, and an egregiously oppressive reaction to it, marginalised those who viewed modernity as opportunity as well as threat, as something to be engaged rather than ignored. Despite the achievements of the Second Vatican Council, 'supernaturalism' has reasserted itself and insists on presenting the church as a redoubt of stability in the midst of secular delusion. Gabriel Daly memorably puts it: 'In this atmosphere, the medium overshadows the message, clericalism is reinforced, alternative viewpoints ... are condemned as unorthodox or disloyal, and fear controls relationships within the institution.'[4]

Modernity cannot be evaded since it is part of our own mindset. Questions which might have been resolved long ago present themselves again. To an extent, they come from disciplines properly extraneous to the Christian tradition. Yet they form part of our own mental constructs and evoke different reactions within ourselves. Paradoxically, it is a tribute to the extensiveness of the *traditio fidei* that it is challenged on such a wide front – from social justice to bioethics, from environmentalism to feminism. For some, the easiest solution is rigidly to dissociate faith and critical reflection. The problems attached to this have been

4. Gabriel Daly OSA, 'Table d'Hôte Catholicism', *The Furrow* 42 (1991) 407-414; 409.

frequently rehearsed and require no elaboration here. For others, regression towards a golden age provides a bulwark against uncertainty. Unfortunately, an unseeing move backwards leads only to disaster. Golden ages were never quite so golden as is imagined: in any event, they can never be recreated. For yet others, embattled defensiveness within a strictly regimented institution promises security and order. But this is fatally to underestimate the life-enhancing potential of Christian faith. If the search for truth and authenticity are disqualified, a situation arises where few care what the church says since it is no longer a credible partner in serious discourse. These dangers have been well examined in David Lodge's *Paradise News*.[5]

The signal merit of thinkers like Daly is that they remain open to the challenges of modernity – not in a spirit of compromise but in generous appreciation that truth is ultimately indivisible. Like Augustine and Aquinas, Newman and Teilhard de Chardin, they endeavour to appropriate modern insights – in the first place, insofar as these are true and, in the second place, so that theology may breathe and grow. It requires confidence in one's tradition to maintain commitment to reasoned argument in face of multiple questioning. For Aquinas, the doctrines of faith were signposts to mystery: as verbal formulations they were not ends in themselves. For Teilhard de Chardin, the teaching of faith was not a strait-jacket. Rather, it was a growing tree which, although it changes, remains identical with itself. Thus, new and sometimes threatening data should be met, assimilated, and allowed to challenge our cherished formulations – precisely in order that faith may survive. In a lecture to the Irish Catechetical Association, Gabriel Daly quoted with approval a statement by Henry Sidgwick that 'philosophy and history alike [teach us] to seek not what is "safe" but what is true.'[6] Daly's fine book, *Transcendence and Immanence*,[7] amply documents the loss of nerve which damaged the church for decades and caused untold pain to sincere men like George Tyrrell.

5. David Lodge, *Paradise News*, London: Secker and Warburg, 1991. See the discussion by Anthony Draper, 'Watching Our God-Language,' *Doctrine & Life* 47 (1997) 204-212; 204. In a seminal address Gabriel Daly highlights the matter, 'The Problem of Original Sin,' *The Furrow* 24 (1973) 13-26; 19.

6. ibid., 20.

7. Gabriel Daly OSA, *Transcendence and Immanence: A Study in Catholic Modernism and Integralism*, Oxford; Clarendon Press, 1980.

II QUESTIONS TO OUR CREATION 'STORY'

New models of cosmic origination/development question the inner cohesion of our creation story. As every teacher knows, there is a great difference between the biblical narratives and the postulations of a Stephen Hawking or a Niels Bohr. What are we to make of Jacques Monod's question about the relation of chance to necessity? Can theology – can anyone – answer what happened before the 'Big Bang'? (To the latter question, science of every kind, including theology, does well to remain mute.) Other questions have to do with purpose, randomness, value. Those who hold to Judaeo-Christianity may be perturbed by Richard Dawkins' assertion that nature is neither benevolent nor malevolent – it simply does not care. Dawkins' repeated dismissal of the religious question is itself questionable and no one has better expressed this question than Gabriel Daly. Without rekindling the old antagonisms between religion and science, Daly maps out their proper methodologies in such a way that both faith and science can, minimally, co-exist and, maximally, learn from each other. There are problems about a creator God which theologians must consider anew. Does God care? Does God accompany God's creation? Is there a 'history of salvation'? Can we do more than remain silent in face of mystery? Do we expect theologians to be scientists? Or shall we ask them also to develop Patrick Kavanagh's assertion that 'God is in the bits and pieces of everyday'? A good treatment of these questions is given in Daly's writing, particularly *Creation and Redemption* where one notes his courteous approach not only to science, but also to the arts.[8]

Biotechnology is an especially pressing example of these new questions. It may well be an advance of human endeavour and, as such, requires critical evaluation. With its potential for hitherto unsuspected innovations, it can alter life as we have known it before now. In regard to people, animals and plants, genetic engineering confronts us with frightening vistas. As well, considerations of financial gain have attracted the attention of transnational corporations in the pharmaceutical and agribusiness sectors. Hence, the field urgently requires agreed ethical guidelines. Questions arise. Is it not an arrogance, an example of *hubris*, to claim ownership of life? Which values will guide this

8. Gabriel Daly, OSA, *Creation and Redemption*, Dublin: Gill & Macmillan, 1988.

endeavour? Which motives will shape its operations? Will the world's poor suffer as transnational corporations corner yet another area of 'intellectual property'? Are there unforeseen results, damaging to people and habitat, in the longer term? In 1993, an extended comment by the Catholic Institute for International Relations argued that, with the driving force behind the biorevolution being an industry avid for global sales, increased uniformity is likely to be the dominant trend. In any case, biotechnology has the means to destroy biodiversity. Hence the importance of a critical theology of the kind Gabriel Daly has for long practised.

Then there is a prevalent breakdown in the shared meaning of history. Post-modern philosophy casts doubt on aspirations to justice and solidarity with the oppressed. All too frequently, the hope that history and justice can 'rhyme' is deemed naïve and ideological. In the search for an appropriate Christian *weltanschauung* (which means broadening the theological purview on creation/eschatology), our alternatives cannot be automatic repetition of inherited formulae, or careless disregard of the tradition. A middle way is what Daly calls 'the often uncomfortable quest for *actualité,* for a contemporary understanding of what God is saying to the human race.'[9] Such an understanding would be impossible if theology were forbidden to reappraise its own sources. Thus, from the 1970s, Daly's application of theological 'models' or 'metaphors' was immensely helpful. It enabled critical yet loyal reappraisal of church teaching, analogous to new methods of biblical interpretation. Theologians now speak of St Paul's 'forensic' model of soteriology, of Trent's 'genetic' model of original sin. In *Creation and Redemption,* Daly helpfully envisages creation/redemption in the model of a broken world which needs healing – the earth is a hospital with a promise of full healing on the other side of death. To speak thus of theological models only is not reductive but signally helpful. Theological reflection can go behind the 'model' to what the model intends. In a second innocence (Ricoeur), we can move beyond literalised mythology and avoid the problems issuing from a confusion of models.

More than ever, creation theology is challenged to due humility and retention of nerve. Due humility: theology is neither surrogate science nor 'queen of the sciences'. If it is to communic-

9. Daly, 'The Problem of Original Sin,' 19.

ate, its language has to be more open to mystery and less arrogant, more experiential and less ideological, more genuinely searching and less dogmatic where dogmatism only alienates and discourages. In addition, science itself recognises the ultimate and perhaps intractable mystery of the cosmos. On the other hand, retention of nerve is required, especially if we believe that our creation story has a worthwhile purpose, namely to communicate 'a fully human and humanising Christian *Weltanschauung*' (Teilhard de Chardin). Gabriel Daly has developed this observation with elegant imagination. Clearly, he shares Teilhard's optimism although he transcends the latter's anthropological concentration. For example, with Teilhard he refuses to see humankind 'as a whipped cur brought to heel by an avenging history'. He rejects the suggestion 'that history [should] play the sadist to man's masochism.'[10] And, ever more urgently, he enjoins recognition that our co-inhabitants of creation must be respected for themselves rather than their use-value. Yet Daly is Augustinian on 'the scandalising phenomena of historical existence'. He re-echoes Paul in asserting that: '*homo in seipso divisus* is a fact of social and historical observation and individual introspection.'[11]

Again, one notes how frequently he alludes to Pascal's view of humankind as the 'glory and scandal of the universe'. This combination of optimism and realism strengthens Daly's reminder that

> [w]e are a species that builds hospitals and concentration camps. We are a species that can make the desert bloom. By the same token we are a species that also reduces blooms to deserts.[12]

Again, in a more recent article he asserts that Christian revelation is centred on divine acceptance/forgiveness, despite the worst that we can do.[13]

---

10. Daly, 'The Problem of Original Sin,' 25.
11. Daly, 'An Ecofeminist Contention Examined,' *Irish Theological Quarterly*, 60/3, (1994) 216-224; 222.
12. ibid., 223.
13. Gabriel Daly, 'Conscience, Guilt and Sin' in Seán Freyne, ed., *Ethics and the Christian*, Trinity College Dublin, Studies in Theology, Dublin: Columba, 1989, 58-74, 69.

III JUSTICE, POWER AND CREATION

Despite its achievements, the 'first' Enlightenment has run into some trouble. Its insistence on critical reason has more than once led to hard-nosed individualism. Critical reason is rarely consistent in self-criticism. It has been remarked that the hardest thing is to turn one's demythologising impulse upon the assumptions which enable it.[14] Hence, many groups, classes and countries remained outside the benefits of the Enlightenment. To adapt the phrase of Karl Marx, the *Aufklarung* concentrated on critique of knowledge rather than on transformation of society. In recent decades, excluded groups have demanded the overhaul of unjust structures. Their critique, mainly from a liberationist perspective, has been a marked feature of the last four decades. Theologically, the liberation perspective has moved on from answering the objections of religion's 'cultured despisers'. Latin American theologians heavily criticise European and north American ideologies and speak of collusion by *soi-disant* liberals.

Thus, the 'second' Enlightenment is, indeed, based on critical reason but even more on commitment to justice, on solidarity with the poor, the excluded and the victims of an unjust world order. Splendid publications (and splendid acts of heroism) marked the practice of 'contextual theology'. In all this, the great symbols of creation, redemption and eschatology were re-examined so that creation theology became more an element of 'praxis' than purely theoretic endeavour. To their surprise, European theologians (even those sympathetic to liberation movements) found their own critical presuppositions strenuously questioned. They were accused of viewing reality from the professorial rostrum and of favouring the questions of 'educated European man'. On the surface at least, it was a clash between the 'first' and the 'second' Enlightenment in the sense mentioned above.

The call from theologians of liberation practically to apply creation theology is indeed urgent. With their several – now converging – emphases, these theologians explicate the imperative of economic, sexual and environmental justice. Gutiérrez, Sobrino and many others emphasise the scandal of grinding poverty. They effected a revolution in their 'theology from the underside of history' and their insistence that theology is inseparable from action. Feminist theology stressed that man and

14. Terry Eagleton, unpublished paper, Desmond Greaves Summer School, Dublin 1996.

woman are created equal. Hence, age-old oppression based on gender is intrinsically wrong. In a further extension of feminist analysis, theologians such as Sallie McFague and Rosemary Radford Ruether undertake a 'revision' of traditional concepts of God. They criticise even progressive theologians as supporters of patriarchy. Again, environmental theology applied neglected strands of Christian tradition to the issue of the earth's survival. Here one notices the work of the Irish theologian/anthropologist, Seán McDonagh, whose studies have been pioneering contributions to a theology of the environment. These voices, even in their diversity, raise a challenge every whit as pressing as the scientific/technological revolution of other days.

There has also been a proliferation of stances more loosely based on a theology of creation. These run a wide gamut in which their performance has been varied. Some (for example, various forms of 'New Ageism') marry ambiguous understandings of 'the new physics' to an arbitrary selection from Christian theology. No matter how sincerely intended or attractively presented, they have drawbacks in regard to the total affirmation of Christian belief. Even more problematic is their tendency to esoteric theory and adherence to new, sometimes dubious, 'authorities'. On the necessity for critical reason and on the indispensible relation of creation/redemption/eschatology, some of Gabriel Daly's remarks may sound untypically conservative. Yet they are all the more credible given his own rejection of fundamentalism and his suspicion of doom-laden theological menaces. The task, he says, is 'to give a statement like "Jesus died for us and for our salvation" reference and *resonance within the context of a theology of creation* and to show that it need not be given a fundamentalist interpretation.'[15] An admixture of optimism and realism emerges in the same article: 'Creation is indeed to be celebrated, but not at the cost of hearing its groanings for liberation from its bondage to decay, including the ecological decay inflicted on it by sinful human beings. Allelluias are all the more resonant for not being premature.'[16]

Insofar as Daly has expressed such reserves, they apply to manner of argument rather than the demand for justice. Daly's view that social justice is a Christian imperative emerges from his *Creation and Redemption*. There he observes that '[W]e could

15. Daly, 'An Ecofeminist Contention Examined', 221-2.
16. ibid., 224.

feed and house every man, woman and child on our planet, but instead our representatives and rulers speak of free market forces and of the undesirability of interfering with these forces.'[17] On the ecological question he has already made clear his position. Respect for creation is a spiritual imperative not reducible to 'a cunning self-interest of the kind that recognises the diminishing returns ... of over-fishing the seas or chemically dependent farming.'[18] In an interchange with Anna Primavesi he signals his recognition of the justice within the feminist canon. By its critique of patriarchy, feminist theology is a powerful reminder that in proclaiming God's sovereignty over all nature, we have sometimes gone on to draw the false conclusion that omnipotence and sovereignty necessarily mean control.'[19] Yet, he utters a *caveat*: 'Patriarchy is one element accounting for what has gone wrong with our attitude to the environment. Greed, indolence, stupidity and our desire for a comfortable lifestyle make equally significant contributions to the crisis. Not even ecofeminists are immune from these less engaging features of being human.'[20]

This is of a piece with Daly's conviction that theological discourse takes place within an interpretative community. To both conservatives and radicals he insists that such a community is not a club which one must quit if one does not agree with all the rules. In an interpretative community, truth is sought by open-minded communion of free subjects. Even the most urgent truth can be distorted if it is imposed by 'power-based communication.'[21] Daly rejects all situations where 'only one version of the true or the good is allowed expression.'[22] Doubtless, such a perception underlies his remark that 'one instinctively quails before a prophet conscious of possessing … a just cause who advances on one with the light of rectitude in his or her eyes, proclaiming in a loud and peremptory voice "We talk and you listen".'[23] Here, too, must be situated his insistence on the necessity to

17. Daly, *Creation and Redemption*, 208.
18. ibid., 44. See also Denis Carroll, 'On Not Jumping on the Green Bandwagon,' in Freyne, ed., *Ethics and the Christian*, 127-137; 129-30.
19. Daly, 'An Ecofeminist Contention,' 224.
20. ibid., 218.
21. Daly, 'Table d'Hôte Catholicism', 414
22. ibid., 414.
23. Daly, 'Conscience, Guilt and Sin,' 68.

respect freedom of conscience in face of demands from hierarchs and, even, prophets. (In fairness, it can be argued that Daly's fear lest theologies of liberation place commitment above reflection is addressed by their dialectical notion of praxis as critical interplay of theory / practice.)

Edward Schillebeeckx's reference to the church as interpretative community and theology as conversation between tradition and modernity remains valuable. Taken seriously, it is a difficult programme when demands for commitment or 'loyalty' override the irreplaceable function of critical reflection. Such a conversation between tradition and modernity can be associated with Gabriel Daly's own style of writing. In a culture subject to bewildering change, his courageous search for a renewed articulation of the Judaeo-Christian *Weltanschauung* is timely. In what is now called a 'post-modern' context, the great symbols of creation, redemption and eschatology, the work for justice and the imperative to respect the environment, are as necessary as ever.

It has to be said that 'modernity' and 'post-modernity' are fluid, even ambiguous, concepts. Some theologians view post-modernity as not merely the friend of Christian faith, but 'a cultural wavelength' in which faith can live and be credible today.[24] Yet, even our Sunday newspapers show that the wavelength is also one where self-interest and arrogant consumerism strangle justice and compassion. In such a context it would be a tragedy if the churches lost the critical edge of prophetic discourse. To challenge prevalent social injustice and environmental irresponsibility, Christian faith needs to re-appraise its own foundational symbols and, in particular, its theology of creation. Further, it has to earn its *droit de cité* by its seriousness of intent and its commitment to the attainment of truth. Here, Daly has contributed valuably. In face of 'power communication,' whether from the right or the left, he continues to argue for expansion of theological imagination and an 'educated conscience.' His reiterated defence of human rights 'within' and 'without' the church provides an antidote to institutional arrogance. If we are to 'keep hope alive,' our own discourse must reflect the Christian *Anschauung* on creation, redemption and eschatology, in a way that is at once loyal to the tradition and critically in touch with our own day.

---

24. See, Michael Paul Gallagher, SJ, *Clashing Symbols: An Introduction to Faith and Culture,* London: DLT, 87-100.

Daly's seminal article on 'Table d'Hôte Catholicism' effectively sets out the problem. Here, he argues that what is happening in the Catholic Church scandalises many outside its ranks and profoundly discourages loyal Catholics. The scandal, he tells us, is not the Pauline scandal of Christ's cross, but rather 'partial, dictatorial and unjust' exercise of power.[25] One takes the impression that Daly's indignation is reserved, not for those who emphasise commitment to justice, but for those who have tried to reverse the achievements of Vatican II. The casualties have been open communication and respect for diversity within unity. Gabriel Daly has spoken of the dangers inherent in a managerial attitude to truth. The truth about creation-redemption-eschatology is not subject to ecclesiastical *diktat*. Rather, it is wilfully truncated by 'partial, unjust and dictatorial exercise of power'.[26] Nor in the end can the Christian message be fully encapsulated by doctrines or decrees.

One returns to Aquinas's reminder that doctrines are best understood as signposts to mystery. An implication of this is that truth is sought rather than imposed. Aquinas never shirked the burden of critical reflection; yet he practised, in the last analysis, 'an agnosticism of reverence'. Without fear of correction, I would suggest that Gabriel Daly's service to truth has been of this order. In emphasising the role of imagination as part of the educated conscience, he provides a stimulus to growth where a credible voice from the world religions is more than ever needed. When he speaks of reinterpretation within creation theology he does well to insist on the evolutionary concept of nature and the necessity for ethical imagination, if we are to lay the foundation for developments as yet unforeseen.

25. Daly, 'Table d'Hôte Catholicism,' 410.
26. ibid., 410.

CHAPTER 2

Faith and Ideology in the Old Testament*

A. D. H. Mayes

The title of this chapter is the title of an article by P. D. Miller,[1] and my objective is a very limited one: to react to this article in the light of some further study in the following twenty-five years.[2] There will be four sections to this discussion: first, a summary account of Miller's article; second, a critique of the article; third, a development of the critique in the light of studies on ideology by Clifford Geertz and Paul Ricoeur, with particular reference to our understanding of the religion of Israel as ideology; and, fourth, a critical reaction to the study of Israelite religion as ideology, with particular reference to the question of faith.

I

Miller's study is concerned with the relation of religious thought to social context, particularly in view of Mannheim's argument that 'no human thought is immune to the ideologising influences of its social context.'[3] If this is the case, then the presence of ideological factors in the faith of Israel is to be expected.

The term 'ideology' may mean, in a neutral way, 'a description of the way things are in a society, the values, ideas and con-

* It is a particular pleasure to offer this short study as a tribute to a scholar and friend who, through his writing, teaching and conversation, has done much to enrich our understanding.

1. P.D.Miller, 'Faith and Ideology in the Old Testament,' *Magnalia Dei: The Mighty Acts of God: Essays on the Bible and Archaeology in Memory of G. Ernest Wright*, ed. F. M. Cross, W. E. Lemke and P. D. Miller, New York: Doubleday, 1976,464-79

2. See also A. D. H. Mayes, 'Deuteronomistic Ideology and the Theology of the Old Testament,' *Israel Constructs its History: Deuteronomistic Historiography in Recent Research*, ed. A. de Pury, T. Römer, J.- D. Macchi (JSOTS 306), Sheffield: Sheffield Academic Press, 2000, 456-80; J. Barr, *History and Ideology in the Old Testament*, Oxford: Oxford University Press, 2000, 102-40.

3. K. Mannheim, *Ideology and Utopia*, New York: 1966, 6.

ceptions of a society which cause it to do or act as it does.'[4] But it commonly has a pejorative sense: it is a partial view of the way things are, a view which is a function of the conditions of the person who holds it; the ideas expressed are to be interpreted in the light of those conditions and are not to be taken at face value. Two quotations are given, both of which tend to emphasise the partial nature of ideology, the one more strongly than the other: 'An ideology is a selective interpretation of the state of affairs in society made by those who share some particular conception of what it ought to be,'[5] and, 'that composite myth by which a society or group identifies itself, not only for itself but also for other societies and groups. An ideology posits the group's goals and the justification of these goals in terms of which the group deals with other groups and with conflicts within the group; it defines and interprets the situation; aims to overcome indifference to the common good; it reduces excessive emphasis on individual action. It makes possible group action.'[6]

Ideology thus defined is to be traced back to Israel's old election and covenant theology; it becomes clearly articulated, however, in the Yahwist's notion of a chosen people and belief in divine promises. Here is reflected the partial view, Israel's self-interest, a selective, ideological interpretation of Israel's past.

Faith, on the other hand, is that which goes beyond or transcends self-interest. It is marked by self-criticism, by a positive relationship between Israel and other nations, and by the demand for justice and righteousness. An expression of faith need not be marked by all three of these characteristics at the same time; in the case of each of them, the exclusive interest of the group is criticised or transcended.

Israel's early poetry, as it comes to expression particularly in Ex 15, Deut 33 and Judg 5, is thoroughly ideological. The material interests of Israel, particularly its acquisition of land, are projected as the interests of Yahweh also. There is no self-criticism, and relationships with other groups are hostile.

In J, ideological elements are also present: especially the notion that Israel is descended from a common ancestor who received

4. Miller, 'Faith and Ideology in the Old Testament,' 465.
5. W.White, *Beyond Conformity*, New York: 1961, 6; quoted in Miller, 'Faith and Ideology in the Old Testament,' 466.
6. J. L. Adams, 'Religion and Ideologies,' *Confluence* 4, 1955, 72; quoted in Miller, 'Faith and Ideology in the Old Testament,'466.

divine promises of land and descendants. But the criteria of faith are also to be found in J: the divine blessing on Israel is fully realised only in the context of universal blessing (Gen 12:1-3), and the demand for justice and righteousness in Israel is also to be found (Gen 18:17b-19). In J, therefore, pure self-interest is transcended; faith and ideology are intertwined.

The deuteronomic conquest traditions in Joshua represent an ideological presentation of the past, a justification for certain actions and practices on the basis of Israel's self-understanding as the chosen people. Israel's actions in dispossessing the former inhabitants is projected as the fulfilling of the purposes of Yahweh. A certain check is kept on ideology, however, insofar as the framework for the presentation is that of the covenant, with its demand for Israel's obedience.

The prophets 'perceived that the popular or national theology was simply an ideology without controls, without any checks and balances.'[7] So, while standing in continuity with the old ideology, they changed and criticised it from a faith perspective. Amos used the ideology of election and promise as a basis for criticising Israel ('You only have I known of all the families of the earth; therefore I will punish you for all your iniquities' – Am 3:2); Jeremiah interpreted the gift of the land to imply the possibility of the removal of the gift (Jer 7:3). The prophets are not non-ideological, but the old ideology is changed and transcended. Their faith consists in their radical treatment of the old traditions, a reinterpretation of national ideology within a universalistic and self-critical context.

II

There is much in this article which is, clearly, very reasonable and convincing, but it does present some problems. In the first place, the relationship between the neutral understanding of ideology as simple description and ideology as selective interpretation remains unresolved. Miller admits that ideology may mean simply 'a description of the way things are in society', but his article effectively works with ideology in its pejorative sense only. So the question of the definition of ideology remains a general problem.

Second, insofar as the article contrasts faith and ideology, it clearly presupposes that faith is non-ideological. But if faith is

7. Miller, 'Faith and Ideology in the Old Testament,' 473.

non-ideological, does this mean that faith then is some form of pure knowledge or understanding, knowledge or understanding which is somehow immune to the ideologising influences of its social context? How, then, can this be reconciled with Miller's apparent acceptance of Mannheim's argument that 'no human thought is immune to the ideologising influences of its social context,' and with Miller's own admission that 'it may be ultimately an impossible task to distinguish between ideology and faith'?[8] So the definition of faith is a particular problem.

Two writers, Clifford Geertz and Paul Ricoeur, have contributed much towards a resolution of these issues,[9] and in a way which has a fruitful impact on our understanding of the faith of Israel. In the light of these, it is clear that the problems present in Miller's article may be defined in a different way. First, that ideology, at least in its pejorative sense, is understood as an expression of material interests: so, insofar as the religion of Israel identifies Israel's material interests with the will of Yahweh, it is ideological. This could be held to imply that the ideological is characterised by a causal relationship between the physical, material conditions experienced by an individual and the thinking of that person; where the relationship between the material conditions and thinking has a direct causal nature then that thinking is ideological. So, Israel's material and physical conditions, her possession of the land, caused the ideology of the divine promise of land to the patriarchs.[10] That 'ideology' should then be understood in negative terms is not surprising: it is thinking which is caused by material interest and so is essentially selective, partial, distorting. Second, however, despite that assumed causal relationship, Miller does not feel it necessary to discuss ideology in terms of its fundamental, causal, social and material conditions. That is to say, ideology is seen as an intrinsic characteristic of certain statements and beliefs in themselves, rather than as a characteristic of certain statements in relation to social and material conditions. Thus, the belief that Israel is the

8. Ibid., 477 n. 10.

9. C. Geertz, 'Ideology as a Cultural System,' *The Interpretation of Cultures*, New York: 1973, 193-233; P. Ricoeur, *Lectures on Ideology and Utopia*, Columbia University Press, 1986.

10. Such a view is indeed implicit in much general scholarly study of this topic, going back to A. Alt, 'The God of the Fathers,' *Essays on Old Testament History and Religion*, Oxford: 1966, 3-77 (esp. 65).

people of Yahweh is an intrinsically and essentially ideological statement. Both of these points require more substantial development.

III

1. That ideology is a direct reflection of material circumstances and interests is a materialist view which has often been traced back to Marx. Its antecedents are, however, pre-Marxist. In modern times it appears in the work of the American anthropologist Marvin Harris,[11] and from him it has also been adopted by Norman Gottwald[12] to account for Israel's religion: according to Gottwald, the social-egalitarian system of Israel initiated the rise of Yahwism.

This understanding, a materialist one of a very mechanistic type, was in fact fundamentally criticised by Marx, and that critique has been developed by Geertz and Ricoeur. The essence of the critique is this: how can physical conditions be transformed into mental conditions? Physical causes will have physical effects, not mental effects. The idea that a causal relationship exists between physical conditions and thought cannot account for the transformation of the one into the other. Marx, in his theses on Feuerbach, said: 'The chief defect of all hitherto existing materialism (that of Feuerbach included) is that the thing, reality, sensuousness, is conceived only in the form of the object or of contemplation, but not as sensuous human activity, practice, not subjectively.'[13] In our present context, this can be taken to mean that the problem with the materialism of Harris and Gottwald is that it does not reckon with subjective, conscious human activity in the creation of those conditions which are reckoned to be basic, in a causal sense, to human thinking. Material conditions are not only the cause of thought, they are the product of thought.[14]

11. Marvin Harris, *Cultural Materialism: The Struggle for a Science of Culture*, New York: Vintage Books 1980.
12. N. K. Gottwald, *The Tribes of Yahweh: A Sociology of the Religion of Liberated Israel: 7250-7050 BCE*, London: 1980, 637ff.
13. Cf D. McLellan (ed.), *Karl Marx: Selected Writings*, Oxford: OUP, 1977, 156.
14. On a basic problem in Gottwald's presentation, involving a conflict between his mechanistic materialist theory and his idealist practice, see A. D. H. Mayes, *The Old Testament in Sociological Perspective*, London: 1989, 95ff.

It is precisely this which has been developed by Geertz and Ricoeur.[15] For Geertz, reality is conceived in thought and action not as pure object but in symbolic form. We can understand how ideas arise, an ideology is formed, only if at the most basic level of human existence there is a symbolic dimension. That is to say, physical reality does not just impinge itself on the human mind; if it did do so we would exist in a state of chaos. Rather, physical reality is recognised by the human mind. This recognition is the symbolic ordering of reality in perception from the beginning. This symbolic ordering is ideology, and it functions to make social life possible. Ideology is, then, a symbolic system. The basic function of ideology is to integrate, and it does so in a dual sense: in the first place it integrates phenomena into a coherent system, and, second, it integrates those who share in that system into a coherent group. An ideology is 'a coherent body of shared images, ideas and ideals which … provides for the participants a coherent, if systematically simplified, overall orientation in space and time, in means and ends.'[16] It is a culture pattern which provides 'a template or blueprint for the organisation of social and psychological processes, much as genetic systems provide such a template for the organisation of organic processes.'[17]

This basic function of ideology – to constitute and integrate the human community – is, according to Ricoeur, fundamental to any other role ideology has. In all cases, ideology is representation, representation of reality, that through which reality is experienced, expressed and mediated. Insofar as ideology carries a pejorative sense, this is because it has come to be recognised as performing a distorting role in relation to 'reality'. In Marx, in whose work the pejorative understanding of ideology is now really rooted, the basic idea is that of reversal, and its first point of application is religion. Reversal is the treatment as autonomous of ideas that have human origin. The divine is a human idea, objectified and alienated from its originator to become the active subject; that which man produces is alienated from him, and to it in the end he is enslaved. Ideology is distortion in that it is a representation of distorted social relationships, or a distortion of the real. It is the means by which the process of real life is obscured; it conceals self-interest in terms of divine mandate.[18]

15. Cf n.9.
16. Cf Ricoeur, *Lectures on Ideology and Utopia*, 258, quoting Erik Erikson.
17. So Geertz, *The Interpretation of Cultures*, 216.
18. Cf Ricoeur, *Lectures on Ideology and Utopia*, 4f., 38ff.

Ricoeur[19] argues that the distorting function of ideology presupposes a prior integrating function; ideology can distort only because it originally constituted. Moreover, there is a connecting link between these two functions of ideology. This is the point at which ideology serves not to integrate nor to distort reality but rather to legitimise. As soon as a differentiation appears between a ruling group and the rest of the community, ideology comes in to legitimise and to justify the authority of the ruling group. Ideology is now the claim to legitimacy made by the ruling group.[20] Weber's analysis of forms of domination or authority according to three types: legal-rational, traditional and charismatic, is important here, for these are the three modes by which ideology, as claim to legitimacy, comes to expression.

By way of summary then: ideology is not to be understood as mental superstructure to a material infrastructure. Rather, it is symbolic representation through which reality is experienced and brought to expression. Thinking, symbolic representation, is active at all levels, including the most basic level of material infrastructure. In its most basic function ideology is integrative, providing the symbolic system which constitutes the community; division in the community leads to the need for the ruling group to justify its authority, and now ideology functions to legitimate; at a further remove, ideology functions to distort by obscuring the real process of life. These three roles or functions of ideology stand not merely in a logical relationship but in a temporal relationship: 'logically if not temporally the constitutive function of ideology must precede its distortive function.'[21]

As far as Miller is concerned, therefore, we may say that ideology is not merely a reflection of material circumstances in a pejorative sense, but can be this only because it also functions in a constitutive or integrative way: it is that function which is distorted. Thus, the definition of ideology given by Miller may be set in a more comprehensive framework.

2. The second issue is this: that Miller does not in fact discuss ideology in terms of its social and material context, and this despite the fact that he views ideology as standing in a causal relationship to social and material conditions. Instead he tries to

19. ibid., 12ff.
20. ibid., 183ff.
21. ibid., 182.

define ideological statements in terms of their intrinsic content and significance. Not only is ideology defined in terms of its intrinsic content and significance, so also faith: faith is self-critical, it is universalistic, it speaks of justice and righteousness. In the end, both ideology and faith are understood objectively as inherent qualities of certain types of statement. Now, if Karl Mannheim is right (and Miller seems to agree that he is) that 'no-human thought is immune to the ideologising influences of its social context,' then Miller's contrast between faith and ideology cannot be accepted too quickly, and one must ask if it is because the issue of the social and material context of human thinking has been neglected that it has been possible to make the contrast, or at least to make the contrast in those terms.

The point with which we begin to approach this issue is this: Israelite faith, as part of Israelite thinking, is to be analysed in the first instance as ideology. In fact, Israelite faith illustrates the functioning of ideology at all three levels: the integrating, the legitimating and the distorting.

On the level of integration, Israelite faith operates as that symbolic system which maintains community. The wider framework within which this functioning of Israelite faith belongs is the understanding of the nature of religion put forward by Robertson Smith and taken over from him by Emile Durkheim, and in turn adopted by Norman Gottwald. Robertson Smith wrote:

> A man did not choose his religion or frame it for himself; it came to him as part of the general scheme of social obligations and ordinances laid upon him, as a matter of course, by his position in the family and in the nation ... A certain amount of religion was required of everybody; for the due performance of religious acts was a social obligation in which everyone had his appointed share ... Religion did not exist for the saving of souls but for the preservation and welfare of society.[22]

We find this clearly echoed in Durkheim's argument that religious beliefs

> ... are always common to a determined group, which makes profession of adhering to them and of practising the rites connected with them. They are not merely received individually by all the members of the group; they are something be-

22. W. Robertson Smith, *Lectures on the Religion of the Semites* (3rd Edn. 1927), Ktav: 1969, 28f.

> longing to the group, and they make its unity. The individuals who compose it feel themselves united to each other by the simple fact that they have a common faith.[23]

Religion belongs to what Durkheim calls the collective representations of society; individuals are born into these collective representations which are imbued in the consciousness of those individuals. So Durkheim then defined religion in these terms:

> A religion is a unified system of beliefs and practices relative to sacred things, that is to say, things set apart and forbidden – beliefs and practices which unite into one single moral community called a church, all those who adhere to them.[24]

Religion is thus an ideological system whose function is to unify and to integrate through articulating the fundamental common beliefs of the group.

This same function, in relation to the religion of Israel, is described by Gottwald. Moreover, this is explicitly recognised as an ideological function.

> Ideology serves as a useful cipher to describe religious ideas as integral aspects of total social systems ... When I refer to ideology in ancient Israel, I mean the consensual religious ideas which were structurally embedded in and functionally correlated to other social phenomena within the larger social system, and which served, in a more or less comprehensive manner, to provide explanations or interpretations of the distinctive social relations and historical experiences of Israel and also to define and energise the Israelite social system oppositionally or polemically over against other social systems.[25]

> The religious cult and ideology are potent organisational and symbolic forces in establishing and reinforcing the social, economic, political and military arrangements normative for community.[26]

This integrating function of ideology and religion in an egalitarian context is both the logical and the temporal basis for the functioning of ideology in any other form. The other functions of ideology reflect social and economic changes in the original egalitarian community. These changes took the form of the

23. E.Durkheim, *The Elementary Forms of the Religious Life*, Allen and Unwin: 2nd Edn. 1976, 43.
24. ibid., 47.
25. Gottwald, *The Tribes of Yahweh*, 65f.
26. ibid., 489.

emergence of a distinction between a ruling group and the remainder of the community, a ruling group whose role had to be justified and legitimated if the unity of the community was to be maintained. In Israel, the rise of charismatic leadership and then of the institution of the monarchy represented threats to Israel's unity which had to be averted by a process of legitimation. Ideology as legitimation is the claim which re-unites the ruler and the ruled. The charismatic leaders attracted a following and their role is legitimised through the claim that they are designated and raised up as leaders in Israel by Yahweh. The king, too, is nominated by Yahweh as his appointed leader of Israel. Ideology performs an increasingly distorting role, however, the more extravagant became the claims that were made. The king is not only designated by Yahweh, he is the son of Yahweh; he stands in an exclusive covenant relationship with Yahweh; Yahweh defeats all his enemies; the kings of the earth tremble in fear before Yahweh and his anointed ruler. At this stage, ideology distorts, and it does so in at least two interconnected respects: first, in that it presents Yahweh's designation as an autonomous act of Yahweh, so indeed enslaving Israel, whereas in truth that is a reversal of the true state of affairs, the reality that it is a wholly human action; second, in that it obscures the real conditions of power politics that lie behind the exercise of royal rule in Israel.

When the comprehensive understanding of ideology and its threefold role are fully exploited then we have a good framework for understanding Israelite religion. This is not a matter, of course, of a materialistic explanation of religion for, as we saw, the idea that there is a *causal* relationship between material circumstances and thinking is inadequate. Human thinking is present at all stages, even the most basic, of human existence in the world. Only if this is so is it possible to relate human thinking to material circumstances. That relationship is to be understood in motivational rather than in causal terms. However, the question with which we end this section is: does this offer a full account of Israelite religion, or is there more to be said that might justify Miller's juxtaposition of faith and ideology?

IV

In this concluding section, there are two topics to be addressed, by way of response to the question at the end of the last section. The first of these is: is the account just given of Israelite religion, understood in ideological terms, satisfactory and adequate; and the second, what then are we to say of Miller's discussion of faith as something different from, standing over against, ideology? The answer to which we shall come in relation to the first question is: No, this is not an adequate account. Out of that answer, the attempt will then be made to develop a response to the second question which will involve some modifications to Miller's discussion of the nature of faith.

1. To question the adequacy of this account of Israelite religion understood in ideological terms is not necessarily to imply that there is something about Israelite religion which is not covered by this account, that there is some non-ideological residue which may be looked on as the pure essence of the religion of Israel. Rather, it is to suggest that there is a problem within this ideological account of religion. This problem relates in the first instance to the supposed basic level of ideology, that level at which ideology functions simply in an integrative way, 'like a sort of social cement, binding members of society together by providing them with collectively shared values and norms,'[27] the level at which it 'is first and foremost a cluster of symbols and representations which facilitate the meaningful constitution and social integration of action ... a positive phenomenon, expressing the necessity for any group to give itself an image of itself, to fill the gap between its origin and its actuality.'[28]

Now, there are two points which arise here, both of which create a serious problem for this perception of the role of ideology. First, certainly as far as modern industrial societies are concerned and surely also with respect to ancient Israel, there is little evidence to support the idea that there was a fundamental range of common values and beliefs, common symbols and representations, which functioned simply to express the unity of society. The extent to which 'people of Yahweh' and empirical Israel were ever co-extensive is a major problem of current concern. The model of the amphictyony introduced by Noth, and the more recent model of the segmentary society which has tended in recent years to replace it, seemed to offer the possibility

27. J.B. Thompson, *Studies in the Theory of Ideology*, Polity Press, Oxford: 1984, 5. The following criticism of the notion that ideology has a primary integrative function is taken from Thompson.

28. ibid., 174.

of giving a social description to pre-monarchic Israel which one could accept as the social context for such an integrative and constitutive interpretation of the function of ideology. Now, however, both of these models are very much out of favour, and instead the tendency is to think of pre-monarchic Israelite society as a chiefdom or a number of chiefdoms. It is the chiefdom stage which is the first for which there is clear evidence. If this is the case, then ideology cannot be understood to function primarily in an integrating or constitutive role; rather, its function will be to legitimate and to justify relationships of domination.[29]

Second, it is clear that for Geertz and Ricoeur on the general problem of ideology, and for Gottwald on the specific issue of the role of ideology in Israel, there is a definite question mark over the validity of seeing it in terms of integration. At one point, Geertz writes:

> In ... truly traditional political systems the participants act as ... men of untaught feelings; they are guided both emotionally and intellectually in their judgments and activities by unexamined prejudices, which do not leave them hesitating in the moment of decision, sceptical, puzzled and unresolved. But when ... these hallowed opinions and rules of life come into question, the search for ideological formulations, either to reinforce them or to replace them, flourishes ... It is ... at the point at which a political system begins to free itself from the immediate governance of received tradition, from the direct and detailed guidance of religious or philosophical canons on the one hand and from the unreflective precepts of conventional moralism on the other, that formal ideologies tend first to emerge and take hold.[30]

Ricoeur indeed says at one stage, as already noted: 'logically if not temporally the constitutive function of ideology must precede its distortive function;' but elsewhere[31] he argues: 'while ideology serves as the code of interpretation that secures integration, it does so by justifying the present system of authority,' and again[32] he asks 'whether we are allowed to speak of ideologies outside the situation of distortion and so with reference only to the basic function of integration. Is there ideology where

29. Cf ibid., 130ff.

30. Geertz, *The Interpretation of Cultures*, 218f.

31. Ricoeur, *Lectures on Ideology and Utopia*, 13.

32. ibid., 259.

there is no conflict of ideologies? ... integration without confrontation is pre-ideological.' It is wholly in line with this that Gottwald says that the Israelite religious ideology functioned 'to provide explanations or interpretations of the distinctive social relations and historical experience of Israel and also to define and energise the Israelite social system oppositionally or polemically over against other social systems.'[33] The whole force of Gottwald's argument indeed is that Israel emerged in the context of a conscious social revolution directed against the hierarchic state system of the environment. 'Israel's tribalism was politically conscious and deliberate social revolution.'[34] Clearly, then, the role of ideology cannot be understood simply in terms of integration and constitution; rather, from the beginning, it belongs in a conflict context, a context of opposition to other ideologies, and thus has the role of justifying and legitimating.

What effect does this revision of our understanding of ideology have on our perception of Israelite religion? An answer to this question should emerge out of a discussion of our final topic: Miller's discussion of faith as something different from, standing over against, ideology.

2. We must remember that Miller defined faith not only as something different from, standing over against, ideology, but essentially as that which criticises ideology. The three characteristics of faith, that it is marked by self-criticism, by a positive relationship with other nations, and by the demand for justice and righteousness, share the common factor that they go beyond or transcend self-interest. In effect this means that faith is essentially a critique of, a rejection of, ideology in that the latter is characterised by self-interest. There are three points to be made here.

First, the relationship of faith with ideology is closely parallel to that of utopia with ideology, as described by Mannheim and Ricoeur. The definition of utopia corresponds to that of ideology. Like ideology, so utopia is non-congruent with reality. Just as ideology operates at three levels, so also does utopia: where ideology is distortion, utopia is escapist fantasy; where ideology is legitimation, utopia is an alternative to the present power or an alternative to power or an alternative form of power; where ideology is integration and identification, utopia is an explor-

33. Gottwald, *The Tribes of Yahweh*, 66.
34. ibid., 325.

ation of the possible. In summary, while ideology is at all levels concerned to preserve and conserve the existing system, utopia is concerned with opening up to new possibilities. Utopia, in its rejection of the presently existing, is a critique of the presently existing.[35]

Second, that utopia can be imagined is no indication or demonstration that one can escape from ideology or stand outside ideology. Utopia is a creation of the imagination which itself proceeds from the context of ideology. Karl Mannheim's conclusion that no human thought is immune to the ideologising influences of its social context is not to be forgotten. Utopia is an expression of values which cannot be divorced from social context. Nevertheless, the fact that it is possible for us not only to recognise the ideological as ideological but even to say that the identification of a belief as ideological is itself an ideological identification means that we are not in fact caught up in a vicious circle. We do have the capacity to reflect on our situation, even if in an ideological way, and this capacity for a certain distancing implies that we are not wholly bound by our situation. Utopia may be an ideological creation, but as an ideological critique of ideology it breaks open the otherwise vicious circle of ideology.[36] Social context, the relationship to which makes human thinking ideological, is a *motivational* framework for thought, not a *causal foundation* for thought.

Third, and it is at this point that we return finally to Miller with some fundamental modifications: it is clear that ideology, and indeed faith, is a form of thought, discourse, speech or writing, which is essentially related to social context. Miller, however, does not really acknowledge the essential nature of this relationship. Instead, the character of any given statement as ideological or as faith is recognised solely on the basis of its intrinsic nature and content. Thus, the belief of Israel that she is the people of Yahweh descended from the patriarch Abraham and the result of promise to Abraham, is understood to be an inherently ideological statement in which the goals and purpose of Israel and the goals and purposes of Yahweh are identified, an ideological belief reflecting the integrative functioning of ideology.

There are, however, alternative possibilities of interpretation, alternative possibilities which take on the appearance of proba-

35. Cf. Ricoeur, *Lectures on Ideology and Utopia*, 310ff.
36. ibid., 312.

bility once such beliefs are, as they should be, related to social context, particularly when that social context was not, as we have noted, an egalitarian society. A hint at the nature of this alternative interpretation is, in fact, provided by Gottwald:

> Once the wider social context of early Israel is held in view, the work of the cult can be seen more realistically as a way of mediating between the chaotic conditions and circumstances of Israelite experience and the need for ordering the chaos institutionally and ideologically ... there always existed a hiatus between what the traditions claimed and what the people experienced. The traditions asserted the massive unity of early Israel, but the community knew very well from its contemporary experience that existing Israel was torn with inner divisions and tensions and repeatedly exposed to dangers from without. That the divisions and tensions could be overcome and the external dangers turned aside was the conviction and affirmation of the great centralised traditions.[37]

And again:

> Side by side with the claim of total unity stood stories of disunity and parochial achievement. This is why the 'fiction' of the cult ideology must be seen in its vital dialectical interplay with the 'reality' of the social system in the context of the historical struggles it faced.[38]

Israel, the people of Yahweh, the focus of promise to the patriarchs, is, in other words, possibly best understood not as an integrative ideology reflecting self-interest, but as a utopian critique of the social and economic divisions which characterised existing Israel; it is a statement of faith, forcing Israelites to push beyond the horizons of their divisive economic interests towards an ideal of becoming the people of Yahweh.[39]

37. Gottwald, *The Tribes of Yahweh*, 122.
38. ibid., 124.
39. A quotation from Karl Barth (*Dogmatics in Outline*), which appears at the end of the introduction to E. Jungel, *Theological Essays* (translated with an introduction by J. B. Webster, Edinburgh: 1989), is not inappropriate: 'God is the essence of the possible.'

CHAPTER 3

Returning to Origins and Initiating Dialogue: Jews and Christians faced with their Shared Heritage

Seán V Freyne

One of Gabriel Daly's abiding theological interests has been the ecumenical movement and the challenge it poses to Christian self-understanding in all the churches. One aspect of that challenge which has not always received the attention it deserves is the manner in which Christian origins are constructed. Too often one encounters ecclesiastical pronouncements which operate with stereotypes of the past, which suit the present situation, and are useful for excluding in advance any discussion of issues which are deemed to the establishment to be either inappropriate or dangerous. While ecumenical discussion between the Christian churches is today at a seeming standstill, a much greater and more urgent task – that of inter-religious dialogue – awaits us in our perilous global situation. In this chapter I would like to explore the implications for such a dialogue that a re-consideration of origins might provide, confining myself to Jewish and Christian relations. A consideration of the mutual relations with Islam that these two older members of the Abrahamic family might develop in the light of such a discussion of their own tangled and often painful history must await another occasion. Nevertheless, the exercise of re-considering how origins are constructed, as exemplified in a discussion of the Jewish and Christian developments from the first to the fourth centuries of the Common Era, will hopefully point to several ways in which such future inter-religious dialogue might fruitfully take place. Indeed it might also offer a new lifeline to the now faltering discussions of inner-Christian ecumenism, an issue which has informed so much of our honoree's distinguished academic career.

Jewish scholar Jacob Neusner's comment that 'majorities will always persecute minorities' appears as a realistic, if disappointing appraisal of Jewish and Christian relations in the first to the fourth centuries, a period which he rightly describes as 'foundational' for both religions.[1] The first century saw the emergence of the Jewish reform movement, initiated by Jesus of Nazareth, blossom into the early Christian Church, which by the end of the century had put down roots in all the major cities of the Mediterranean, as well as eastwards to the borders of the Roman Empire beyond the Euphrates. On the other hand, the fourth century witnessed this new movement's consolidation as Christendom, a religio-political world power, following Constantine's victory over his enemies at the battle of the Milvian bridge in Rome in 312 CE, and the subsequent adoption of the Christian faith as the official religion of the empire.

The claim that this same period, the first to the fourth century, could be described as foundational for the Jewish religion may come as a surprise to most Christians, and probably to many Jews also. There are several reasons for this misunderstanding. For Christians, the stereotype of Judaism that has persisted for centuries is that of a religion based on what they call the Old Testament, which effectively came to an end, or at least became fossilised, with its rejection of the messiah, Jesus. This act merited the punishment meted out by God in terms of the destruction of the Jerusalem temple and the dispersion of the nation. Judaism ought to have withered up and died, so the stereotype goes, were it not for the fact that its continued existence is witness to the truth of Christian claims. If Christians have their biased stereotypes, Jews can be equally myopic when it comes to giving an account of their own origins and history. There has been a strong tendency in orthodox circles to push the foundations of Judaism back to the Babylonian exile in the sixth century BCE in such a way that all subsequent development is ignored, especially in terms of the major restructuring that had to take place after the failure of the two revolts against Rome in 66 and 132 CE.

There are, of course, reasons why both Jews and Christians have distorted views of each other's origins. Origins become all-important when competing claims to a shared patrimony surface. One is then faced with the option of either creating a past to suit one's own claims, thereby legitimating the present by pushing it back into the past, or alternatively ignoring the past altogether, deeming it a burden as an obstacle to 'progress'. As Paul Ricoeur perceptively suggests, the ethics of remembering is al-

1. Jacob Neusner, *Judaism and Christianity in the Age of Constantine*, Chicago and London: University of Chicago Press, 1987.

ways demanding, because the past, when critically examined, confronts us with images of ourselves that very often we do not want to have to deal with. Forgetting or distorting becomes the easier option.[2]

The 'journey down memory lane' that I propose to take is not, therefore, nostalgic, but critical. I want to identify key aspects in the emergence of Jewish and Christian identities in their formative periods, partly to uncover many of the distortions under which some people from both traditions operate, and partly to ask the question of how these two world religions might today legitimately re-image their past with a view to their present and future. By presenting a more nuanced account of the origins of both religions than the stereotypes I have just sketched, I want to enquire about the freedom for dialogue that both enjoy in order to adapt both internally and externally to the changing circumstance in which they find themselves, while remaining faithful to their own founding experiences. For dialogue to be fruitful, however, it has to be respectful of the other as *real*, not as *projected other*. By hearing the other as other, aspects of the self that have been lost, forgotten or deliberately repressed, especially when that other is someone very close, are rediscovered; and genuine, as distinct from contrived differences, are revealed and can be acknowledged.

Jews and Christians in the First Century

It is essentially correct to see the beginnings of Judaism in the sixth century BCE when, as part of a general policy, the Persian king Cyrus allowed various ethnic groups, which the previous Babylonian regime had exiled, return to their various homelands. Among these returnees were the *Yehudim,* or descendants of those from Jerusalem and its immediate environs (the territory inhabited by the ancient tribe of Judah), who had been living by the waters of Babylon for some seventy years. In that period of exile many of the rituals that later became associated with normative Judaism originated as a means of protecting their separate identity. Thus, if as the psalm puts it, they could not sing the songs of Zion in a foreign land (Ps 137), they nevertheless gathered in assemblies for prayer, reading of the books of Moses and

2. Paul Ricoeur, *Time and Narrative,* 3 vols, London and Chicago: University of Chicago Press, 1988, 3, 240-74; David Tracy, *Dialogue with the Other: The Inter-Religious Dialogue,* Louvain: Peeters Press, 1990.

observing the Sabbath. The sense of separateness that was thereby achieved has remained with Jews to this day, so deep was, and still is, the experience of exile in Jewish consciousness.

The aura of excitement and high hopes of restoration from exile that are reflected in Isaiah (chapters 40-56) still remained unrealised by the first century CE. The intervening centuries had seen the Jews encounter the power of Greek culture in the wake of Alexander the Great's conquest of the east. For some of the temple aristocracy in Jerusalem this was a good experience, leading ultimately to an attempt to transform the cult of Yahweh into that of Zeus, the head of the Greek pantheon. Despite the successful resistance to this radical challenge to all that they stood for, divisions were soon to emerge, divisions that were religious, social and economic. This situation was the seed-bed for the emergence of the parties we meet in the gospels – Pharisees and Sadducees – as well as the Essenes, about whose way of life we now know so much because of the accidental discovery in 1948 of the Dead Sea Scrolls. To complicate matters further, the Romans had replaced the Greeks as the controllers of the east, including Palestine, installing as client rulers the Herodian regime, in order to control the territory of the Jews and ensure that the region would remain loyal. It was only after two bitter revolts in 66-70 and 132-135 CE that the Jewish desire for self-rule in their own land was finally broken, thereby demonstrating that of all the indigenous peoples of the east, they were by far the most intractable in refusing to bow to Roman imperial desires. Their temple lay in ruins after the first revolt, a victory celebrated on the Arch of Titus in Rome to this day, and after the second revolt they were banished from Judea to Galilee, there to begin the painful process of rebuilding the national and religious identity on the institutions first developed in Babylon six hundred years earlier.

This brief account of the history of Judaism in the Second Temple period must suffice by way of background to the emergence of the reform movement initiated by Jesus of Nazareth early in the first century CE, some thirty years prior to the revolt against Rome. Within two generations this movement had emerged as quite separate, having broken with the parent religion, in what must have been acrimonious circumstances, judging from what we read in almost every page of the New Testament. Ironically, however, it was Jewish rights that Rome continued to recognise as a *religio licita,* despite having its authority so seriously challenged. The Christian movement, by contrast, had no such juridical standing – its founder had been put to death as a criminal under Roman law, and his followers had repeatedly drawn the ire of Roman emperors, most notably Nero, who in 64 CE had made them scapegoats for the great fire in Rome and inflicted the most appalling tortures on them. This was a pattern of treating the Christians that would repeat itself for two centuries, since in Roman eyes the Christians were to be classed an 'odious superstition', and therefore prey to the whims of local governors or imperial decree.

One way to characterise the Jewish religion of the Second Temple period out of which the Jesus movement emerged is to describe it, following Neusner, as a system of interlocking symbols which was invested with sacred meaning and represented what the Jews believed about their God and his dealings with them. The most typical understanding of this God was that of king, in common with ancient near eastern mythology generally. Other images, at once more gentle and less war-like were also possible, as we see in various prophetic writings – lover, nurse, shepherd, builder for example – combining both male and female traits. However, as a royal figure, this God's authority was expressed in and through the symbols of temple, land and Torah. The temple represented his abiding presence, the land the range and extent of his authority and the Torah the written expression of his will. These stable elements of the Jewish symbol system had been variously understood over the centuries, each receiving special attention at different times or among various circles. Thus in the first century, we can speak of the priest and temple, the freedom-fighter and the land, and the scribe and the torah scroll as being representative of these various and often competing strands. It was the failure of these embodiments of the symbol system, either collectively or separately, to generate for some Jews long-lasting moods of confidence and trust – the primary function of all religious symbols and their ritual enactment – that gave rise to the discontent out of which the Jesus movement arose and which it sought to address.

Before examining Jesus' particular understanding of this symbol system, it is important to recall that his was only one such reform movement that the Herodian age in particular had spawned. It is noteworthy that the term messiah, or anointed one, occurs more frequently in the literature from this period than at any other time, either before or after. This impression has been further confirmed by the recent publication of more Essene fragments from Qumran, which make it clear that messianic speculation had become intense in the first century, usually taking the form of commentary on, and reinterpretation of, various texts from the scriptures which promised God's future total deliverance of Israel.[3] Side by this with this élite, academic speculation about the future, there were also popular movements of protest which took on a messianic or end-time colouring in their style and approach. These took two different forms. One was for prophet-like figures to offer various signs of God's imminent intervention to right the wrongs of Israel just as he had done in the Exodus from Egypt, and the other was for militant figures to take on themselves the role of liberator, leading armed gangs in guerrilla-style attacks either on the Roman presence or on the Jewish aristocracy, who were seen as collaborators with imperial rule.[4] That these two types could easily merge is evident from one incident in the fourth gospel where, after Jesus' performance of a sign that recalled God's action in feeding Israel in the desert, the people were convinced that he was a prophet, and wanted 'to take him by force and make him king' (Jn 6:14f).

The gospels make clear that Jesus refused, there and elsewhere, to be cast in such a role. Yet the image of this type of messianic pretender was so strong, in the minds of the Jewish aristocracy and the Roman administration alike, that he was eventually crucified for claiming to be 'King of the Jews'. The action must be understood against the background of a climate of fear and suspicion that prevailed in first-century Palestine, especially in the wake of Herod's reign of terror, combined with Roman imperial claims that the emperor was destined to rule the world and restore peace and harmony to humankind. The precise contours of Jesus' vision of the future, and his own contribution to it, are the subject of endless debates over the last two hundred years.[5] Suffice it to say that in terms of the three symbols already

3. John J. Collins, *The Scepter and the Star: The Messiahs of the Dead Sea Scrolls and Other Ancient Literature*, New York and London: Doubleday, 1995.

4. Richard Horsley and John Hanson, *Bandits, Prophets and Messiahs: Popular Movements in the Time of Jesus*, Minneapolis: Winston Press, 1985.

5. Seán Freyne, *Texts, Contexts and Cultures: Essays on Biblical Topics*, Dublin: Veritas, 2002, 106-21.

mentioned, namely, temple, land and Torah, he offered a radically new understanding of how each might function in practice, while retaining their essential point of reference, namely God's care for Israel (and humanity), the fact that his will had been revealed to Israel and that his presence was indeed very near. Gerd Theissen has recently made the helpful suggestion that the Jesus movement might be characterised as a 'democratisation' of the messianic hope, thereby dis-empowering those within Judaism who felt responsible for the maintenance of the Jewish symbols. This description captures the revolutionary nature of Jesus' insights, while also pointing to his indebtedness to early Israel's sense of being a tribal collectivity, based on the promises to Jacob and Moses.[6]

There is no denying that this new vision and the practical programme that it enjoined set the Jesus movement on a collision course with those who were charged with official care for the symbol system. To speak of God's presence and God's forgiveness being accessible among Galilean peasants undermined the centrality of Jerusalem, its temple and its priesthood; to claim that God's wisdom could be learned by observing the processes of nature as much as by intense study of the torah scrolls appeared to make the scribal schools redundant; and to claim that God's kingship was not restricted to this nation alone, but included all people, as Isaiah had long ago envisaged (Is 2:2-4; 49:6) was to disenfranchise the self-appointed messianic freedom fighters whose slogans of 'freedom for Zion' and 'for Jerusalem the holy,' stamped on their coins, had fostered a decidedly xenophobic attitude towards all non-Jews in the region.[7] But the Jesus movement was also on a collision course with Rome, if not in the obvious way of a militaristic revolt. The meek who turned the other cheek were the real peace-makers, not those who imposed the *pax Romana* by force; status and honour were not the preserve of the wealthy, rather it was the poor who were blessed, and real wisdom belonged to the 'little ones,' not those who enjoyed the luxury of the Roman upper-class education. This radical reinterpretation of Roman imperial values

6. Seán Freyne, 'Messiah and Galilee' in *Galilee and Gospel: Collected Essays*, Tübingen: J. C. B. Mohr, 2000, 230-70.

7. Andrea M. Berlin, and Andrew J. Overman, *The First Jewish Revolt: Archaeology, History and Ideology*, London and New York: Routledge, 2002.

was a far greater threat than that posed by the Zealot freedom-fighters, and Pilate obviously sensed it.

Christians in a Jewish World

Since Jesus' movement involved such a democratisation of values and sharing of roles with his followers, its insights and impulses were continued after his death. It is in Jerusalem, not Galilee, that we find them reassembling to continue the challenge which his life and teaching had posed. They were allowed to do so by the Roman authorities, who clearly felt that once the threat of insurrection had been removed the matter was an inner-Jewish one that did not concern them. Soon, divisions that later were to have a far-reaching influence on the movement itself began to emerge, based on cultural differences to which the labels Hellenists and Hebrews are applied (Acts of the Apostles, ch 6). It is important to realise that both these groups were Jews, many of them gathered from the Diaspora in order to experience 'redemption in Zion,' or at least to await its coming. The Hellenists, through their spokesperson Stephen, are represented as speaking against the temple and the law of Moses, thereby no doubt continuing the critique of Jesus, and they were forced to disperse; whereas the Hebrews remained in Jerusalem and, in the figure of their spokesperson James, 'the brother of the Lord', continued a presence there for over thirty years until shortly before the Jewish revolt of 66 CE. The importance of this episode here is the recognition that the Jesus movement did not initially have to involve a radical break with official Judaism. Dissent, critique and dispute were very much part of the Jewish religious experience, even prior to Jesus, and a 'broad church' approach could be adopted provided the institutions as they were known and revered were left intact.

In Jewish eyes Paul is sometimes seen as the great betrayer of his own heritage, the one who transformed the renewal movement of Jesus into a new Hellenistic-style religion. This portrayal of Paul goes back to nineteenth-century German Christian scholarship, with its strong anti-Jewish bias, seeking to explain the rise of Christianity as the result of Greek enlightenment and owing little to its Jewish roots. Ironically, therefore, those Jewish scholars who saw Paul in an un-Jewish way were unwittingly buying into a set of deeply anti-Jewish prejudices. But there are signs of a real change in more recent Pauline scholarship, both

Jewish and Christian. Christian interpreters challenge the image of Paul, the Hellenist, at least insofar as it seeks to deny his Jewish identity. Thus, for example, Martin Hengel, whose *magnum opus* on Judaism and Hellenism might appear to put him in the camp of those nineteenth century German despisers, has stoutly defended the claim that Judaism in all its branches had absorbed many aspects of Greek thinking and philosophy (just as it had previously absorbed Babylonian and Persian influences also) while remaining true to its essential insights and beliefs. He reminds us that we tend to interpret Paul through Luke's eyes, following him on his journeys to the west only and ignoring entirely the fourteen years that Paul spent in the region of Damascus and Arabia, where he certainly was moving in Semitic rather than Greek circles, possibly motivated by Jewish ideas about the restoration of Israel.[8]

Indeed it was with the first Jewish revolt that the deeper differences began to emerge. The involvement of the various branches of Judaism in Palestine, including the erstwhile collaborators, the priestly aristocracy, in the struggle with Rome, meant that those who opted out were suspect. Thus, James, the leader of the Jerusalem community was put to death by the Jerusalem sanhedrin, and soon afterwards the community itself was forced to flee to Pella in Transjordan, presumably to avoid further reprisals. Meanwhile, Peter and Paul were victims of Nero's pogrom against the Christians of Rome, and hence the new movement was in danger of becoming leaderless as the first generation of Jesus' followers passed on. It was in this apparent break that the move to writing an account of 'the things that were brought to fulfillment' among them were recorded for posterity, as Luke in the prologue to his gospel informs us (Lk 1:1-4). Mark's was the earliest of the four gospels that later became authoritative, based, it was claimed, on Peter's preaching in Rome. Nevertheless, its clear message of non-involvement in the struggle against Rome, warning the community to beware of false messiahs and false prophets (Mk 13:22), suggests an original au-

8. Martin Hengel and Anna Marie Schwemer, *Paul between Antioch and Damascus*, London: SCM Press, 1997. See also Edward P. Sanders, *Paul and Palestinian Judaism*, Philadelphia: Fortress Press, 1977; Alan F. Segal, *Paul the Convert: The Apostolate and Apostasy of Saul the Pharisee*, London and New Haven: Yale University Press, 1990; Troels Engberg-Pedersen, (editor), *Paul Beyond the Judaism/Hellenism Divide*, Louisville and London: John Knox Press, 2001.

dience closer to Palestine and the events leading up to the first revolt. This development illustrates the difference of understanding among different groups of what Jewish restoration involved. In contrast to the nationalistic and territorially-based perception of many Jews based on the ancient texts, the early Christians, following Jesus' example, had opted for a prophetic and universalistic interpretation as indicated in such writings as Isaiah. Thus the first decisive steps of what has been aptly described as 'the parting of the ways' had occurred.[9]

The after-effects of the revolt had serious consequences for Jews as well as Christians. At one fell swoop, the temple, priesthood and land had been removed, and all that remained was the torah scroll and the scribes, who were now called on to leave the ivory towers where they pored over ancient texts and lead the beleaguered remnants of the community. It was inevitably a time of ingathering, self-examination, recrimination and boundary-making. For Christians, it meant that their timescale for God's decisive intervention in terms of the return of Jesus had now to be revised. The nations had not come streaming to Zion as Isaiah had envisaged. Instead they had entered the new movement in the cities throughout the Mediterranean world in sufficient numbers to alarm Roman officialdom in provinces such as Bythinia on the Black Sea, North Africa and Asia, giving rise to new persecutions under the emperors Domitian (81-96 CE) and Trajan (98-117 CE). A new model or models of expressing the relationship to the parent had to be developed, now that the very definition of Jews and Judaism was being refashioned by political circumstances.

These turbulent relations are clearly mirrored in both Christian and Jewish sources in the period between 70 and 135 CE. On the Jewish side, most scholarly attention has been devoted to the discussion of the famous *Birkath ha-minim*, the curse on the heretics, banning the Christians from participating in synagogue worship, something that is reflected in the gospel of John also (Jn 9). There is some debate as to whether or not the earliest form of this curse was directed against all Jewish heretics, not just Christians or Jewish Christians.[10] A later version has a spec-

9. James D. G. Dunn, (editor), *Jews and Christians: The Parting of the Ways AD 70-135*, Tübingen: J. C. B. Mohr, 1992.

ific reference to the *Nozrim*/Nazoreans, the usual name for Christians in the Jewish sources, and several references in the second century Christian writer, Justin Martyr, to Jews 'cursing Christ', are indicative of the climate of animosity and hatred that had developed.

On the Christian side, several different responses can be traced in the later writings of the New Testament. While the gospel of Matthew seeks to present the Christian movement as the *fulfilment* of Jewish hopes, especially in its presentation of Jesus as the true messianic teacher of Torah (chs 5-7), the fourth gospel and the epistle to the Hebrews present the new movement as *superseding* an outmoded, 'earthly' Judaism. In the gospel, the temple and the Jewish feasts provide the symbolic framework for the author's lofty theological ideas about Jesus as the incarnation of God, thus developing and applying to Jesus the symbolic notion of the temple as the locus of divine presence. The rituals of the various feasts, particularly those of the feast of Tabernacles/*Succoth,* are used to express in symbolic form what Jesus has to offer as the giver of the Spirit, an outpouring of which was expected in the messianic age. In this presentation there is no denigration of the Jewish background as such, simply the claim that as the *Logos* incarnate 'who had pitched his tent in our midst' (Jn 1:14), Jesus had finally realised the temple's symbolic meaning.[11] The author of Hebrews goes one step further, using a contrasting typology to show that the Jewish rites of the Day of Atonement/*Yom Kippur*, are outmoded and worthless because of the fact that they had to be repeated each year, whereas Christ's death, now interpreted as a sacrifice for sin, occurred once only, but was valid for all time.[12] The third element of the Jewish system, the land, does not feature so prominently in these developing claims of the Christian within a Jewish framework of reference, but Luke, in presenting his ac-

10. William Horbury, 'The Benediction of the Minim and Early Jewish-Christian Controversy' in *Jews and Christians in Contact and Controversy*, Edinburgh: T & T Clark, 1998, 67-110.

11. Adele Reinhartz, 'The Gospel of John: How 'the Jews' Became Part of the Plot' in Paula Fredriksen and Adele Reinhartz (editors), *Jesus, Judaism and Christian Anti-Judaism: Reading the New Testament after the Holocaust*, Louisville and London, 2002, 99-116.

12. Harry Attridge, 'The uses of Antithesis in Hebrews 8-10' in George Nickelsburg and George MacRae, *Christians among Jews and Gentiles*, Philadelphia: Fortress Press, 1986, 1-9.

count of the early Christian mission, especially in the Acts of the Apostles, shows how the centre has shifted from Jerusalem to Rome, 'the end of the earth'. The episode of Stephen and the Hellenists (Acts 6-8) marks an important moment in this transition, and to explain its significance Luke places a speech on the lips of the accused Stephen which claims that God's election is not tied to the land, since his calls to both Abraham and Moses took place outside the land in Mesopotamia and in Egypt.

The backdrop of the Jewish War and its calamitous results for Jews in the homeland lies behind these portrayals. Before we attribute them to Christian *Schadenfreude*, however, we should recall that the fall of Jerusalem and the destruction of its temple was something that was deeply disturbing for all branches of Judaism. As messianic Jews, as the name '*Christianoi*' signifies, they, like other branches of the parent faith, were searching for an explanation of this divine tragedy, God's apparent abandonment of his own and allowing Rome the 'great beast' to be all-conquering (Rev 13). Nevertheless, the self-definition among Christians inevitably meant denigration of the other, especially since the Christians had not taken part in the revolt. Thus, in these early Christian writings, the destruction becomes a sign of God's judgment, a cessation of the promises of the covenant and a punishment for the rejection of God's prophet, Jesus. There were plenty of literary forerunners for this in the Hebrew Scriptures – Isaiah, Jeremiah and Ezekiel had all issued dire warnings in the past and these were seen as realised in the destruction of the first temple by the Babylonians. The fact that gospels like Matthew and John appear to be so stridently anti-Jewish has sometimes been attributed to the fact that they represent a gentile Christianity, which has cut its ties with Judaism and has chosen the path of Greek philosophy rather than on-going dialogue with the Jewish world that gave it birth.[13] However, that construal of Christian theological reflection has to be abandoned for several reasons, not least because Judaism itself did not represent a totally other world of thought separate from Greco-Roman philosophical speculation.

The more appropriate image for the process of differenti-

13. Seán Freyne, 'Vilifying the Other and Defining the Self: Matthew's and John's Anti-Jewish Polemic in Focus' in Jacob Neusner and Ernest Frerichs, (editors), *To See Ourselves as Others See Us: Jews, Christians and 'Others' in Late Antiquity*, Chico, CA: Scholars Press, 1985, 117-44.

ation that was taking place is that of the child who is deeply rooted in a family which itself is going through a major crisis, and who is struggling to get free, while feeling somewhat guilty and therefore strident in dealing with the parent. In this context it is noteworthy that whereas almost every early Christian document of the period between 70 and 135 CE is deeply concerned in one way or another with the Jewish question, the Jewish sources, apart from the Eighteen Benedictions, do not seem to be overly concerned with the issue of the Christians. The emerging pharisaic/rabbinic branch, which alone had survived the crisis and was to be the bridge generation, had another, larger task on its hands, particularly with the failures of the Jewish revolts in Egypt, North Africa and Cyprus in 114 CE, and even more tellingly, the failure of the messianic war of Bar Cochba in 132-35 CE, which had been supported by some at least of the influential rabbis. Whereas there was a past precedent for overcoming the destruction of the first temple, namely, the fact that it had been rebuilt again after 70 years in exile, the final defeat of Bar Cochba, just 70 years after the first revolt, and the building by the emperor Hadrian of a pagan temple to honour Jupiter on the very site of the Jewish temple, presented a new and unprecedented challenge to the Jewish religious imagination. The rabbi/scribe now replaced both the priest with his altar and the freedom fighters with their messianic wars of liberation; only the humble search for God's will in the revealed Torah could point to another way that had to be taken.

Jews in a Christian World: The Fourth Century

Much had occurred in both Jewish and Christian circles between the end of the Bar Cochba revolt and the victory of Constantine in 312 CE which cannot be discussed here. Suffice to say that while both religions were busily engaged in the tasks of sorting out inner struggles and debates, the on-going relationship between the two never receded too far into the background.

The dominant, though not the only strand of Judaism to emerge was that which eventually produced the Mishnah, the foundational Jewish law-book, that was promulgated for all Israel by Rabbi Judah ha-Nasi in Sepphoris in about the year 200 CE. As described by Neusner, this work embodied the insights of the priests, was the work of the scribes and was addressed to Jewish householders living in the land – thus, in a sense, incorporating in one, all three separate symbols from the pre-70 period.[14] It avoided all talk of messiahs or end-time scenarios, ignored the fact that the temple had been destroyed, and proposed a way of sanctification based on the observance of the Torah as this was spelled out to cover every area of life. It was a system built on the idea of bringing one's life into conformity with the perceived order that the creator God had established in the cosmos. It thus attempted to arrange things, people, food and other objects into specific categories and classifications. Impurity or uncleanness was the result of ignoring the rigid boundaries which these classifications established. Thus, grey areas were to be eliminated by exploring the logic of the law to what might appear to an outsider as rather fanciful lengths. Holiness, leading to participation in the world to come, was to be achieved through observance of these various regulations as expressions of the divine will and purpose for the universe. It was, therefore, the result of the exercise of free will by humans, not something that was achieved through sacramental action as in Christianity.

The Mishnah itself consists of six divisions and some seventy tractates, thereby essaying as comprehensive a coverage as possible: agricultural laws to do with the offerings that were to be set aside according to temple practice; festivals and their celebration; contracts; vows; commercial activity in the market place; ways of incurring uncleaness and restoring purity. In many ways this was a highly utopian programme, attempting to live in home and village as though lay persons were priests and observing the degree of purity expected when serving at the temple. The domestic sphere of home and village was thereby transformed into a sacred space. It is by no means clear that the population of Galilee, where the rabbinic schools were now located, accepted such an idealistic agenda at least in whole. There is evidence to suggest that a separate, more popular form of adherence to the Jewish way of life continued in the synagogue worship, the impressive remains of which are now strewn around the countryside, but mainly in Galilee. The architectural style of these buildings, especially the mosaic floors, indicates a greater openness to outside influences than would have been possible at an earlier period when extreme nationalism, bordering on xenophobia, had sought to prevent any contacts

14. Jacob Neusner, *Judaism: the Evidence of the Mishnah*, Chicago: University of Chicago Press, 1981.

between Jews and non-Jews. In addition, there is the mystical strand of Judaism, which is difficult to document for this period, but which certainly existed, and was carried on orally, to resurface later in the middle ages in the great cabalistic compilations of the *Hekhalot*, or Chariot literature.[15]

This potted account of the emerging Jewish worldview must alert Christians, even well-meaning ones, that far from being an outdated religion of the Old Testament, Judaism of the second to the fourth century – as represented in the rabbinic writings – was a living and vibrant tradition, representing a highly creative and imaginative reworking of its own priestly heritage, to meet the challenges of the new situation that faced it after the destruction of the temple. The Mishnah gave rise to intensive study and commentary, culminating in the Palestinian Talmud, and later still the Babylonian Talmud. In addition, commentaries on those parts of the Bible that were significant for the rabbinic point of view, especially Genesis, Leviticus, Numbers and Deuteronomy, were produced. Various rabbis also composed philosophical tractates dealing with many of the issues that were being debated at the time in Greco-Roman circles. Meantime, of course, Christianity had also been developing its own philosophical and theological system. In the second century it had seen off the threat of Gnosticism, with its dualistic understanding of the universe. Trinitarian and christological speculation had been developed under the influence of the Greek philosophical tradition, and awaited further precision that was to come with the Councils of Nicaea (325 CE) and Chalcedon (451 CE).

Theological debate is never far removed from political realities, however, and suddenly the legal standing in the Roman world of the two religions was to undergo both dramatic and subtle changes. As already mentioned, Constantine had opted for the Christian religion, not because of his startling personal conversion, as is often asserted, but because it offered him the best option of uniting both parts of the empire under one state religion. The choice was all the more dramatic because his predecessor, Diocletian, had conducted the most vicious persecution yet on the Christians throughout the east in the years 303-11

15. Lee I. Levine, *Judaism and Hellenism in Antiquity: Conflict or Confluence*, Peabody, Mass.: Hendrickson Publishers, 1998, is an excellent account of these issues.

CE.[16] The fact that Christians were being successful in terms of conversions, even at the highest echelons of Roman society meant that they had to be taken seriously, whereas the Jews had a long-standing position of being tolerated by Roman law, which had never been rescinded despite the two revolts. Jews had rarely aspired to top administrative posts within the empire, and hence, for influential pagans within the imperial court, they did not pose the same threat to their status as did 'the nefarious race' of Christians.

A century earlier, this Christian self-confidence had expressed itself robustly in the words of the former Roman lawyer, turned Christian, Tertullian:

> We are but of yesterday and we have filled everything you have: cities, tenements, forts, towns, exchanges, yes! and camps, tribes, palace, senate, forum. All we have left to you is the temples! (*Apology* 37.4-5)

By contrast, the Jews, especially after the two revolts, posed no such political threat. The following conversation between three rabbis from the Palestinian Talmud shows the contrast with the Christian point of view just cited:

> Rabbi Judah began. 'How splendid are the works of this people [the Romans]. They have built market-places, baths and bridges.
>
> Rabbi Yose said nothing.
>
> Rabbi Simeon bar Yohai answered him: 'Everything they have made they have for themselves: market places for whores; baths to wallow in; bridges to levy tolls.'

Whereas the Christians have a self-confident air in terms of Greco-Roman society, at least in Tertullian's account, one detects the note of resignation in the rabbis' conversation. For them it is a matter, not of taking over Roman popular institutions, but of ignoring their baneful moral influences.

How was the Jewish position altered in the change to a Christian empire? At first there seems to have been no legal change in their status, though pretty soon certain restrictions begin to be imposed. Thus Jews were not allowed to own Christian slaves in case of proselytism from as early as 336 CE. Inter-marriage with a Jew or Jewess was prohibited and by the end of the fourth century Jews were debarred both from acting

16. Ramsey McMullen, *Christianising the Roman Empire, AD 100-400*, New Haven and London: Yale University Press, 1984.

as legal counsels and of testifying against or accusing Christians before a magistrate. Legislation such as this was clearly the beginning of the process whereby Jews would become second-class citizens in a Christian empire, eventually leading to their ghettoisation, even though a decree from the Christian emperor Theodosius I in 393 CE declared that 'the sect of the Jews is forbidden by no law'. The fact that such a decree had to be issued tells its own story.[17]

Apart from the legal situation, there were also other consequences of the arrival of a Christian empire that had a negative impact as far as Jews were concerned. As had happened in the past when Jewish identity was under threat during the Babylonian captivity, the response was an extraordinary outpouring of literature: the Palestinian Talmud, a composite commentary on the Mishnah was produced in the schools of Tiberias and Sepphoris, as were several of the great biblical commentaries already mentioned. Not merely were these works produced, however, as a means of cherishing and preserving for the future their traditions, but their content shows clearly how the Jewish intellectual establishment in Palestine was responding, implicitly at least, to Christian claims, especially through the reintroduction of the notion of the messiah which had been noticeably absent from the Mishnah a century and a half earlier. There, the footprints of the messiah were described as bringing desolation to Galilee and the Golan – a clear reference to the messianic wars against Rome – but, in the later Talmud, the messiah is presented as a teacher figure, Rabbi David rather than King David.[18] This is in striking contrast to the way in which Constantine was being presented as a Christ-like figure by Christian propagandists. The Christ-victim of earlier times had now become the Christ-victor, and Constantine was his embodiment on earth.[19] Likewise, the commentaries on the scriptural texts that were important to the rabbinic system should be

17. Robert Wilken, 'The Jews and Christian Apologetics after Theodosius I's Cunctos Populos' *HTR* 73 (1980) 451-71; Bernard Bachracht, 'The Jewish Community in the Later Roman Empire as seen in the Codex Theodosianus' in *To See Ourselves as Others See Us*, 399-421.
18. Jacob Neusner, *Messiah in Context: Israel's History and Destiny in Formative Judaism*, Philadelphia: Fortress Press, 1984,
19. Alisdair Kee, *Constantine versus Christ*, London: SCM Press, 1982 and H. A. Drake, *A Historical Study and New Translation of Eusebius' Triennial Oration*, Berkeley: University of California Press, 1973.

been noted that the rabbinic system opted for the priestly texts of the pentateuch – Leviticus, Numbers and Deuteronomy in particular – whereas the Christians found that the prophetic texts, especially Isaiah, were the more important. Each set of texts already determined to some extent the hermeneutical perspective of their readers/users. The rabbinic system was based on achieving harmony within an already established order, and therefore looked backwards rather than to the future. The extent to which this choice was determined by the historical experiences of Jewish nationalist aspirations and their eventual eclipse under the Romans, is a moot point. It serves to illustrate the reality that there is no 'pure' religious experience, but one that is always culturally and socially conditioned. In such a situation the danger to be avoided is a reductionism that collapses the experience into social and political realities only, with no enduring significance beyond its transient expression. The distinctive Christian choice of the prophetic tradition was future-oriented, based presumably on Jesus' own consciousness of the imminent coming of God. Thus, the hermeneutical perspective with which the sacred texts were approached was that of promise and fulfilment, emphasising the new reality that was already being experienced and the relegation of the past to a pale shadow of the anticipated completion.

These two strands represent the mainstreams of both faith traditions, but they are by no means exclusive. As Christianity became more at home within the empire from the early fourth century onwards, it lost its prophetic edge; and concern for order, corresponding to that of Rome's, became more important for its new-found role as the state religion. Corresponding to the order that was Rome, was the order of God's city, and the pentateuch with its strong priestly orientation provided the sacred script for this development. Hierarchy became institutionalised and the sacred realm was made to correspond to that of the empire. This was a highly ironic development in view of Christianity's origins as a prophetic movement of protest against the power of the Jerusalem priestly aristocracy. Normative or Rabbinic Judaism was innately suspicious of prophetic movements of protest, since it was these that embroiled the nation in the struggle with Rome, with such disastrous consequences. Yet the prophetic impulse continued to function through the synagogue worship, where readings from the prophets were included with those from the Torah as part of the regular cycle. The Aramaic paraphrases of these readings are preserved in the Targumim, suggesting that the prophetic / apocalyptic voice was not quenched, but found its own channels that would continue to flow – well below the surface, it would seem – until it eventually emerged in the *Hekhaloth* literature of later times.[23]

This return to the origins of Judaism and Christianity has much to contribute to contemporary inter-religious dialogue, since it disabuses us of the idea of a 'golden age' of tolerance and understanding between two world religions. Once this is realised, no unitary model can or should apply, and yet there is much that both traditions can learn from encountering the other as other, since a proper understanding of difference should lead to a deeper appreciation of one's own distinctive features combined with respect for the other. This approach to the history of the relationship in the formative period for both traditions should lead to some reconciliation of memories, without attempting to obliterate the scars of ancient and more recent animosities. Within Judaism itself, the rediscovery of the messianic and mystical traditions, by scholars such as Scholem and Idel, has opened up new possibilities for Christian reappraisal of its own christological formulations. It should no longer be necessary to emphasise a triumphalist christology, especially in view of the rediscovery of the historical Jesus as a thoroughly Jewish figure, by both Christian and Jewish scholars. Here the Islamic witness to Jesus as a prophet, second only to Mohammed, is an interesting contrast to the early Jewish vilification of him as a sorcerer and deceiver. This in turn should lead to a consideration of the strong monotheistic tendencies in all three Abrahamic religions, and to an examination of how this might function to generate an ethic of care for the whole of creation and a sense of respect and inclusiveness for all God's peoples.

23. Moshe Idel, *Messianic Mystics*, New Haven and London: Yale University Press, 1997.

CHAPTER 4

Celtic Culture and Christianity: The Beginnings of the Irish Experience

Terence P McCaughey

In the last decade or two, in spite of all the scientific work done on the extant texts, there has been a remarkable revival of romantic enthusiasm for what is called the 'Celtic Church'. The spiritually parched and jaded, both inside and outside the bounds of the churches, have turned for sustenance to what they understand to be the unpolluted spring water of the early Christian past of these islands. New books, claiming to give access to that past come out each month, it seems – making fanciful but most often unverifiable claims for the peculiar character of that period.[1]

While it is true that Christianity, as it developed in Gaul or Britain or Ireland, did take on a peculiar profile (as it has done in South America, in Asia and in Africa), the fact is that in its essential character, it is most often simply a variant of the Christianity of the Western Empire during the period in question. Furthermore, it should be stated straight away that the term 'Celtic Christianity', which is so often referred to in the past tense only, can probably best be used to mean Christianity as it has been and continues to be, in communities of people speaking one or other of the Celtic languages from the fifth century right down to the present. The forms that Christianity has taken among Welsh speakers in Patagonia or in Nova Scotia among Scottish Gaelic speakers, in Man or in Ireland, in Gaul among the romanised aristocracy, or among the Scottish crofting communities of today (both Catholic and Presbyterian), are as various as the communities themselves. What they have in common is a basic Christian profile and the fact that they spoke or speak a Celtic language. Accordingly, it is probably much better to throw out the unhelpful term 'Celtic Church' and speak instead of the Irish, Welsh, Gaulish or Highland churches.

1. Donald Meek has given a sound critical assessment of this phenomenon in *The Quest for Celtic Christianity*, Garten, Scotland: Handsel, 2000.

If we are to address the subject outlined in the title to this chapter, i.e. 'Celtic culture and Christian faith: the beginnings of the Irish experience', we could do no better than first to address the question: 'What kind of Christianity was it that came to Ireland in the mission of the fifth century?'

I IN SEARCH OF PATRICK

Responding to that question is made an easier task by the fact that the man who appears to have been the most significant figure in that mission has left us two documents he wrote himself.[2] That man is of course Patricius/Patrick, and it is probably the case that those scholars are nearest the mark who consider that he arrived here circa 458-60 CE. Those two writings are, of course, in Latin – but, in the light of what we have already been saying, it is important to note that he was himself a Celt. His first language was British, i.e. a Celtic language. His *Confessio* appears to have been written late on in his time as bishop in Ireland, and it is addressed to his confrères in the church in his native Britain. The second (and shorter) document is an angry letter addressed to a British chief whose name he latinises as 'Coroticus', castigating him for carrying off and enslaving some of Patrick's newly-baptised converts. From these two documents, and from material found in the Irish annals and the *Chronicle of Prosper of Aquitaine*, we can build up a fair amount of hard fact:

1. It appears that Patrick was born and reared on the small estate of his father (a *decurio*) in or near the little Roman town he calls Banna Venta Berniae. It must have been near the coast, possibly not far from the larger Roman town we know as Carlisle.

2. His father was a deacon, and Patrick gives his name as Calpurnius. Deacons at the time had considerable prestige and were excused taxation. His grandfather, Potitus, had been a presbyter.

3. At the age of barely sixteen, Patrick tells us he was cap-

2. These two documents have attracted a great deal of scholarly attention. See Liam de Paor, *Saint Patrick's World: The Christian Culture of Ireland's Apostolic Age*, Dublin: Four Courts Press, 1993, which includes translations into English of Patrick's writings and a number of other relevant more or less contemporary documents, as well as a select bibliography. A more comprehensive, though earlier, bibliography is to be found in J F Kenney, *The Sources for the Early History of Ireland: Ecclesiastical: An Introduction and Guide*, 1929; Dublin: 1979.

tured by Irish raiders and 'carried off into slavery, along with a great number of people'. As an old man, looking back at this time, he saw it as no more than they deserved, considering how indifferent many of them had become to the teaching of their bishops. In old age, of course, and at the end of his spectacular mission in Ireland, he saw his captivity as providential, laying upon him the obligation 'to make known God's wonders to every race under heaven.'

Of the conditions of his service as a slave in Ireland he tells nothing except that he was for six years a herdsman somewhere near a wood called 'Foclut', itself 'near the western sea'. Later writings than his own encourage us to identify this wood as having been on the western shore of Killala Bay in Co Mayo. After six years as a slave, he escaped and after a walk of (he says) two hundred miles, he reached what was presumably the south-east coast. After some difficulties negotiating his acceptance, he secured his passage on a boat carrying dogs to either Gaul or Britain.

4. After some time at home with his own people, in obedience to a dream (which, as told, resembles Paul's night-vision of the young man from Macedonia), Patrick obediently prepared himself to go to Ireland. In spite of objections made (by whom?) against him (on grounds of poor or insufficient education?) Patrick was eventually ordained bishop for Ireland.

5. He gives us some account of his activities in Ireland. But, embedded as they are in his general defence of his ministry here, what he says is often hard to interpret. There is no chronology and no map, and he gives no explanatory notes on the population-groups he refers to by name. However, he does distinguish in Ireland between three named groups: first, the *British* – 'our own people' as he says, writing to fellow-Britons at home; second, the *Scotti* some of whom were clearly Christians long before Patrick was sent to be their bishop; and third, the *Hiberionaces*, among whom he had been a slave, who seem *not* to have been Christianised, and whom he was determined to bring to Christ.

It was almost certainly to the people called the *Scotti* that Patrick came as bishop. However, we can be certain that he was not their first bishop. For, as early as the year 431, a good quarter of a century or more before Patrick returned to Ireland as a free man and a bishop, a deacon of Auxerre called Palladius had been sent by Pope Celestinus *ad Scottos in Christum credentes,* 'to the *Scotti* who believe in Christ'. We do not know how there came to be Christian believers among these *Scotti* at this time.

As far as those in Ireland of British birth and language are concerned, we have a reference in Patrick's *Confession,* where he writes to his own people in Britain about 'those of our race who were born [in Ireland] – we do not know their number'. Nor do we today – any more than we know how they came to be in Ireland in the first place. Perhaps they came in the same way as Patrick himself had done at first, i.e., as captives, or it may be that some were the descendents of deserters from the army or were evading imperial tax-gatherers in Britain. Many of these could be more or less Christian. They and the converts they made – more often as a result of marriage into the local population than of proselytisation – had originally been 'free' persons in the province of Britain and would therefore be eligible in the eyes of church authorities in Britain to ask for a bishop.[3] Pope Celestinus, who sent Palladius in 431, had himself laid it down that a bishop should be sent only to a community who wanted one. It follows, therefore, that there was in existence in Ireland at the end of the third decade of the fifth century, a community of Christian *Scotti,* small perhaps, but sufficiently substantial to make such a request or application.

But there is another important point about bishops at this time, i.e., that bishops in the fifth century were pastoral, *not* missionary figures. So Palladius in 431, like Patrick in c. 458, was not sent as a missionary. No Pope earlier than Gregory the Great (d 604) is known to have sent people out on missionary work.

Certainly Prosper of Aquitaine, in his *De Vocatione Gentium,* does speak of the way Christians managed to cross the imperial frontier. In one of his letters (*Ep* 199) Augustine speaks of tribesmen from the interior of Africa who were telling him of countless barbarians who had never heard the gospel. He is, however, gratified to learn that, where Roman prefects have been appointed to replace traditional leaders, the people are inclined to take on the religion of the prefects. Clovis and the Franks appear to have been won over at the very end of the fifth century, and, at the other end of the Empire, a Saracen leader on the imperial border

3. See C. Thomas, *Christianity in Roman and sub-Roman Britain to 500 AD,* London: 1979; R. P. C. Hanson, *St Patrick: His Origins and Career,* London: 1968.

was baptised in 512. But, by and large, there was no formal mission, and certainly none beyond the frontiers, during the fifth century.

It is certain, therefore, that it is as a pastoral bishop to the *Scotti* that Patrick returned to Ireland in c. 458. His *Confession*, written some thirty years later, is in large measure his response to those in his native Britain who questioned the decision he had apparently made after reaching Ireland, to extend his mandate by becoming an actual missionary to those tribes in Ireland who had not previously heard the gospel.

II PATRICK'S CULTURAL BACKGROUND

But let us return for a moment to a consideration of Patrick's home background. He grew up in a world which, from north Africa to northern Britain and eastward to the Holy Land itself, was uncertain about what the future might hold. Everywhere there was anxiety about what would happen if or when the unthinkable came to pass – as it did, when Alaric entered the city of Rome in 410.

Families like Patrick's in northern Britain, who formed the leadership in their little *civitas* in Banna Venta Berniae, had begun the process of accommodating themselves to life without the Roman military presence and infrastructure a good while before Rome itself fell to Alaric. The Roman presence in a place just south of the wall of Hadrian in north Britain was probably never as significant as it had been in the south of the island since the beginning of the third century. Certainly we know that the Christian community was strong enough in Britain for it to send British bishops in the fourth century to the councils held in Arles, Rimini and Sardica. There were Christians in south Britain wealthy enough to be villa-owners, e.g. at Lullingstone in Kent, with house churches on their estate. A fourth century roundel mosaic at Hinton St Mary in Dorset has at its centre what is said to be one of the first 'portraits' of Christ to be found anywhere in the Empire.[4]

We may guess that Patrick's home place in the north-west was a good deal less affluent than the romanised centres of the south. But, in a modest way, his people too were romanised.

4. Charles Thomas, *Britain and Ireland in Early Christian Times AD 400-800*, London: Thames and Hudson, 1971, 72-75, and plates 53-56.

But in 409 CE, i.e., five or ten years before Patrick was born, the Emperor Honorius had brought himself to write to the British Roman towns, urging them to arrange for their own defence. Patrick's father and grandfather and their contemporaries would scarcely have needed the Emperor's warning, however – even supposing that they ever actually heard it. For, as early as 367, according to the annals, the Picts had breached Hadrian's wall – even though they were subsequently pushed back to the north. In 383 Magnus Maximus, the Spaniard who was Roman commander-in-chief in the province of Britannia, actually left Britain for Gaul, to pursue his personal ambitions on the mainland of Europe. He took most of the garrison with him.

Even before the Roman withdrawal, life and schooling in the likes of Banna Venta Berniae were probably simpler or more basic than they were further south. Nevertheless, we may assume that the education a boy like Patrick was offered, up to the time of his capture at sixteen years of age, was essentially a peripheral or provincial version of what was on offer in more sophisticated centres in southern Britain or in Gaul. Experts on the Latin of the period are agreed that Patrick's Latin is not of the highest quality, but Dr Ludwig Bieler was of the view that it is of a kind with the Latin written by many of his contemporaries in Western Europe.[5] Thirty-five years ago, Nora Chadwick warned readers against taking Patrick's presentation of himself as *peccator/rusticus/rusticissimus* too seriously. She pointed out that, in so doing, Patrick actually shows himself to be a person perfectly at home with the self-deprecatory epistolary conventions of the time.[6] The learned Gaulish Paulinus of Nola and his spouse Therasia, end the letters which they signed jointly, 'Paulinus et Therasia, *peccatores*'.

Three points about Patrick's own particular education and experience should be noted: first, his education was arrested suddenly at 16 years of age; second, he tells us himself that he had not been paying a lot of attention to his teachers; and third, he was growing up at a time when British leaders (whether romanised or not) were seeking to fill the power-vacuum caused by

5. Bieler makes this observation at several points in *Libri Epistolarum Sancti Patricii Episcopi, Part II: Commentary,* Dublin: Irish Manuscripts Commision, 1952.

6. N. K. Chadwick, *The Age of the Saints in the Early Celtic Church,* Oxford: OUP, 1961.

Roman withdrawal. It is likely too that native culture and religion were reasserting themselves among the young in the abandoned provinces.

III THE CHURCHES IN BRITAIN AND GAUL

The Christian churches of Britain and Gaul were essentially urban. A bishop had his *sedes* in the *civitas*, and it was not expected that he would move from it. Kathleen Hughes describes fifth century Gaulish Christianity as 'a socially respectable religion, professed by many of the well-to-do and well-born'. Gaulish bishops appear to have been drawn from a limited circle of families, 'well used to performing a number of social services. So it was that, when the Romans left, they were the natural leaders to fill the administrative vacuum and even arrange defence.[7]

The Christian families of Gaul had earlier, over the generations, made the transition from Gaulish to Gallo-Roman culture fairly painlessly – identifying their own deities with those of Roman religion. The transition to Christianity had not been traumatic either; they dumped as little as possible of classic learning when they embraced the new faith.

Nora Chadwick has assembled a delightful portrait of one such fourth-century romanised, Christianised Gaul – Ausonius of Bordeaux, son of a local senator, educated in the Roman school of rhetoric – in himself a harmonious blend of Christianity and classic Latin literary culture.[8] But, already in Ausonius' old age, a new movement was sweeping northwards through Gaul, calling in question the civilised *modus vivendi* which Ausonius represented. It was to sweep northwards, ready (as it were) to confront the barbarians infiltrating into Gaul from the north and east. It was a movement made up of church people who had committed themselves to the rigours of the ascetic movement. It is represented, in urbane form, by Ausonius' own pupil Paulinus of Nola and, in more militant form, by Martin the ex-soldier turned ascetic who, on being elected bishop of Tours, refused to live in the former bishop's house, preferring the discomfort of the nearby cave which is still to be seen on the bank of the Loire.

---

7. Kathleen Hughes, *The Church in Early Irish Society*, London: Methuen, 1966, 17f.

8. N.K. Chadwick, *Poetry and Letters in Early Christian Gaul*, London: 1955. See also Hagith Sivan, *Ausonius of Bordeaux: Genesis of a Gallic Aristocracy*, London: Routledge, 1993.

The asceticism of people like Martin aimed, of course, to recapture the single-mindedness and supreme commitment of the martyrs of two hundred years earlier, by imposing upon themselves the greatest mortifications they could think of. This movement was spreading northward from the monasteries of Marseilles and of the island of Lérins which lies off the coast from the modern Cannes.

While the Gallo-Roman bishops of good family were organising the Gaulish *civitates* to defend themselves in the wake of Roman withdrawal, the ascetics, fanning out from Lérins were internalising the faith and summoning their adherents to another kind of battle altogether. Faustus of Riez, in one of his sermons addressed to the monks of Lérins, identifies their monastery as itself a *castra* (military camp), but of a new kind, inviting the conclusion that, in the administrative defence preparations undertaken by the Gallo-Roman bishops on the one hand, and in the call out of the world and on to the spiritual battlefield on the other, we are observing two alternative responses to the great challenge of the time, already referred to.[9] And that challenge was about how to cope, how to sustain Christian obedience, in a world controlled by the barbarians.

As everyone knows, these were not the only responses offered by people contemplating this appalling abyss. Far away in north Africa, Augustine the bishop of Hippo, watched what was happening and, in 413 – three years after the sack of Rome – and for the next thirteen years wrote his long book *The City of God*. This book was in part a rebuttal of the view that Rome had fallen because the Christians had encouraged citizens to foresake the old gods of the city. Augustine identified the causes in a different way, in the sins of the city. He was as acutely aware as Faustus of the part their sins had played in the disaster. But he recognised that there was and is another city which survives the disaster. For the city which, as he says, 'gave us birth according to the flesh' and which still survives in ruinous state, he prays 'that it may receive a spiritual birth and, together with us, pass into eternity'.

Patrick's childhood and youth were passed in the twilight following Rome's irreversible withdrawal from the British

9. For a helpful discussion of Faustus (died c. 492) see Henry Chadwick, *The Church in Ancient Society: From Galilee to Gregory the Great*, Oxford: OUP, 2001, 646-647.

province. He then spent six years as a slave on the western coast of Ireland beyond which, of course, it was believed no one lived. According to the evidence of his own writings, Patrick came excitedly to entertain the possibility that to him (of all unlikely people) it had fallen to fulfil the prophecies of scripture, by bringing these remotest and most peripheral of all people to Christ. It is hardly an accident that he rounds up his anthology of scripture texts cited to defend this unprecedented mission of his, with this one: 'This gospel shall be preached throughout the whole world as a testimony to the nations: *and then the end shall come*' (Mt 24:14). Did he dare to believe that he was the one called to be the instrument of the End? Was this his particular response to the *angst* of the time?

We know (because he tells us) that among the *Scotti*, to whom he was sent as bishop before ever he took the further step, for which he was criticised back home in Britain, of striking westward to evangelise the *Hiberionaces*, that from the beginning of his sojourn, he had received 'sons and daughters of the Irish (*Scotti*) Kings and underkings' to be 'monks and virgins of Christ'. He singles out one 'mature and [sic!] most beautiful lady of the *Scotti*' for mention, whom he baptised and (perhaps following Jerome's example) set her apart as a 'virgin of Christ'. And there were also British widows and women living in chastity.'[10]

Unfortunately, he tells us very little about his mission to the *Hiberionaces* which so radically broke with the practice of the time. He mentions that he sometimes went in danger of his life, but from whom he does not say. He does tell us, however, that he was accompanied on his travels by 'the sons of kings' and that he engaged in the exchange of gifts. These facts seem to have surprised and even shocked his fellow-countrymen in Britain. He explains the giving and receiving of gifts by reference to his having sold up his patrimony at home to finance himself in Ireland, in a culture which subsisted on the patterned exchange of gifts. But the accompanying 'sons of kings' suggests the travel arrangements of the *filid*, jurists and leeches who, accompanied by their *dámh* (company), alone of all classes, traversed the numerous borders between the 150-200 *túatha* (tribal units) into which Ireland was divided. Patrick had observed this practice during his captivity. It may be that he had recognised

10. Liam de Paor, *Saint Patrick's World*, 104

that travelling in the guise of a *fili* was the condition of travelling the length of the land at all.

He has left us no account at all of how he approached the pagan Irish or how he made his appeal to them. How did he convince them to abandon the gods who (often in heavily euhemerised forms) peer out at us in some of the sagas, and whose images have survived here and there in remote corners of the country, like Boa Island on Loch Erne? Insofar as they had served the people well, how was it possible to persuade the people to forsake them and risk their wrath and punishment?

In one of Gregory the Great's letters to Augustine of Canterbury, he counsels that pagan practices should be changed only gradually. Otherwise, the main means should be (1) preaching, and (2) coercion. Only preaching was open to Patrick; coercion was presumably out of the question. Besides, coercion sooner or later provokes reaction, and if there is one over-ridingly significant fact about early Irish Christianity, it is that there were no martyrdoms. By and large, the new faith slotted into Irish society without causing the serious social dislocation which inevitably provokes martyrdoms. It is hard to resist the conclusion that the absence of martyrdoms is in large measure due to the peculiar experience and acquired wisdom of Patrick himself, who, in the course of six years spent as a slave, had mastered the language and had had the opportunity to observe how Irish society worked from a vantage-point at the very bottom of the social scale.

Professor E. A. Thompson discourages the notion that Patrick was helped in his proselytising activities by 'the enormous reputation of the Roman Empire among the barbarians who crowded on its frontiers'.[11] However, with due deference to his view, we may note that there is now sufficient evidence to suggest that some people in Ireland were aware at least of the Roman/romanised civilisation on the island to the east and perhaps on the mainland beyond, and were sufficiently aware to raid it for slaves and artefacts. Liam de Paor goes so far as to claim that 'Roman influence was to be the principal agent of change in the transformation of society', and points to the archaeological evidence for export and import trade with the province of Britain at this very period.[12]

12. Liam de Paor, *Saint Patrick's World*, see especially chapter 3.
11. E. A. Thompson, *Who Was St Patrick?* Woodbridge: 1985, 14.

Furthermore, it appears to be the case that confederations of the small tribal units known as *túatha* began to form in the Ireland of the fourth and fifth centuries. They may have been formed precisely to engage in the kind of raiding of Britain to which the youthful Patrick fell victim. Many of the slaves they brought back to Ireland were Christian. By the mid-fifth century, however, the leaders of these Irish raiding-bands began to find themselves deprived of plunderable Roman settlements on west-coast Britain and, probably as a result, turned inwards to engage in internal conquest and expansion. This would certainly explain the growth of confederations at this time, in which an over-arching *dynastic* organisation began to be superimposed upon the earlier patchwork of *túatha* or small tribal units. The evidence suggests that this political change was at a fairly fluid stage of development during and just after Patrick's ministry.

Patrick and his colleagues came to Ireland at a time of drastic internal change when the new dynasts were beginning to control areas which comprised a number (sometimes quite a large number) of *túatha*. The famous penannular brooches which the Irish upper orders began to wear were probably adapted from the gap-ring bronze pins which Romans of the military province fastened their cloaks with. Other apparent adaptations include the heavy belt-buckles, straps and harnesses etc. of half-Roman, half-barbarian fashion. The relatively new Irish over-kings were developing a style and a confidence which judicious Christian bishops with Patrick's kind of background – in Britain and perhaps Gaul – could and no doubt did assist by helping to plug them into a higher civilisation. The inclination to do just that may explain the remarkable fact that the learned class of Ireland who had, from time immemorial, passed on and cultivated the great body of learning (*senchus*) which comprised what we would call law, poetry, genealogy, medicine, prophecy and much else, seem to have adopted eagerly and quickly the new communication medium of reading and writing which the Christian missionaries brought with them.

The new dynasts of this period have been culturally described as 'post-Roman' without ever having been Roman! (This may be the first of many times in Irish history when we have felt the after-effects of a paradigm-shift we actually *missed*.) The new political entities they were creating, however, needed more than mere wealth and learning to give an ideological basis to the new polity. It seems more than likely that an increasingly self-confident church saw itself as providing just that.

Many of the rulers of these emergent confederations of *túatha* (*mór-thúatha*, as they came to be called) belonged to families which had been head-men or kings of individual *túatha*. Perhaps most of them had been. Each *rí*, or head-man, was a sacral figure who had been cultically 'mated' with the sovereignty or goddess of the land at his inauguration. The title of this inauguration ceremony was *feis* (spending the night with) or *banais* (marriage). In it, the part of the deity of the land was, it seems, played by the *ollamh* or *fili*. It appears that the 'mating' (symbolic, but perhaps not entirely so) took place at this ceremony – as is described, in the twelfth century, perhaps in exaggerated terms, with reference to the inauguration of the chief of the Cenél gConaill, by Giraldus Cambrensis.[13]

Clearly a ceremony of this kind was going to be difficult or almost impossible to Christianise. However, an opportunity to do so by at least slotting a bishop into the proceedings seems to have offered itself in the fifth-sixth centuries. The new confederations of *túatha*, which were emerging during this period, clearly required a broadly supportive ideology to undergird them, as well as new rituals and ceremonies to legitimate them. Many inauguration-sites of small units survive, but the new confederations required their own, and it would appear that they often found one at a site within their sphere of influence where the other world had from time immemorial been deemed to be specially and even dangerously present, e.g., Cruachu in the west or Tara in the east. This appears to be the case with the Uí Néill, from whom Colum Cille came, and the Uí Chonchubhair in Connacht, with reference to Tara and Cruachu respectively. One thing is clear, however. By the time what scanty accounts as we have of inauguration came to be written, the bishop was established as fully participant, side by side with the *ollamh*, and the proceedings had long been Christianised.

Earlier, as we read in a contemporary account, the *fili* (poet) alone went into the inauguration place with the one to be proclaimed and inaugurated. With reference to the inauguration of Ó Conchubhair, circa 1450, one source states that, although bishops and *comharba* (successors of ecclesiastics) were in attendance

13. For an account and discussion of this, see F. J. Byrne, *Irish Kings and High-Kings*, London: Batsford, 1973, 7-27.

together with sub-kings of Connacht, 'it is Ó Maolchonaire [the poet] who is entitled to give the rod of kingship into his hand at his inauguration, and none of the nobles of Connacht has a right to be with him on the mound save Ó Maolchonaire who inaugurates him and Ó Connachtain who keeps the gate of the mound.'[14]

Recently, an attempt has been made to identify a considerable number of inauguration-sites across the country – most of them of great antiquity. But no such site was on offer to those who crossed the sea from north-east Antrim in the fifth century to establish a new political entity in the new Dál Riata in western Scotland. In Adomnán' s *Life of Columba,* written in 597 to mark the first centenary of Colum Cille's death, we have an account of how Colum Cille rose to the occasion, and provided in Iona an inauguration-place of a novel kind for the leaders of the Scottish Dál Riata. He inaugurated Aedán mac Gabráin, we are told, not according to ancient pre-Christian rites, but by anointing him at Iona in imitation of the inauguration of the Kings of Judah.[15]

Colum Cille was alive to the changes that were taking place in Ireland and Gaelic Scotland, and particularly to the possible ways in which the ambitious expansionism of his own Uí Néill and the aims of an expanding monastery-centred church could be made to serve one another. Within the territories controlled by the northern Uí Néill (to which he himself belonged) and the southern Uí Néill (which stretched right down into the midlands) he set up a network of monasteries which were well-established by the time he left Ireland for Scotland in 563. The Uí Néill were probably expected to protect the monasteries and the monasteries in return were expected to provide the Uí Néill with something of an ideological and religious support-frame.

Much ink has been spilt on the alleged change from an episcopally-centred church of Patrick's time to the monastery-centred church of succeeding centuries. Recent scholarship is less inclined to say that bishops lost out to abbots in the post-Patrician church or anything of the sort. Wherever the truth may lie in that controversy, it is worthwhile to recall: first, that there were in the fifth century (and for a long time thereafter), no urban centres in Ireland in which a 'bishop' as the contemporaries of Patrick in Britain or Gaul would have understood the

14. ibid., 15-16.

15. Adomnán of Iona, *Life of St Columba,* translated by Richard Sharpe, London: Penguin, 1991, 355-6.

office, could have his *sedes*. Second, that, as we have seen, Patrick himself was a bishop without a *sedes* and presumably ministered to a very scattered flock of *Scotti* at first. Third, Patrick was not unaware of the ascetic and monastic movement, as it had taken root in Gaul and Britain. His *Confession* alludes to such in his own church in Ireland.

Physically, the early Irish monasteries of the centuries after Patrick seem to have resembled the homestead of a *bóaire* ('cow-lord', a substantial representative of the free class), living within his own *lios* or pallisaded hill-fort, of which so many have survived round the Irish countryside. The practice of succession in secular society was not primogeniture, and this meant that it could be applied more or less without alteration to succession in the abbacy. The set-up of an early monastery was (with obvious differences, like the all-male character of it) so like that of a *bóaire* that abbots were sometimes tempted to behave in a way that was altogether too like the conduct of their secular cousins – even to the extent of taking up arms against their neighbours. They had come to be conformed to the surrounding world.

Insofar as the monastic church of early Ireland was so well slotted into the aristocratic patriarchal pastoral society, under a leadership drawn almost exclusively from the higher echelons of that society, it was no doubt tempted to succumb to an attitude of uncritical worldliness. However, two things at least militated against this. First, it is a fact that, deep within the self-awareness of the ascetic movement to which the monasteries were committed, was a critical and counter-cultural strain – which was its origin and which it never wholly lost. There are many examples of this. One notable example would be the way in which the practice of setting guilty or suspected persons adrift in a boat to allow the sea to take the voyagers where it would, or even to drown them, was transformed by the ascetic movement into *peregrinatio pro Christo* (becoming a voyager for Christ). The voyager came to be seen as abandoning home and loved ones and allowing the spirit to take him to some unknown destination, as what they called a *miles insulanus* (an island soldier), and all for Christ's sake.

Second, it is important to remember that the monasteries were operating within and yet on the edge of a warrior society. Many (perhaps most) of the monks came themselves from the warrior caste, but the self-consciously aware among them had joined the monastery precisely in order to take part in the spiritual warfare to which Faustus and Cassian had summoned the monks of Lérins and Marseilles.

Those who went on *peregrinatio* were, as has been noted, often referred to as 'island soldiers'. The literature again and again gives expression to a seriously critical attitude towards the assumptions and the practices of the warrior society. One has only to think of the story entitled *Buile Shuibhne/The battle-frenzy of Suibhne* in which Suibhne, King of Dál nAraide levitates out of the battle of Magh Rath (Moira) and achieves a kind of ambivalent sanctity (and sanity?) which he did not have before, living in the trees and in the wild.[16] Or one may think of the Old Irish poem, often sung in churches today in Eleanor Hull's version, which begins, 'Be Thou my vision …' But the word translated by Eleanor Hull as 'vision' is in fact the word used of 'battle-frenzy' in *Buile Shuibhne* and other texts. It is the frenzy that fills Cú Chulainn and many another before battle. What the Old Irish poet, who was probably a monk, is praying for in the poem is that he should be filled with that kind of frenzy as he engages in the battle of faith. He goes on to ask (st 5) that God should be his battle-shield and his sword (st 6), his shelter and fortress. Certainly, in st 14 he speaks of 'victory', but this is a paradoxical victory in which the victor laments and rejoices at once:

> Beloved Father, hear my lamentation –
> timely is the cry of this miserable wretch.

The victor in this battle does not look for loot or for power over others (st 10):

> O God, you be my noble estate!
> I do not seek men or dead wealth (captives or loot).

By this frenzy the poet hopes to see things as they really are:

> O heart of my heart, whatever befalls me,
> O ruler of all, be my battle-frenzy! (*Roptu mo boile*)[17]

The *Amra* (i.e., elegy) on Colum Cille, composed in 597 on hearing of his death, by Dallán Forgaill, chief poet of Ireland, and commissioned by Colum Cille's cousin the high-King, speaks of

---

16. J. G. O'Keeffe ed, *Buile Suibhne Geilt: A Middle-Irish Romance*, Irish Text Society, Vol 12, 1913.

17. See Terence P McCaughey, 'Social World as Sacrament,' in David Brown and Ann Loades, eds, *The Sense of the Sacramental: Movement and Measure in Art and Music, Place and Time*, London: SPCK, 1995, 189-199.

him in revealing terms.[18] He praises him in accordance with the rhetorical norms of the panegyric of kings and warriors, i.e., in terms of his genealogy and descent, as 'descendant of Conall', as 'son of Feidhlimid', as 'kinsman of Niall'. He praises him as a 'wise man' and 'teacher', but he also calls him a *nia* (champion), thus indicating perhaps the sphere in which this champion's valour found expression.

Those who entered the monasteries of early Christian Ireland, as we have seen, were setting themselves under a regime of suffering and endurance comparable with what the martyrs had endured in earlier centuries at the hands of others. Their communal life, however often it fell short of its own highest ideals in learning, prayer or practice, was nevertheless by intention a lived-out counter-cultural critique of the warrior society, in the midst of which the members of monastic communities were set and from which they had come.

Their way of life may perhaps be seen as their answer to the question which the bishops of Gaul, the members of the ascetic movement, and individuals like Augustine, Pelagius, Jerome and Patrick had answered in other ways, i.e., What is to be done when or if ever the barbarians take over?

18. See Brian Lacey, ed., Manus O'Donnell, *The Life of Colum Cille*, Dublin: Four Courts, 1998, 210f.

CHAPTER 5

Internalising the Primal Other: Aboriginal Religion and European Christianity*

John D'Arcy May

The discovery the 'I' makes of the 'others' inhabiting it is accompanied by the more alarming assertion of the disappearance of the 'I' into the 'we' characteristic of all totalitarian regimes.

— Tzvetan Todorov[1]

There exist records – photographic and even cinematographic – of the moment of contact between Europeans and peoples who had hitherto had no knowledge of a world outside their own geographical areas. These pictures, capturing expressions of mingled fear and curiosity, of limitless wonderment and the courage to face the radically new, invite profound meditation. In the case of the arrival of European colonists in what was variously known two centuries ago as *terra australis incognita, Tierra Australia del Espiritu Santo,* or simply New Holland, only written records survive alongside some pen and ink drawings, but they enable us to reconstruct much of what was thought and done in those first fatal weeks and months after the landing of the First Fleet at Botany Bay on 18 January 1788. The outer story of first contact is instructive enough, and we will return to it presently; the historian of the convict settlements, Robert Hughes, speaks of Europeans discovering their 'geographical unconscious'.[2] But the real aim of this chapter is to penetrate to the inner story of contact between Europeans and Aboriginals. We will see that in a very real sense this first contact is only now beginning to take place.

*This chapter anticipates the discussion in John D'Arcy May, *Transcendence and Violence: The Encounter of Buddhist, Christian and Primal Traditions*, London and New York: Continuum, 2003, 25-41.

1. Tzvetan Todorov, *The Conquest of America: The Question of the Other*, New York: Harper & Row, 1989, 251.
2. Robert Hughes, *The Fatal Shore: A History of the Transportation of Convicts to Australia 1787-1868*, London: Pan Books, 1988, chap. 3.

The Europeans in question were almost exclusively inhabitants of Britain and Ireland and adherents of the main Christian traditions (though there were also some Jews; the first Irish convicts left on the *Queen* in 1791, and 50,000 had been transported by 1852).[3] For me, of Australian birth but Irish descent, living as a Pacific Islander on this European island, this creates a peculiar ambivalence in my relationship with both the Old World and the New: I am not unambiguously 'European'. Though this, in turn, complicates my relationship to Australia and its Aboriginal people, it does not remove my responsibility as an ecumenical theologian to try to come to grips with this paradigmatic European encounter with the radically 'Other', both human and religious.

None of the terms in my title can be taken for granted; each needs explanation, which it will receive in reverse order: first the failure of European Christianity in this encounter, then the resilience of Aboriginal religion until today, and finally the task still awaiting 'us' – Europeans and Australians – of confronting the 'primal Other' which we thought we had outgrown, but which re-entered our awareness during the era of colonial conquest and still remains to be 'discovered', no longer as a zoological curiosity but as a component, in some sense, of our own humanity.

1. The Failure of European Theology

There is a story to be told here. I can only sketch a part of it, for I wish to move beyond it to concentrate on its significance for our Christianity, our theology now. We need have no illusions about the Christian convictions of those whom the First Fleet under Governor Phillip deposited on the 'fatal shore' of Botany Bay on that fateful January day in 1788. His successor, Governor Hunter, wrote that 'a more wicked, abandoned and irreligious set of people have never been brought together in any part of the world.'[4] The officers were as appalled as the convicts at the harshness of the landscape, the severity of the climate, and their inability to make contact with the New Hollanders, as the Aborigines were then called. The best educated and most ideal-

3. Cf John N. Molony, *The Penguin Bicentennial History of Australia: The Story of 200 Years*, Ringwood: Viking, 1987, 6, 16-17.

4. Cited by John Harris, *One Blood. 200 Years of Aboriginal Encounter with Christianity: A Story of Hope*, Sutherland: Albatross Books, 1990, 37.

istic among the settlers were children of the Enlightenment; indeed, they were self-conscious in their application of its humanitarian principles, and Phillip was under explicit instructions 'by every possible means to open an intercourse' with the Aborigines and to 'conciliate their affections', enjoining everyone to 'live in amity and kindness with them' and punishing anyone who should 'wantonly destroy them'.[5] This he conscientiously tried to do, and his admiration for them was as genuine as his ignorance was profound. The result was tragedy. As the weeks slipped by, and incomprehension turned into exasperation, some of the convicts reacted violently to what, in their fear of the unknown, they took to be provocations by the Aborigines, who promptly retaliated by spearing cattle and men. According to John Harris,

> [a]lthough it can no longer be proven, it is virtually certain that the first acts of aggression in the long war between whites and blacks were committed by white colonists, and that the first deaths were Aboriginal, unrecorded like the majority of subsequent Aboriginal deaths ... It was the general opinion ... that 'the natives are not the aggressors'.[6]

The Governor resorted to that well-tried standby of colonial rulers, the punitive expedition. The officer entrusted with carrying out the first of these, Captain Watkin Tench, was a humane and thoughtful Christian. He remonstrated with Phillip about the morality of such harsh retaliation, and when he failed to find any culprits in the impenetrable bush, nothing more was said. But two precedents had been set: crime, even on the part of ignorant savages, merited punishment; but under the extraordinary circumstances then prevailing, such retribution raised moral issues which had yet to be debated. It also raised the issue of simply understanding a way of life so utterly different from anything Europeans had encountered before, even after three centuries of colonialism.

Two fundamental misconceptions bedevilled the 'theology' which marked out the first settlers as children of their time, and they continued to characterise the much more explicit theology of the first missionaries to the Aborigines, who did not arrive till

---

5. Cited by W. E. H. Stanner, 'The History of Indifference Thus Begins', in *White Man Got No Dreaming: Essays 1938-1973*, Canberra: Australian National University Press, 1979, 165-191; 165.
6. Harris, 37.

more than thirty years later. The first was the Enlightenment ideal of the Noble Savage, the child of nature unspoiled by what a later author was to call 'the first taint of civilisation' in the Pacific.[7] This idea of an ideal humanity proved impossible to reconcile with the reality of Aboriginal life as abundantly documented by the whites, even the most highly principled among them, in overwhelmingly negative terms. The Aborigines were almost unanimously located at the lower end of the Chain of Being. There was earnest debate about whether they were human at all.[8]

The second misconception concerned the relationship between civilisation and evangelisation. There were those who debated which should come first, but most of the educated Christians simply assumed their interdependence and regarded civilisation – which invariably meant Europeanisation; attempts were soon made to 'Europeanise' even the landscape and the fauna – as the indispensable precondition for receiving the gospel. The conclusion was easy to draw that the Aborigines (like the Irish in the eyes of the first Jesuits to land in Donegal!) were 'as yet beyond the power of Christ to save'. Samuel Marsden, the most forceful and influential clergyman of Sydney's early days, declared:

> The Aborigines are the most degraded of the human race ... the time is not yet arrived for them to receive the great blessings of civilisation and the knowledge of Christianity.[9]

To their credit, the missionaries never went to the length of exonerating the brutality of pastoralists and the hostility of the secular press by acquiescing in the prevailing view that the Aborigines were sub-human and could therefore be disposed of like the native flora and fauna. Archbishop Polding, among others, firmly asserted that they had immortal souls, and the verse from the Acts of the Apostles, 'God hath made of one blood all nations of men for to dwell on all the face of the earth' (17:26), is cited again and again in letters and diaries of the period.[10] There

7. Francis X. Hezel SJ, *The First Taint of Civilization: A History of the Caroline and Marshall Islands in Pre-Colonial Days, 1521-1885*, Honolulu: University of Hawaii Press, 1983.

8. See the extensive documentation compiled by Henry Reynolds, *Dispossession: Black Australians and White Invaders*, Sydney: Allen & Unwin, 1989, especially chap 4.

9. Cited in Harris, 22.

10. Cf Harris, 33-4.

were even those who raised the question of the Europeans' right to invade the continent in the first place.[11] The standard biblical apology for racism was that the darker races stand under the curse of Ham (Gen 9:10), which was given a global interpretation, and the imagery of black for evil, white for virtue occurs frequently.[12] The terminology of denigration was often taken directly from the simian imagery used to portray the Irish as brutish savages.[13] The Aborigines, in short, had to be civilised, and the best means to achieve this was to take people away from their land, on which they performed unspeakable ceremonies, and to 'rescue' children from their benighted parents. Thus began the sorry story of Aboriginal reserves and children's homes which was to continue well into the 1960s. The unquestioned assumption that assimilation was prerequisite for salvation never ceased to determine both missionary and government policy towards Aborigines.

The enormity of the tragedy that sprang from this failure to recognise the humanity of the Aborigines and the integrity of their culture is only now being revealed. As Harris rightly points out, '[t]he missionaries' own belief system presented them with an almost insurmountable barrier to the achievement of their aims',[14] just as their instinctive ethnocentricity prevented them from understanding Aboriginal culture. No one in the early nineteenth century had any clear conception that the small bands which made up the kinship and language groups had to keep moving in order to follow the seasons and the location of game, for they were nomadic hunter-gatherers who had no need of agriculture or the domestication of animals.[15] In the eyes of the settlers, however, this fact alone made them uncivilised, for everyone knew that, as Marsden put it, people who had no material wants and lived by sharing rather than owning property must be savages (the Irish, by this time, were regarded as 'sav-

11. See Reynolds, chap 3, and the first history of Australia written entirely from the point of view of the Europeans' moral right to occupy the land: David Day, *Claiming a Continent: A History of Australia*, Sydney: Angus & Robertson, 1996, chaps 4-7.

12. See Harris, 27-28.

13. On this see the thought-provoking essay by Stanner, 'Caliban Discovered', in his *White Man Got No Dreaming*, 144-164; 150.

14. Harris, 71.

15. See Stanner, 'History of Indifference'.

age but civilised!).[16] The invaders, in Harris's words, 'wanted it all', and the squatters' maxim was 'niggers and cattle don't mix'.[17]

The Enlightenment had proclaimed the equality of all, and the figure of the Noble Savage was comprehensible because it fitted this European preconception. Aboriginal reality, however, was incomprehensible, which is why even the more humane among the settlers looked upon the Aborigines as sub-human.[18] As white settlement inexorably progressed and the Aborigines sank into despair dulled by alcohol, this too was rationalised as further proof that they were lazy and degenerate, a view the clergy reinforced by preaching that it was obviously the hand of Providence that was causing them to 'fade', 'melt away' and 'perish' as a 'doomed race'.[19] The few Aborigines who became Christians learned to cherish hope for the next life, not for this. By the middle of the nineteenth century it was widely felt that Australians should 'draw the veil' over the atrocities of the early years of settlement, thus inaugurating what the anthropologist Stanner was later to call 'the great Australian silence', 'a cult of forgetfulness practised on a national scale'.[20]

The men and women who thus dismally failed to understand the Aboriginal cultures they had stumbled upon were, in many cases, 'the best the nineteenth century had to offer', and 'without them, the plight of Aboriginal people would have been immeasurably worse'.[21] They were for a long time utterly unable to grasp that the primary aggression was white presence itself, with its thoughtless invasion of the land that was life to Aboriginal people and the immediate introduction of venereal and other diseases against which the Aborigines had no resistance (Governor Phillip recorded that half the population of the Sydney area died of chickenpox in the first fourteen months of settlement.)[22] Over and above the outright violence of 'punitive

16. Cf Harris, 72-75.
17. See Harris, 148.
18. See Harris, 23-24.
19. See Harris, 182.
20. Stanner, *After the Dreaming*, 24-25, cited in Denis Edwards, 'Sin and Salvation in the South Land of the Holy Spirit', Peter Malone, ed., *Discovering an Australian Theology*, Homebush: St Paul Publications, 1988, 89-102, 96-97.
21. Harris, 184.
22. See Harris, 39-40.

expeditions', poisonings and random shootings, there was the cognitive violence which eroded and largely destroyed an intact and functioning view of the world. By the middle of the nineteenth century the birthrate had plummeted as people literally lost the will to live and the motivation to reproduce. In the area around Port Phillip 'it was reported that there was an "indifference to prolonging their race, on the ground as they state of having no country they can call their own"'; or, in the more eloquent words of an Aboriginal witness: 'No country, no good have it piccaninny. No country now for them and no more come up piccaninny.'[23]

It is time to ask ourselves how we react to this story ('we' meaning both Europeans and Euro-Australians). If we are honest, I suggest that we will find ourselves saying that it is all very tragic, but understandable in view of the mentality of the time. But to what extent is their time our time; how much of their mentality do we still share? These nineteenth-century Christians were 'enlightened', and their knowledge of and dedication to the gospel were at least as great as ours. There may well be lessons to be learned from their failure. Let us see if we really can understand Aboriginal religion.

2. The Resilience of Aboriginal Religion

The memory is only now being retrieved of just how tenaciously Aboriginal groups in many parts of Australia fought to defend their land against the incursions of whites.[24] The land was their life, and against overwhelming odds they clung to it until they were forcibly removed or, anticipating the cost of resistance, acquiesced in relocation and drowned their despair in drink. It is only now that the realisation is beginning to dawn on white Australians that the land has *religious* significance for Aborigines; that although they probably never numbered more than a few hundred thousand at any one time[25] they had humanised the entire continent, covering it with a seamless web of meaning which, though invisible to whites, on the latest archaeological evidence may have endured for 100,000 years.[26]

23. Cited by Harris, 150.
24. See Henry Reynolds, *The Other Side of the Frontier*, Ringwood: Penguin, 1982.
25. Molony, 11, estimates 750,000, though lower figures are also given.
26. Personal communication from the priest-archaeologist Eugene Stockton, since confirmed by Day, *Claiming a Continent*, 8, who considers 120,000 years to be a likely figure.

For most nineteenth century Christians, religion meant theism of a morally robust kind (unless they preferred the more abstract and rationalistic deism proposed in the previous century). In the face of what they saw as the moral depravity and infantile intelligence of the Aborigines, they could not imagine that they were dealing with anything remotely resembling 'religion'. The young science of anthropology, for its part, was equally incapable of seeing anything religious in Aboriginal culture, for different but related reasons. There were those – notably the German anthropologist Wilhelm Schmidt SVD – who assumed that religion, if discernible at all in such 'uncouth savages, would consist in faint traces of the monotheism from which all religion originally derived, and the most zealous researchers uncovered evidence of "high gods" or "supreme beings" (among them Baiame and Daramulun) on the deist pattern; but as a student of this period remarks, "the place these beings have found in anthropological literature is disproportionate to their place in Aboriginal religion".'[27]

For the pioneers of the discipline such as Tylor and Frazer, the religion of 'primitive' peoples remained fixated at the childish stage of evolution and was more properly categorised as 'magic'. Durkheim, utilising the earliest first-hand reports of Aboriginal customs and ceremonies supplied from central Australia by Spencer and Gillen, tested his theories of the origin of society on what he took to be these 'elementary forms' of religion and thus of society. Though his was 'the first attempt to take Aboriginal religion seriously', he was compelled by his own theory to present Aboriginal religion as a function of society, thereby postponing for many years the fundamental insight that virtually the opposite is the case: 'one might almost say that society exists for the sake of religion rather than religion for the sake of society'.[28] Malinowski's functionalism, in the modified form of the structural-functionalism proposed by Radcliffe-Brown, Australia's first professor of anthropology, set the pattern for the scientific investigation of Aboriginal cultures in the first half of this century.

27. Tony Swain, *Interpreting Aboriginal Religion: An Historical Account*, Adelaide: Australian Assoc. for the Study of Religions, 1985, 14; see also 75 ff., 102-3, 106-123.

28. Max Charlesworth, introducing the anthology edited by him with Howard Morphy, Diane Bell and Kenneth Maddock, *Religion in Aboriginal Australia*, St Lucia: University of Queensland Press, 1986, 2, 4.

Religiously sensitive anthropologists such as Strehlow, Elkin and Stanner were eventually able to transcend the Durkheimian premises of functionalism and to discern a non-theistic religion which, while vividly aware of transcendence and couched in terms of spirit beings, is primarily centred on Life, Land and Community as its pre-eminent religious values. Elkin was prepared to speak of Aboriginal 'philosophy', Stanner to use the word 'sacrament' of the Aboriginal relationship to the land.[29] This epoch-making paradigm shift opened the way towards the realisation that Aboriginal religion flows through the physical landscape as the symbolic-sacramental point of contact with the deeds of ancestral beings whose emergence from a timeless state, beyond yet encompassing human time, established the Law and brought into being the present order of things.

Stanner called this timeless state 'what many Aborigines call it in English: The Dreaming' (deriving from Spencer and Gillen's translation of the central Australian Aranda word *alcheringa*).[30] Remarking that he had never found Aboriginal words for 'time' or 'history', he characterised this time-beyond-time as an 'everywhen'. Each individual and each lineage group has a specific Dreaming, which can be symbolised by virtually any aspect of physical nature but is usually a plant or animal (which thereby falls under a taboo for the individuals concerned). In traditional culture people carried a kind of 'Dreaming map' in their memories, imparted as secret-sacred knowledge at the time of initiation, which defined their relationship to a particular stretch of country and allowed them to negotiate kinship relationships with neighbouring groups and rights to travel through their country. The continent was thus 'a world full of signs',[31] a 'speaking land'.[32]

Our present situation *vis-à-vis* Aboriginal religion is well summarised by Charlesworth:

> Australian Aboriginal religion is a non-theistic religion based on the sacred and sacramental character of the land, and it re-

29. See Stanner, 'Some Aspects of Aboriginal Religion', Robert Crotty, ed., *The Charles Strong Lectures 1972-1984*, Leiden: E. J. Brill, 1987, 3-20.
30. Stanner, 'The Dreaming'' in *White Man Got No Dreaming*, 23-40; 23.
31. Stanner, 'Aboriginal Religion', 4.
32. Roland M. Berndt and Catherine H. Berndt, *The Speaking Land: Myth and Story in Aboriginal Australia*, Ringwood: Penguin, 1988.

quires a considerable effort of mind and imagination for a European to come to grips with it.[33]

It may help us to make this effort if we remember that the mythical stories are not so much ontological statements about the nature of the universe as what the Berndts call 'guides for action', distillations of traditional wisdom designed to address the perennial choice between good and evil and provide 'a charter for the whole pattern of human existence'.[34]

Today, we see the emergence of a post-traditional Aboriginal culture which calls itself 'Aboriginality' (comparable perhaps to the *négritude* of West Africa or the 'black consciousness' of South Africa) and is coming to terms with a more mobile urban lifestyle. According to Swain, 'it seems Aborigines today increasingly define Aboriginality in terms of *how* they relate to land rather than *to which* lands they are related. Theirs is a *sense* of place rather than a *knowledge* of their specific site.'[35] The tough political battles over land rights, better health care and humane treatment in prisons have brought about a new sense of emancipation and self-confidence. This is producing Aboriginal literature, including theology. But before we proceed to a brief review of this, we need to pause and take stock of our position as European Christians with regard to this remarkable story of apparent cultural eclipse and unexpected renewal. Now that we are painfully learning to decipher the meaning of Aboriginal religion, can we – may we, Europeans and Australians with our historical responsibility for the Aboriginal tragedy – transpose that meaning into Christian theology in a wider ecumenical context?

3. *Confronting the Primal Other*

The Australian priest-archaeologist Eugene Stockton is surely not far wrong when he says that the arrival of Europeans in

---

33. Charlesworth, 7.

34. Roland M. Berndt, 'Good and Bad in Australian Aboriginal Religion', in Crotty, ed., 21-36; 22-3; for a discussion of the Berndts' 'charter theory' of the Dreaming, cr Swain, 112-114.

35. Tony Swain, 'Reinventing the Eternal: Aboriginal Spirituality and Modernity', in Norman C. Habel, ed., *Religion and Multiculturalism in Australia: Essays in Honour of Victor Hayes*, Adelaide: AASR, 1992, 122-136; 130.

Australia initiated 'the most severe culture clash in history'.[36] The scale of the physical violence may have been greater in Latin America or East Africa, but in the case of the Aborigines the cognitive violence was extreme, the cultural incompatibility almost incalculable. Even if we allow for the extraordinary situation in which Europeans from these islands found themselves, we must ask what lay at the root of their failure to comprehend. In particular, where was their implicit or explicit Christian theology deficient in ways that might still have something to teach us? Can we probe the subconscious depths of their dilemma and learn something about our own relationship to primal religion – which is, after all, the way in which the vast majority of humankind *is* religious?

We begin to discern a dialectic of ' sameness' and 'otherness': in the nineteenth century, the European urge was to make what was different the same as us and what we are used to; today, it could perhaps be said that we are happy to assert otherness as a basis for incompatibility and incommunicability, thereby absolving ourselves from trying to establish a relationship. In reacting as they did to Aboriginal reality as they perceived it, the colonists, I suggest, were encountering themselves, but to a degree of 'otherness' greater than they could cope with. Their inability to acknowledge this 'Other' as in some sense a forgotten dimension of themselves very soon led them to project their terror of it onto the Aborigines – and the land itself – in the form of naked aggression and destruction. There are testimonies by Aborigines who preserved the memory of what the encounter looked like from their side which reveal their moral outrage at these strange beings who were as helpless as children in a land where sustenannce abounded, yet would listen to no advice and lashed out vengefully at every Aboriginal protest against their wanton selfishness:

> When whites first came to this land ... they did not come to it as proper human beings. They came in here bloodthirsty. They fought their way across the whole island of Australia. The missionaries, also, who took up positions here – they were not real Christians because most had hatred in their hearts for the Aboriginal people. When I think back over the

36. Eugene Stockton, *The Aboriginal Gift: Spirituality for a Nation*, Sydney: Millennium Books, 1995, 18.

> stories of my grandfather and great-grandfather, I know the whites did not have love in their hearts.[37]

It has taken two centuries for this irreparable hurt to begin to be understood.

White Australian artists have begun to fathom the depths of this psychic 'first contact'.[38] Sidney Nolan and Russel Drysdale in their severe depictions of the land and its legends; Roland Robinson in his translations of Aboriginal poetry;[39] poets such as Les Murray and Bruce Dawe;[40] Patrick White (*Voss, A Fringe of Leaves*) and Thomas Keneally (*The Chant of Jimmy Blacksmith*) in their imaginative reconstructions of traumatic historical incidents;[41] films such as Peter Weir's *Picnic at Hanging Rock* and *The Last Wave* have insisted on the wider human dimensions of the European encounter with the land itself as the 'sacred site' of Aboriginal religion. Perhaps this is nowhere more vividly captured than in Xavier Herbert's sprawling epic *Poor Fellow My Country*, in which the great mythical figures of Aboriginal cosmology such as the Rainbow Serpent are, in a sense, characters. But no one, in my view, has plumbed these depths more sensitively than David Malouf. In *An Imaginary Life* he uses the fictional autobiography of the poet Ovid, exiled from imperial Rome to the wild shores of Dalmatia, to examine the re-education of a sophisticated European as he learns to communicate with a

37. Guboo Ted Thomas, 'The Land is Sacred: Renewing the Dreaming in Modem Australia', Garry W. Trompf, ed., *The Gospel is Not Western: Black Theologies from the Southwest Pacific*, Maryknoll: Orbis Books, 1987, 90-94; 93.

38. David Tacey, *Edge of the Sacred: Transformation in Australia*, North Blackburn, Vic.: Harper Collins, 1995, has traced the rediscovery of the sacred in a wide range of Australian artists, both European and Aboriginal, in the framework of Jungian psychology. Of particular interest is the profound disturbance evoked in the visiting English novelist D. H. Lawrence by his intuition of the sacredness of the Australian landscape, which inspired his novel *Kangaroo*; see Tacey, chap 4.

39. Some are reproduced in Les Murray's *Anthology of Australian Religious Poetry*, Blackburn: CollinsDove, 1986.

40. See Peter Kirkwood, 'Two Australian Poets as Theologians: Les Murray and Bruce Dawe', Malone, *Discovering an Australian Theology*, 195-216.

41. See Veronica Brady, 'A Properly Appointed Humanism: Australian Culture and the Aborigines in Patrick White's *A Fringe of Leaves*', *Caught in the Draught: On Contemporary Australian Culture and Society*, Sydney: Angus & Robertson, 1994, 139-152.

captured boy who had lived wild, privy to the secrets of nature. In *Remembering Babylon* the theme is varied to probe the reactions of settlers in western Queensland to a white boy who has lived with the Aborigines, who is both 'of us' and 'of them'. Reviewing these works, the critic Veronica Brady says that they embark on a journey into the self which bears comparison with the quest for the *atman* in Indian religious philosophy.[42]

These imaginative encounters with the primal Other invite Euro-Australian theologians, for the first time, to embark on a true *dialogue* with Aboriginal religion in which the Enlightenment sensibility of the European Christian confronts the repressed and forgotten 'archaic Other', the 'cosmic religion' which, though it lacks virtually all the characteristics of European civilisation, may turn out to be crucial for humanity's survival.[43] White Australian theologians such as Denis Edwards, Eugene Stockton, Frank Fletcher, Martin Wilson, Don Carrington and Robert Bos are experimenting with different approaches, some philosophical, others biblical, to this lost dimension of European theology.

To take just two examples, Eugene Stockton reminds all 'new Australians' that they are 'grafted like a branch on to a living mature stock', the native gum tree of Aboriginal culture, which implies 'not only participating in the social, political and economic life of the nation, but also a deliberate effort, a sort of spiritual conversion – what I have elsewhere described as "coming home to this land".'[44] Aboriginal religion still holds in readiness a 'spiritual gift' which could make the once so self-confident 'lucky country' from a merely 'clever country' into a 'wise country'.[45]

Frank Fletcher, drawing on recent cultural criticism such as Tacey's *Edge of the Sacred* and the philosophical theology of David Tracy and Bernard Lonergan, sets out to locate 'the inner story as well as the outer history of our dealing with the Aborigines'[46] with its 'unresolved inner conflict':

---

42. Brady, 'Malouf's An Imaginary Life', *Caught in the Draught*, 233-257.
43. This is developed by David Tracy, *Dialogue with the Other: The Inter-Religious Dialogue*, Louvain: Peeters Press, 1990, Ch. III.
44. Stockton, *Aboriginal Gift*, 4.
45. Stockton, *Aboriginal Gift*, 169
46. Frank Fletcher, 'Finding the Framework to Prepare for Dialogue with the Aborigines', unpubl. ms., 2 (since published in *Pacifica* 10

> the Euro-Australian is drawn deeply toward a primal feeling evoked by this land but remains so wedded to the human-centred historical worldview that the primal is habitually suppressed or repressed.[47]

He calls this 'the sealing off of the primal by the modern colonial mentality in and outside the church', whose price has been 'a sense of loss afflicting both psyche and spirituality'.[48]

> The early settlers were unready culturally and psychically for the depths where the *Tremendum* awaited them in this land, the numinous snake beneath the waterhole ready to arch up into the clouds to bring earth and heaven together. The affliction of the Euro-Australian soul has been in the ongoing frustration of the primal sacredness, the loss of the earth-heaven passion. As such we remain still colonialist strangers in dread of the Mystery that is here.[49]

In the words of Denis Edwards, we are all 'in apprenticeship to the Aboriginal view of the land'.[50]

What of the Aborigines themselves? On the burnt-out stump of their culture the fresh shoots of new growth are appearing. The pope's phrase in his speech at Alice Springs, 'you have endured the flames', has become a catchcry among Aboriginal activists. The immemorial rock carvings and cave paintings, the body and bark decorations have been successfully transposed from traditional ceremonies to more durable media such as acrylic paint and screen printing. The resulting paintings and sculptures have captured the imagination of the international art world, and they have become the most successful medium of expression for Aborginal religion. Though by no means all levels of meaning in these paintings are disclosed to whites, 'Aborigines appear more adept at expressing themselves in painting than in words, when it comes to deeply felt convictions.'[51] The poetry of Kath Walker (Oodgeroo Noonuccal) has

---

(1997) 25-38; see also id., 'Towards a Dialogue with Traditional Aboriginal Religion', *Pacifica* 9 (1996) 164-174).

47. Fletcher, 3.

48. Fletcher, 12.

49. Fletcher, 16.

50. Cited in Stockton, *Aboriginal Gift*, 113.

51. Stockton, 95. For a religiously sensitive interpretation of Aboriginal art, see Rosemary Crumlin, ed., *Aboriginal Art and Spirituality*, Blackburn: Dove Communications, 1991.

compelled the attention of Australians for decades, but now there are vigorous new voices such as Bill Nedjie, whose *Story About Feeling* is widely read by concerned Australians, as is Sally Morgan's autobiography *My Place*. In theology, the patient work of the Anglican and Uniting Churches at Nungalinya College near Darwin has produced leaders such as Bishop Arthur Malcom and Moderator Djiniyini Gondarra, who have been able to interpret the religious significance of land rights claims and the Christian revivalism among northern Aborigines to white Australian Christians. Patrick Dodson, the first Aboriginal Catholic priest, who left the church to become a key figure in Aboriginal politics, has made a powerful theological interpretation of the religious basis of land rights.[52] Miriam Rose Ungunmerr, an Aboriginal Catholic artist, besides giving us Aboriginal stations of the cross which have become a subject of meditation for many Australian Christians, has beautifully explained the Aboriginal term for contemplation, *dadirri*, as 'listening to the stillness' in order to learn the language of the sacred land.[53]

There is now possibly a higher proportion of Aboriginal people actively engaged in 'publishable theological reflection' than whites.[54] Though still strongly influenced by the 'missionised Christianity' implanted by the early missionaries, Aboriginal theologians are slowly finding their voice in the public sphere. They are conscious of their debt to the 'forgotten theologians' of the past: the first converts, beginning with the son of Bennelong; the first ordained ministers (James Noble, Anglican, 1925; Patrick Dodson, Roman Catholic, 1975; Liyapidiny Marika, the first Uniting Church Aboriginal woman minister, 1991); the early Bible translators, whose achievements went largely unrecognised. Aboriginal Christianity still bears the conservative stamp given it by missionary teaching, which is sometimes expressed in evangelistic or pentecostal revival movements.[55] But what Pattel-Gray calls a 'story-telling theology' is also developing, 'a non-western, non-intellectualised model of teaching tran-

52. Patrick Dodson, 'The Land our Mother, the Church our Mother', Malone, *Australian Theology*, 83-88.
53. Reproduced in Stockton, *Aboriginal Gift*, 179-184; see also chap 10.
54. Anne Pattel-Gray and Garry W. Trompf, 'Styles of Australian Aboriginal and Melanesian Theology', *International Review of Mission* 82 (1993) 167-188; 168.
55. Pattel-Gray and Trompf, 172.

scendent truths about creation and life'. She also identifies 'Aboriginal theology' proper, which is

> autonomous (post-western, post-denominational), and emphasises liberation, prophetic obedience, and action. It treasures traditional Aboriginal religion as the divine grounding for contemporary faith and identity. It keeps traditional practices ... as potent reminders of important cosmic and temporal truths. And, it holds the Dreaming as a timeless guide for active engagement.[56]

It will be a test of the authenticity of Euro-Australian reflection on Aboriginal identity that it practise *dadirri*, attentive listening, towards these newly articulate voices of Aboriginal Christians. In this way we may yet be able to receive the rejected gift of Aboriginal spirituality and achieve 'a breakthrough out of the ordinary, where the soul is brought to a spiritual experience for which the land is a sacrament'.[57]

Could the sort of approach sketched here to the European Christian encounter with Aboriginal religion be dismissed as an exercise in pop pyschology? Perhaps; but that would too easily avoid the challenge this encounter presents. Appreciating this is difficult for Europeans in much the same way that psychological counselling or pyschoanalysis is difficult: one can no longer take refuge in generalisation! One must confront oneself in all one's particularity, minus the masks, and face the memories one would prefer to leave buried; in short, one must see one's 'self' as Other. Now that Aboriginals at last have a voice in the public sphere, Euro-Australians hear the repressed primal Other speaking back, proclaiming an unfamiliar and unwelcome version of Western selfhood. We are able to gauge the depth of the hurt and anger caused by the attitude of 'assimilation', which justified the removal of children from their families and people from their land and obliterated memories of language and culture. Confronting this pain are the hostility and resentment of many whites, who do not feel themselves responsible for past and present atrocities and do not want to be reminded of them. It seems obvious to me that this confrontation has a psychosocial dimension which must be addressed by both sides together if there is to be any hope of national reconciliation and healing as the prerequisite to some kind of treaty (*makarrata*). Strictly

56. Pattel-Gray and Trompf, 176.
57. Fletcher, 14.

speaking, nothing can or may be compared with the *Shoah*, the Nazi Holocaust of European Jewry; but it may be permissible to make the point that for Australians, coming to terms with the atrocities perpetrated on the Aborigines and the land that was their life is something like the moral equivalent of European Christianity's responsibility to the Jews.

Theology, however, must go even deeper than psychology. The dialogue with Aboriginal religion and spirituality as expressions of the 'primal Other' constitutive of all humanity must first of all be internalised, must become – in Raimundo Panikkar's felicitous phrase – 'intra-religious dialogue'. The recognition of Aboriginal otherness implies critique of European completeness. Really listening to the 'discourse of the others' means the end of European intellectual sovereignty, for the Others *have* succeeded in surviving humanly and socially and in shaping and reshaping those 'universes of meaning' or 'webs of significance' which have allowed them to live meaningful lives and survive the encounter with an alien culture. But Aboriginal humanity is not *absolutely* 'Other', nor have a century and a half of 'assimilation' made Aboriginal culture in any fundamental way the 'same'. Neither Aboriginal nor European can lay absolute claim on the Infinite, which transcends yet relates both. From the point of their meeting on, whether they like it or not, they are in relationship, and henceforth the Infinite is mediated to them *both* by the quality of that relationship. The short cut of the one's reducing the other to 'the same as us' or 'incompatible with us' is no longer available to either.

Lest we imagine that only European thought is capable of constructing a 'basis' for dialogue in this way, let it be remembered that Aboriginal religion had a profound sense of transcendence (in Stanner's view it was one of the most transcendental of all religions) and even a practice of something like mystical contemplation (*dadirri*). The difficulty it presents to Europeans is the essentially aesthetic quality of its awareness, the mythic consciousness embodied in the metaphorical structures of its stories and the symbolism of its art. What we European Christian theologians need to consider is the loss to all humanity if this consciousness is finally obliterated. It has been the burden of this chapter that in such a case something of ourselves and our relationship to nature would be irreparably damaged at the very time when we are beginning to realise its universal importance.

Aboriginal religion is world religion.[58] If Christianity is ever to break loose from its European captivity, the Aboriginal contribution will be pivotal. If this offer is rejected, we must ask whether we are morally justified in continuing to assert the 'universality' of our tradition and its claim to ecumenical relevance. Even the supposition that we are entitled to 'use' Aboriginal religion for some larger purpose must be subjected to moral scrutiny.

The Christian encounter with the Other is no longer exclusively subject to European definitions of this encounter. The primal Other of Aboriginal religion has a voice, and it is making itself heard in language we can understand. We are obliged to listen, and if we do, our Christian faith and practice will be immeasurably enriched. As Australians, it is perhaps our historic opportunity to have been at least partially dissociated from the dominant European 'We' and to be able, at last, when it is almost too late, to make 'first contact' on the human and religious level.

---

58. Cf David H. Turner, 'Aboriginal Religion as World Religion: an Assessment', *Studies in World Christianity* 2 (1996) 77-96; 'Australian Aboriginal Religion as "World Religion"', *Studies in Religion* 20 (1991) 165-180, in which he argues that Aboriginal religion belongs to all humanity as much as Hindu or Buddhist religion, and has at least as much capacity for peacemaking.

CHAPTER 6

Endangered Identity and Ecumenical Risk: Changing the Theological Terms in Northern Ireland

Geraldine Smyth OP

Two buckets were easier carried than one.
I grew up in between …
Baronies, parishes met where I was born.
— Seamus Heaney

Ecumenism Endangering Identity?

Each July, in Drumcree near Portadown in Northern Ireland, a combined band of Orange Order lodges (culturally Protestant) and the local Nationalist (culturally Roman Catholic) community engage in their annual stand-off. The siege centres upon a Protestant church on a hill, and the annual war of words rehearses well-worn epithets of civil and religious liberties and is accompanied by political brinkmanship and fraught efforts at mediation. In the worst years violence has spilled over in further places spawning further violence and even death. Drumcree has attained almost classical status as a case study of a sectarian interface where conflicting political claims configure around a nexus of cultural and religious identities. Neither official church intervention nor formal mediation services have yet been able to bring the opposed groups into the face-to-face talks that might break the impasse. In Drumcree, identity is territory and the territorial boundary infused with sacral significance.[1]

1. Typically, the Loyal Orange Order is refused permission from the Parades Commission to return from its Somme Commemoration Service in Drumcree Church by their traditional route which in recent decades impinges on a Nationalist housing estate. 2003 once more saw the protest and counter-protest, but less volatile and more controlled than in previous years, despite the same banning of the 'traditional route', not because either group had relinquished right or claim, but rather because the hard core of accompanying violent supporters had during the preceding year been variously imprisoned, exiled or assassinated, mainly as a result of an internecine Loyalist feud. Such is the grim back-drop to the forging of new myths of identity.

At one level, such scenes portray as classic instances of a clash of rights, rooted in contesting memories of resentment and blame, conflicting histories of victimhood and oppression. Particularly noteworthy, however, is the way in which religion lends transcending force to the cultural-political conflict. Thus, following one such outbreak of violence, one Orange leader, seeking to exonerate the Loyal Order, inveighed against its enemies, reserving his strongest epithets for church leaders who were 'corrupting our young people with ecumenism.' Ecumenism was evidently viewed as a contaminating influence on purity of religious identity. There is a certain irony that in his blast against ecumenism, the Orange leader invoked that damnable 'E' word four times in as many sentences, oblivious that his iterations served to re-inscribe what he sought to efface. Perhaps for those deemed guilty by association with the 'E' word, the 'danger' accusation comes as a welcome change from the more usual charge that ecumenism is but a harmless hobby, a sloppy form of church liberalism, or a bewildered ghost hovering around the ruins of modernity. Who knows but this discourse of 'danger' may signal that ecumenism has come of age, noted at last for its subverting of closed systems, whether in church or society? Better surely to be deemed 'dangerous', than despatched to the grey zones of mediocrity ... However, a sense of perspective enters at this point and one must make two concessions to reality: that in Ireland ecumenism remains a minority activity; and that for those who perceive their identity under threat, ecumenical activity is indeed dangerous. Gabriel Daly, one of Ireland's outstanding ecumenical theologians, in a particularly cogent reflection following the massacre at Darkley Pentecostal hall in 1983, offers some searching comment on the dangers and deceptions inherent in tribal religion:

> Neither side listens to the other's conviction and each dreams its own dream, apparently unconcerned that its own dream is the other's nightmare ... Each side gives the impression that to represent to itself imaginatively the other's dream or nightmare would be a species of tribal treason. Yet until they do so there will be no lasting peace.[2]

2. Twenty years later, we can acknowledge the prophetic quality of these words. Noting many of the protagonists to be professed Christians, Daly, in another telling phrase, points to the lack of 'a baptised imagination', lamenting that 'their dreams have not yet been bap-

The above illustrations brings us into that magnetic field of 'identity politics' and 'cultural religion', and offers an opportunity to reflect – in the light of the Ecumenical Decade to Overcome Violence (2001-2011) – on such conflicts where religion, ethnicity and politics intersect.[3] In noting the Ecumenical Decade to Overcome Violence, we acknowledge the call to Christians, whatever their confessional beliefs, to sojourn together across the boundary of historic divisions, particularly where these divisions tear communities apart in violent conflict.

The dynamics of sectarianism, identity and religion can be related to the tension in the Hebrew Bible between the doctrine of the election of Israel as God's chosen people (through Moses), and the universal covenant with Abraham and Sarah and through them with all nations.[4] In Christian theology, one finds

tised by the Galilean dream.' Gabriel Daly, 'Towards an Irish Theology: Some Questions of Method', in Enda McDonagh, *ed. Irish Challenges to Theology: Papers of the Irish Theological Association Conference*, Dublin: Dominican Publications, 1984, 96.

3. See, *Ecumenical Review Special Issue: The Decade to Overcome Violence*, vol 53, no 2, April 2001. For an in-depth general study on the formation of core identity patterns in relation to ethnic conflict, see, Vamik Volkan, *Bloodlines: From Ethnic Pride to Ethnic Terrorism*, Boulder, US: Westview Press, 1997. Volkan speaks of an 'externalization' of good and bad aspects of the self, and the child's emotional investment in 'shared reservoirs' with constant and shared features – songs, flags, colours for example – through which infants bond themselves to a large group (88-91). At a later stage, this shared reservoir expands to include mental images, as children are initiated into crude understandings of 'chosen traumas' and 'chosen glories' in the ethnic myths and history of the group. Volkan's theory is borne out in a recent study in Northern Ireland: Paul Connolly, Alan Smith and Berni Kelly, *Too Young to Notice? The Cultural and Political Awareness of 3-6 year olds in Northern Ireland*, Research Project commissioned by the Community Relations Council, Belfast and Channel 4, England, CRC, Belfast, 2002 gives a hard-hitting analysis of the sectarian socialisation process even in the post-ceasefire generation. See also Yvonne Naylor's, *Moving Beyond Sectarianism: a Resource for Young Adult*, ISE, Dublin and Belfast, 2001, and her, *Who We Are – Dealing With Difference*, ISE, Dublin and Belfast, 2003 – geared towards 9-13 year olds. These creative practical resources are based on the research of Cecelia Clegg and Joseph Liechty's, *Moving Beyond Sectarianism: Religion, Conflict and Reconciliation in Northern Ireland*, Columba Press, Dublin, 2001.

4. Cf Geraldine Smyth, 'Sectarianism – Theology Gone Wrong?' in Alan Falconer and Trevor Williams, eds., *Sectarianism*, Dominican Publications, Dublin, 1995, 52-76.

the same double-edge. The gospel according to Mark – the starkest of the gospels – evokes the sense of otherness and dread in the face of the foreign territory at the other side of the lake. This is a helpful starting point for Christians who seek to be ecumenical within a society divided along ethnic and political rifts and where these rifts serve as Protestant and Catholic identity markers. But it behoves ecumenists and peacemakers to tread softly around the dreams and nightmares of threatened majorities or minorities, and to temper their own impetuosity with a tact and imagination that are baptised into Christ's patience and compassion.

Resisting the Claim of Redemptive Violence

Ecumenists and peace-makers also do well to take account of the fact that divisions in this context are deeply structured whether in unconscious psychological reflexes or ingrained socio-religious practices. Frank Wright designated Northern Ireland as an 'an ethnic frontier society', in which relationships are structurally antagonistic.[5] This is played out at many levels, whether in regard to views on the legitimacy of the border, the courts, the police, or – most fundamentally – on the legitimacy of Westminster or Dublin in the affairs of governance, with many in each group also drawing solace from the powerful position of their respective church. In times of conflict and relative peace alike, social and political relationships have been governed by the threat of violence and repeating outbreaks of violence, and, at times, by a religious sanction for violence.[6] The times of relative peace were somehow defined by violence in what has been described as a 'tranquillity of mutual deterrence'. This systemic pattern was radically disrupted by the Civil Rights Campaign from 1968, to be followed by more than a quarter century of violence and counter-violence executed by rival paramilitary groups and indeed by the state, each protagonist using violence to achieve its own version of social order or controlled tranquillity. The Good Friday Agreement of 1998 has been bedevilled by (as it was in

5. Frank Wright, *Northern Ireland: a Comparative Analysis*, Gill and Macmillan, Dublin, 1992, 20ff; also, Geraldine Smyth, 'Brokenness, Forgiveness, Healing and Peace in Ireland', in Rodney Petersen, *Forgiveness and Reconciliation: Religion, Public Policy and Conflict Transformation*, Philadelphia: Templeton Foundation Press, 2001, 319- 349.
6. Frank Wright, ibid., 112-116.

many ways choreographed around) these oppositional dynamics. A recent example of the inherent frustration and (to many outsiders) the sheer incomprehensibility of this self-defeating repetition emerged in the apparently stubborn refusal of Unionists to accept the *bona fides* of the the IRA's substantial act of decommissioning, reported on by General de Chastelain (Head of the International Decommissioning Body), and the matching stubborn refusal of the IRA to concede to the Unionist demand for exact inventory and 'transparency'. Each publicly claimed the moral high ground as the position of their respective group and attributed deception, if not betrayal, on the part of the other. Despite all the exquisitely planned orchestration, the deadlock repeats itself, as expectations are dashed, and once more, 'hype and history clash'.[7]

Walter Wink has pointed to the need to demythologise and unmask the claim that violence is redemptive, and to expose its dynamics as systemically destructive, in a pattern whereby controlled violence is used to tranquillise trauma, contriving a deceptive lull, that gives way not to peace, but to further retaliation in a relentless cycle.[8]

At this point, the sacral dimension of a repeating cycle of violence moves into view, both internally, insofar as the churches have made available certain legitimising symbol structures for self-superiority and separation, such as 'Chosen People', 'Promised Land', 'God on our Side' or 'Martyrdom as liberation.' In such instances, memory is massaged by quasi-religious re-enactments of past defeat or future triumph. This translates into ecclesiological stances in which truth claims are not so much confessed in a stance of faith as asserted in terms that are arrogant and absolute; in which the sense of community belonging closes off from an eschatological horizon of hope and is expressed in tribal ways; while expressions of social being become at best privatised and at worst oppressive of the other, falling far short of the discipleship of loving freedom enjoined by Jesus as the way of God's Reign on earth.[9]

7. *The Irish Times*, Sat 25 Oct 2003, pp 1 & 7.

8. Walter Wink, *Engaging the Powers: Discernment and Resistance in a World of Domination*, Minneapolis: Fortress Press, 1992, 133ff.

9. Cf Interchurch Group on Faith and Politics, *Boasting: Self-Righteous Collective Superiority as a Cause of Conflict*, Belfast, 1999.

Ending the Sacral Sanction for Separation

From a Christian perspective on peace, churches must withdraw the sacral power of Christian symbol and creed for securing relationships of mutual deterrence, which with little resistance slip into justifications of violence in the name of a transcendent good.[10] This disestablishing move must in turn give way to a creative movement that can hold together self-critique, repentance and some measure of hospitality to the other. In the Irish context, the challenge facing churches is to co-operate in the creation of such a contrast-society in the interests of sustaining civic peace and communion with other Christian churches. To this end also, Christian imagination can retrieve and breathe new life into rituals of healing and forgiveness which can encourage communities to let go of violence, and practise reconciliation.[11]

But, in this process, churches need to probe their own attitudes and behaviour and acknowledge how they, as sacred institutions, actually mirror cultural divisions, re-infusing them with mythico-religious potency. This potency in turn helps to disguise the reality that the churches operate as social entities. Thus, many social activities sited in church institutions function as sectarian in their effect, if not in intention. In the case of the activities of the Orange Order, it rankles not only with Catholics and Nationalists but with many Protestants and Unionists that church buildings are often made available for meetings and marches with church ministers acting as chaplains. The association of Roman Catholicism and cultural nationalism is ritualised at annual graveside commemorations of the Easter Rising of 1916, while the traditional links between Gaelic games and Catholic parochial structures, and at times, personnel, have effectively left Protestants (and, until recently, anyone working for the security services) excluded. It is not sufficient, however, to rest a case on such occasional occurrences that may be peripheral to the lives of the majority. Churches could usefully submit

10. Cf The Interchurch Group on Faith and Politics, *Doing Unto Others: Parity of Esteem in a Contested Space*, Belfast, 1998.

11. Cf Roel Kaptein, with the co-operation of Duncan Morrow, *On the Way to Freedom*, with Introduction by René Girard. Without a total espousal of a Girardean analysis, one finds here some useful diagnostic and analytic methods for understanding the stubborn patterns of violence in the North, and correlating these emergent insights with a gospel vision, as a contrast-culture and a resource for change.

their week-by-week calendar to a simple ecumenical audit, not with any view to eliminating congregation-based activities, but merely to discover whether *any* cross-community or ecumenical contact occurs. Perhaps, following sober reflection, some initiatives might be considered: for sharing readers, or exchanging or conjoining choirs, say, on a monthly basis; for opening church hall facilities for occasional joint social or sporting activities, or for an arranged ecumenical learning series to which members of different local congregations could contribute. In a sectarian society, there is need, too, of a social ecclesiology that would encourage shared gatherings of a socio-ecclesial nature. In this vein, Michael Hurley coined the term, 'ecumenical tithing,' challenging church-goers to worship with occasional regularity in a different church.[12] Another modest proposal from Enda McDonagh relates to the potential of celebrating baptism as an interchurch event.[13] Such thoughtful suggestions also underline the reality that one can open one's church doors occasionally without damage to the confessional ethos, whether in regard to the social-ecclesiological practices of worship or to the rubrics governing parish hall kitchens. Some practices may end up the more cherished as a result of opening them to other's perceptions and experience.

Ecumenism as a Social Movement – its Ecclesiological Significance

In seeking to examine this phenomenon further, we can illustrate with reference to the churches in Ireland the persistent gap between the fixed expressions of 'official' ecumenism expressed in intense confessionalised mores, and ecumenism as a social movement which attracts Christians who are prepared to cross denominational boundaries. Such ecumenical Christians, operating with the dynamic of a social movement, have been prepared to make common cause with other movers and shakers in civil society who wish to break free of imprisoning structures and to interrelate in creative ways. The ethical imperative of overcoming violence has drawn such Christians together with peace activists, human rights agencies and community develop-

12. See, Michael Hurley SJ, 'One Bread One Body': Review Article', *Studies,* Vol 88, No 350, 2002, 225-230, for a recent re-statement of the author's call nearly twenty years ago.
13. Enda McDonagh, 'Invite and Encourage', *The Furrow,* Vol 50, No 1, January 1999, 21-22.

ment groups, on local and regional initiatives of peace and social justice. There is often real ecumenical substance to such co-operation, in so far as it challenges or points a contrast to the sectarian nature of much church activity, but more constructively too, in the testimony of so many who describe it as deepening their sense of Christian identity and as widening the horizons of their Christian community. Models of church associated with the people of God or the priesthood of all believers, and the rediscovery of shared baptism as a basis for renewal of the local community, can still engender fruitful co-operation in re-creating the living connections between the gospel and people's lives, even in situations of social upheaval or ecclesiological indifference.

In this context, one agrees with the statement of the World Council of Churches' study process aimed at a more fruitful connecting of ecclesiology and ethics, that 'the churches have not yet grasped the full implications of this decisive "ecumenical dimension". They have not realised that a costly unity requires a costly commitment to one another'; so too one reads, 'Must we not also say: if the churches are not engaging these ethical issues together, then none of them individually is being fully church?'[14] Clearly also, the rigidity of ecumenical expression often reflects the internal confessional inflexibility which churches seem to be experiencing in the face of the divergent perspectives within their own ranks, and that both rigidities show up the reality that the churches frequently function as social institutions, merely, unwilling to be prophetic signs of Christ the Peace-bringer and Life-giver. One can illustrate this reality and probe it further.

Turning Away From Prophetic Witness

It is a truism to observe that in time of ethnic conflict churches or religious groups can find themselves as front-runners in the parade of cultural identity. In allowing themselves to be so coopted, they in effect choose ties of tribe over courageous prophetic witness. In surrendering their authority to the ancient ethnic impulse, they rein in the potential of grace and goodness

14. *Costly Commitment: Ecclesiology and Ethics,* ed. Thomas F. Best and Martin Robra, WCC, Geneva, 1995, par 17. For a critical assessment of this and related WCC studies on ethics and ecclesiology, see, Simone Sinn, *The Church as Participatory Community: on the Interrelationship of Hermeneutics, Ecclesiology and Ethics,* Columba Press, Dublin, 2002.

that is the creative overflow of proclaiming the gospel. Blood becomes thicker than water – even the water of baptism. So too, the particular authority of a given church's tradition (with its preferred hermeneutical keys to gospel understanding and living) is re-confessionalised. There then develops a plurality of views, but minus the capacity for mutual intelligibility or dialogue across cultures or congregations. The nature and interplay of different communities of interpretation and the possibility for coexistence within and between the churches becomes brittle. Agents of reconciliation are distrusted almost in the very measure of their aim to be ecumenical, with the result that ruptures are hastened, as communities lose the knowledge of how to be creative interpreters of their own identity in new times, undermining the confidence to engage in real dialogue with what is other. The institutional cement of the respective church bodies hardens and they function almost entirely as cultural entities. Questions face us all as to the ways churches weaken the gospel's power to transform minds and hearts as long as they allow it to be held fast by the flying buttresses of political stubbornness. It is as if they have hammered the poet's ironic adage, 'If you must say something; say nothing,' into an iron axiom.

Perhaps more fundamentally, church leaders, in recognising the increasing pluralism within their own traditions, need to find ways of hearing the different voices into speech. In the popular mind, churches are often thought to be out of touch with the concerns of the communities they serve. Churches in Ireland, as anywhere, are themselves grappling with the tension of fidelity to a founding vision in changing generations, and struggling to keep open the fraught relationship between charism and institution. Anti-church bandwagons themselves offer neither shelter nor liberty, railing against a dogmatic past as they trundle towards a thoughtless future. Yet, if churches wish to contribute to open, critical dialogue in the public arena, they need to find fresh ways of speaking as churches with an authority that is eschatologically open to the Reign of God. Without that, while there may be some scope for the odd prophetic voice from the margins, the churches as ecclesial bodies cut themselves off from the wider search for meaning, belonging and social freedom. Until something approaching this inclusiveness is attempted, the church's catholicity is endangered and churches will offer little to the formation of a public culture of respect and reconciliation. Gabriel Daly, true to the ideals of Augustine, his founder, as to the ecumenical imperative of *reformans et semper reformanda,* sees a critical openness to pluralism as a matter of faith that is ever prepared to search further for the truth.[15]

Unsettling the 'Single Identity' Myth

In the fostering of respect and reconciliation attention must be paid to one's own sense of identity. However, it is also true to say that in order to understand ourselves more deeply it is necessary somehow to stand outside ourselves and to integrate something of the Other's perception of us. Identity is intrinsically complex or many-in-one; it is discovered by journeying beyond private worlds; in order to become itself, it must encounter what is deemed other and different; so too, the formation of healthy identity is related to one's capacity to act and give body to theory or vision.[16] To be confronted with another's strangeness evokes an impulse to protect ourselves one way or another (Freud's fight or flight dictum).[17] Developmental and social psychology demonstrates that a self, a nation, or culture define themselves in relationship, both negatively and positively, to some signifi-

---

15. Gabriel Daly, 'Christian Response to Religious Pluralism', in *Studies,* vol LXVII, nos 265-266, 1978. He quotes Augustine's exhortation: 'Let us seek in the conviction that we shall find, and let us find in the conviction that must go on and seek anew' (66-76). In this nuanced but trenchant analysis of pluralism in the context of Irish Christianity, the author challenges the intransigent conservatism that thrives on anti-intellectual authoritarianism, and that evinces a spurious loyalty to the church and makes religion irrelevant. Rather, and revealing Daly's inimitable capacity for the *mot juste,* 'adult Christian faith needs, and will thrive on, the challenge of pluralism, because Christian faith is *not a matter of sanctified inertia* but of constantly renewed decision' (76); italics mine.
16. Cf Geraldine Smyth OP, 'Envisaging a New Identity and a Common Home: Seeking Peace on our Borders', in *Milltown Studies,* vol 46, Winter 2000, 58-84, 62ff.
17. In the context of the current quest for reconciliation between conflicting groups in Northern Ireland, the vogue for 'single identity work' (particularly just now within Unionist and Loyalist communities in beleaguered areas) must be shown to be a contradiction in terms and indeed self-defeating. Nationalists and Republicans, however, need to recognise that in some instances physical threats are real; and even if not, leaders should seek to alleviate fears and create a climate of confidence,

cant other.[18] So also it can be observed that persons in society share in a range of overlapping identities and networks of belonging, inhabiting each other's memories and histories. We are complicit across a boundary that is also a bond structured by human fear and conflict, honed by hidden intimacies and interests.[19]

The vast majority in Ireland, North and South call themselves Christian. One can but hope that after so many years of

---

without which possibilities of fruitful encounter are doomed. But would also that some Unionist politicians refrain from massaging these fears for petty electoral ends, ever ready to re-invest them with mentalities and myths of siege.

18. Cf George Herbert Mead on the role of 'significant others', in *Mind, Self and Society*, Chicago University Press, 1934. See also, Kristeva, *Strangers to Ourselves*, 170, 181-3, and passim. See also, John Macmurray, *Persons in Relation*, Faber and Faber, London, 1961, 86-105, on the necessary rhythm in all relationship of 'withdrawal and return', where the withdrawal is always for the sake of the return: 'My withdrawal from the Other is itself a phase of my relation to the Other. The isolation of the self does not annul the relation; it refuses it ... to annul the relation is to annul oneself' (92).

19. Peter Berger and Thomas Luckmann have also demonstrated that in the process of identity formation and in the maintenance of a symbolic universe, opposition actually helps to constitute that symbolic universe, and embodies elements from the opposite view, and redefines self-understanding according to shifts in the balance of interests: cf *The Social Construction of Reality: A Treatise in the Sociology of Knowledge*, Penguin, Harmondsworth, 1967, 1985, 122ff and passim. See also Julia Kristeva, *Strangers to Ourselves*, on Freud's concept of the 'alien double', with the 'compulsion to repeat', 183-4. On social identity theory in the Irish context, see, Ed Cairns, *Caught in the Crossfire: Children and the Northern Ireland Conflict*, Appletree Press Belfast and Syracuse University Press, NY, 1987, 104-117. On the basis of his empirical research and structural identity analysis, Cairns grimly anticipated that children, 'caught in the crossfire' of ancient conflicts were set not only to repeat the social identity formations of their parents but to reinforce them along negatively segregated lines. He notes the significance of 'the pressure to disassociate' from the other group and the concomitant tendency to exaggerate differences, both cultural and religious. Ironically there is a sameness in both groups, such behaviour being typical of that in any inter-group conflict (114). More evidence here (if any were needed) for the churches to reflect upon the oppositional social construction of cultural and religious identity in Northern Ireland, and their participation and acquiescence in this construction.

intentional and wonted segregation, the active encouragement of contact, mutual questioning and interchange, will enable Christians to discover the communion that underlies their diversity. It is as regrettable as it is ironic that the Pauline text asserting that the life and death of each one of us has its influence on others is heard and preached mainly at funerals. As Christians, we need to accept that it is not alone in our personal and social relations, but as communities of faith, that we need others in order to become ourselves. The grittiness of our differences can unite, even in the moment of standing apart from the other group in a step of critical distance, to reflect on what each brings to the relationship, and how as churches they might be more true to themselves and to what they might become. It will be above all through dialogue that churches and cultural groups discover that their identity is irreducibly relational and that in opening to this truth, their own self-understanding will paradoxically become more robust.[20]

Freedom and Order in Contest: Living in the Tension

The human need for freedom and for security is experienced in ambivalence and contradiction. A frequent tendency is to eschew the inherent polarity. Repeatedly in history, the dynamics of social, political and religious worlds manifest two basic impulses in dialectic pattern – an impulse towards order on the one hand, and on the other, towards freedom. Both impulses find their origin in irreducible instincts and needs. So too, the higher level aspirations to community and to personal authenticity are in alignment with these impulses. When such instinct or aspiration suffers frustration, it can turn to a rage which grasps after 'more of itself', whereas what each needs to fulfil itself is in reality 'more of the other'.

Thus, the rage for order, security and certainty which so

20. Sociologists speak of identity-in-contrast. One can also adduce a narrative hermeneutic here. Students at the Irish School of Ecumenics, who study alongside others from different church traditions, year by year, testify to achieving a new depth of understanding of their own church doctrines and practice as a result of broader base of study, exposure and reflection than had been possible while reflecting within their own denominational family. For an ecclesiological exploration, see also, Alan D. Falconer, 'Beyond the Limits of Familiar Landscape', in Falconer, ed., *Faith and Order in Moshe: the 1996 Commission Meeting*, WCC Publications, Geneva, 1998, 40-55.

often features in the politics of identity refuses what is unfamiliar as threatening or dangerous, and turns in on itself in totalitarian stances of belief, belonging and social control. The rage is played out through cultural, political and religious constructions, designed to seal the personal or institutional system against what is deemed different, and repressing dissidence from within.[21]

Conversely, the rage for freedom, plurality and independence involves a distortion of the human instinct, need and aspiration by the denial of limits and accountability. One expression of this is found in the contemporary market economy, where billions of dollars circle the globe in seconds, without reference to human need or political accountability. In religious and cultural terms, one sees similar extremes of privatised believing without belonging. One might speak of the 'Californication' phenomenon, where religions and spiritualities endlessly invent themselves unencumbered by communities of tradition and service, cut adrift from the exigencies of social and temporal location.[22]

Each rage involves a rejection of limits, a rejection of mutuality, whether cultural, political or religious, that is the condition for self-realisation. Each mirrors the other in its self-destructive pathology. The logic of each pattern is violent: thus, the one who rages after identity operates by the imposition of a particular brand of sameness – claiming that there is no room for 'the other' and insisting on the necessity of ever stronger walls between the in-group and out-group; the other insisting that if only extremist and fundamentalist could be written out and the boundary abolished, then freedom could reign. Each, in fact, shares the refusal to recognise and engage with otherness. The preference is for more of the same.

Surveying the past thirty years of conflict in Ireland, one can speculate that at some unconscious level people and groups – including churches – faced with the choice between negotiating

21. I am playing here upon the underlying image of David Tracy's, *Blessed Rage for Order: the New Pluralism in Theology*, University of Chicago Press, Chicago, 1975, whose title derives in turn from a line in a Wallace Stephens' poem – 'Order at Key West.'

22. For a helpful philosophical exploration of the matter, see, Charles Taylor, 'The Politics of Recognition', in *Philosophical Arguments*, Harvard University Press, USA, 1997, 225-256, or his, 'Cross-Purposes: The Liberal-Communitarian Debate', in the same volume, 181-203.

their lives around the disruption of violence, or the interruption of the stranger, have made the former their default option. In the months following the ceasefire declarations, it was not uncommon to hear people say in an abashed tone that they almost missed the violence. The choice of intercourse with the stranger, of the conversations and relationship that might follow, because it is threatening to old belief systems and to the binitarian symbolic self-understandings of insider and outsider, oppressor and oppressed, is not usually a once-for-all choice. The pull of ancient identities works its seductions again and again. To imagine the world from the point of view of the stranger does invite the risk of responsibility for co-authoring a new social and theological landscape, new sets of power structures within churches, and new interchurch relationships open for sharing faith and life. Ultimately, each group must be prepared to interrupt its own cultural and religious assumptions of normative status, and disrupt the settled expectation that the other group must change and fit in.[23] But neither can dialogue be forced. One must be willing to show patience, and, to borrow a term from Gabriel Daly, 'ecumenical tact'.

Churches and Identity – Between the Already and the Not Yet

Hearkening to stranger, then, blurs boundaries and stretches the limits of dreams and responsibilities. The exigencies of encounter and conversation are rarely without anxiety or contention. Fear and suspicion of the stranger is close to the surface of every culture. In the Judaeo-Christian tradition, however, we find a counter-tradition, whereby the stranger's interruption also

23. Julia Kristeva suggests that the foreigner lives within us as, 'the hidden face of our identity' (1) and that challenge is not so much to live with others as to live as others (*Strangers to Ourselves,* 1). Kristeva unpacks the Jewish understanding of the foreigner as '*ger*', but she warns of certain problems with this term (that are particularly relevant to Northern Ireland). She points out that '*ger*' standing alone can include the idea of 'conversion' or assimilation. Perhaps, as she proposes, the more nuanced '*ger-tochav*' (resident alien) is more precise in maintaining the necessary tension and in insisting on the need not to absorb the stranger, but to refrain from co-opting her or his foreignness as such – respecting and welcoming without demanding conformity. Ruth, the Moabite is, of course, the exemplary *ger-tochav* (67-76).

bears an invitation and a promise.[24] In this vein, Paul Ricoeur, commenting on Emmanuel Levinas, agrees that 'ethics unfolds outside the field of ontology'.[25] This has special significance wherever people – or indeed churches – would infuse identity with an ontological substance which it does not possess. Ricoeur asserts that 'the "one for the other" constitutive of my responsibility for the other is of the order of a "summons", not of manifestation' – again a most significant distinction in its theological reminder of the transcendent otherness of the divine. Ricoeur interprets identity in terms of a tension between the certainties one holds about oneself – the 'saying' of a 'said' – and the process that requires a continual letting go to the future, to the as yet 'unsaid': 'There is therefore in the positing of an identity,' claims Ricoeur, 'an initial forgetting, the forgetting of the saying, lost in the said.'[26] It is Ricoeur's intention to challenge any conferring of substance or status for identity as fixed or as possessing an original meaning as the beginning of all meaning. Churches caught in identity-fixation do well to remember Jesus' constant reminder of the transcendent horizon of identity, as when he exposed the false security among those who would base their religious credentials in descent from Abraham (Mt 3:9), or when he asserted that kinship with him was constituted, not by blood ties, but the 'doing the will of my Father in heaven' (Mt 12:47-50).

Ricoeur's interrelating identity with human consciousness is also *à propos*. Thus, he insists on a distinction between two understandings of identity – identity as *idem* and identity as *ipse*. The first denotes a closed sense of oneself, rooted in some original past, and expressing oneself according to what has already been said, and oriented to 'more of the same.' The second – *ipse* – denotes a more open, restless sense of the self, in process of expressing the not yet said, and inclined, not towards the self-justi-

24. Gen 18 is the *locus classicus* of such a promise-bearing stranger, but others abound: e.g. 1 Kings 17, besides other texts where the stranger stands as an ethical reminder to the people of their own pilgrim history, challenging them to treat strangers bountifully (e.g. Ex 22-23; Lev 17-23). Eph 2:19 gives a vision of the new dispensation in which strangers and aliens are now fully citizens and saints in the household of God.
25. Paul Ricoeur, 'Emmanuel Levinas: Thinker of Testimony', in, *Figuring the Sacred: Religion, Narrative and Imagination,* Augsburg Fortress Press, Minneapolis, 1995, 119.
26. Paul Ricoeur, ibid, 120.

fying, but towards the yet unsaid. One can correlate Ricoeur's analysis to Jesus's announcement that those who would save their life would lose it, and those laying down their life would find it. So also, in what is recounted of his conversation with Mary of Magdala in the garden of the tomb. It is as if in speaking her name, Jesus recognises and affirms her identity in continuity with the fears, sufferings and joys of their past relationship. Nothing of the 'already said' will be lost. But, in bidding her not to cling to him, it is as if Jesus is inviting Mary to let go of the constraints of the previous Master-Disciple relationship. In the power of the Resurrection, *she* is now graced with the responsibility to go and tell – to announce the vision not yet spoken, to the disciples and then to the whole world.

Between the false choice of identity and communion, Christians find their place in the shadows of the empty tomb and are called to turn around and recognise Jesus for who he is; refusing to cling to what is worn out, not seeking the living among the dead; but commissioned to go and preach the news that Jesus is alive, is going ahead, and will be known as the Christ by those who live in his Spirit, who surrender themselves to the not-yet of new creation.

One can read the Philippians hymn (2:6-11) in similar light. Here, Jesus is portrayed as emptying himself, not *clinging* to his identity with God (we find the cognate Greek – *hapton* – in John 20:17). The text breaks open the paradox of authentic Christian identity in terms of self-emptying, and an obedience that surrenders to death and to being raised up by God.[27] But it is important here to see the implications for churches, not simply in those situations (intimated above) where there is a temptation to adopt the role of guardians of particular cultural identities, but equally to confessional identities that have 'crystallised in history as a result of the occurrence of divisions', dis-embedded from that

27. For a critical constructive reading of the Philippians text to take account of feminist misgivings about the inherent danger of *kenosis* in sustaining a demeaning pattern of vulnerability, see Sarah Coakley's interpretation of the transformative potential in this term, in *Powers and Submissions: Spirituality, Philosophy and Gender*, Blackwell Publishers, Oxford, 2002, 3-39.

larger Tradition in which those identities subsist.[28] The ecumenical *Groupe des Dombes* authors indicate that where confessional identities have become ends in themselves, they have given rise to rejection and aggressiveness towards other Christian groups. Accordingly, these negative manifestations confuse the true identity with public image, reducing a legitimate *confessionalité* to a narrow *confessionalisme*, which '[hardens] ... confessional identity into an attitude of self-justification ... [which] withdraws into itself and rejects real confrontation with other confessions or denominations.'[29]

The Dombes text specifically names Northern Ireland, 'where confessional identity is used as a powerful emotive lever at the risk of ending up by quite simply contradicting Christian identity and gospel love.'[30] The central point of the text is to challenge the divided churches to recognise that their divided identity must be grounded in a continual conversion without which their unity cannot even be imagined. It insists that the churches in the context of initiation of conversion to faith through baptism and the constant struggle to undergo conversion – 'celebrated in the proclamation of the Word, and in the sacramental act of reconciliation, as it is likewise in the celebration of the eucharist' (26) – finds its identity in repentance and grace.[31] In this, then, the churches live between the already there (Ricoeur's identity as *idem*) and the not yet (Ricoeur's identity as *ipse*). John Paul II's important words, echoing Vatican II's *Unitatis Redintegratio*, 7) suggest a similar open-endedness in referring to dialogue not simply as a way to finding agreement (least of all, 'facile "agreement"'), but as a '*dialogue of conversion*.'[32]

28. Groupe des Dombes, *For the Conversion of the Churches*, trs from the French by James Greig, WCC, Geneva, 1993, 23. See also, *Ut Unum Sint: Encyclical Letter of the Holy Father Pope John Paul II on Commitment to Ecumenism*, Catholic Truth Society, London, 1995, where the Pope says that the Catholic Church must enter into what might be termed, a 'dialogue of conversion with other churches, which will involve repentance and absolute trust in the reconciling power of the truth which is Christ' (par 82).
29. Groupe des Dombes, ibid, 23-24.
30 Groupe des Dombes, ibid, 25.
31 Groupe des Dombes, ibid, 26.
32. *Ut Unum Sint: Encyclical Letter of the Holy Father John Paul II on Commitment to Ecumenism*, CTS, London, 1995, pars 36 and 35: italics as given.

Relating Identity and Communion

One of the most troubling aspects of the current interchurch controversies in Ireland over intercommunion and eucharistic hospitality was the spirit of animosity which crept into the public discussions (often betraying a surprising degree of ignorance of the respective churches' teaching on eucharist, and certainly an obliviousness of such daring ecumenical texts as *Baptism, Eucharist and Ministry*). Another was the way the specific interpretations of eucharistic doctrine were functionalised and reduced to a fence-post of confessional identity. Such interpretations were all but shorn of sacramental significance as bond of communion and mystery of grace. This reductionism of eucharist to ecclesial boundary-marker was embarrassingly manifest in the 'Letters to the Editor' pages of newspapers, featuring comments from certain Roman Catholic priests and people, some of them more damaging to Christian belief than any doctrinal heresy, while also stunningly gauche in ecumenical terms.[33]

Interestingly, the publication in April 2003 of the encyclical letter, *Ecclesia de Eucharistia*,[34] did not provoke the same level of heated response. In this encyclical, more devotional and at times mystical in tone, John Paul reaffirms the eucharist as both 'the source and the summit of all evangelisation' – again echoing the language of Vatican II and also holding together the easily bro-

33. See the Letters to the Editor, *The Irish Times*, recurring week days, mid February-mid March, 2001, and again in late April 2003 following the publication of the encyclical, *Ecclesia de Eucharistia*. The differing readings of this section in a weekly journal like *The Tablet* during these periods show the matter to be still controversial and indeed neuralgic. The same can be said in respect of the publication of the teaching document emanating in 1999 from the Bishops of Britain and Ireland, *One Bread One Body: A Teaching Document on the Eucharist in the Life of the Church, and the Establishment of General Norms on Sacramental Sharing:* Catholic Bishops' Conference of England and Wales, Ireland and Scotland, Veritas, Dublin, 1999. Here too, one notes in the very title, the intermixing of eucharistic theology and ecclesiology with the more disciplinary language of 'norms', as if lending equal significance to forms of speech and teaching that are usually kept somewhat distinct.

34. *Ecclesia de Eucharistia: Encyclical Letter of His Holiness John Paul II to the Bishops, Priests and Deacons, Men and Women in the Consecrated Life, and All the Lay Faithful on the Eucharist and its Relationship to the Church*, Rome, April 2003, Veritas Publications, Dublin, 2003 (Italics in above citations mine).

ken threefold tension between the eucharist as the goal of unity, as confirmation of the gift of unity already bestowed, and as sustenance on the way to unity.[35] Too, there are clear statements of the eucharist's particular effectiveness in creating and fostering communion (par 40), and in 'promoting communion' (par 41, though here linked explicitly to Sunday Mass). The text also claims (par 39) that 'a truly eucharistic community cannot be closed in on itself, as though it were somehow self-sufficient' (although the specific type of communion here called for is with 'every other Catholic community', which is open to some ambiguity). The key stumbling blocks are not hard to find, with reference made to the requirement that 'the bonds of communion in the sacraments, particularly in Baptism and priestly Orders be real' (par 38); and to the necessity of visible communion with the bishop and with the Roman Pontiff (par 39). The section relating eucharistic ecclesiology to ecumenical life (pars 43-46) does in fact reiterate the positive statement in the encyclical, *Ut Unum Sint* (1995), where the Pope expresses joy in those occasions wherein administration of the sacrament may be permitted according to the fulfilling of three necessary conditions. However, here there is a lingering cautionary legal tone, and language couched in the register of disciplinary norms, largely absent in *Ut Unum Sint*. One notes the apodictic statement that the church's unity 'absolutely requires full communion in the bonds of the profession of faith, the sacraments and ecclesiastical governance', and the insistence on the impossibility of celebrating together the same eucharistic liturgy 'until those bonds are fully re-established' (par 45). There is here too a uniform underlining of 'obstacles' to unity, of '*how far we remain from this goal*' (par 44) and of the terms governing the legitimacy and validity of eucharistic celebrations, without any counter-balancing acknowledgement of how far some churches and ecclesial communions have travelled together on the road to eucharistic communion.

For some this is no more than a re-statement of the official Roman Catholic line, but unfortunately, and however unintended, those who chafe at a nearing prospect of unity have managed to draw from it a certain comfort. Perhaps more unfortunate is the possible effect of a disillusion among the ecumenically-minded

35. The latter aspect is reflected in the title of the encyclical's second chapter in which this reference is found: 'The Eucharist Builds the Church.'

who read in this stringent approach evidence of a widening gap between gifts and gains in the theology and practice of ecumenical reconciliation, and the lack of significant endorsement and integration of these gifts and gains in terms of visible shared expressions of 'a certain, though imperfect communion.'[36]

It is not to our purpose here to do a proper ecumenical analysis of specific Roman Catholic documents, other than to insist that one must read them with a wide-angled, historically-focused and contextually sensitive lens. The point to be stressed relates rather to the concomitant difficulties which may arise in those situations where interchurch relations are culturally fraught or politically freighted, and where it is a *sine qua non* that church representatives avoid the least semblance of arrogance or self-sufficiency in their projection of official church teaching without due attention to varying *genres* of official ecumenical discourse (mystical, doctrinal, didactic, disciplinary), and to the need to preserve such discourse from co-option by the partisan or polemical. St Paul in his address to the church at Corinth was at pains to point out God's displeasure at any kind of self-righteousness rooted in one's historic past or original election:

> I do not want you to be unaware, brothers and sisters, that our ancestors were all under the cloud, and all passed through the sea, and all were baptised into Moses in the cloud and in the sea, and all ate the same spiritual food, and all drank the same spiritual drink. For they drank from the spiritual rock that followed them, and the rock was Christ. Nevertheless, God was not pleased with most of them and they were struck down in the wilderness (1 Cor 10:1-5).

Instructively for Christian churches now, as for the Corinthians, Paul proceeds to draw specific analogies with the subverting of the eucharist for purposes of securing identity or privilege. This

36. *Ut Unum Sint*, pars 80 & 11. Later in this encyclical, interconnections are made between 'this basic but partial unity' and 'the necessary advance towards the visible unity which is required and sufficient and which is manifest in a real and concrete way', and the expression of full communion 'in the common celebration of the Eucharist'. We note here the strong pilgrim impulse in the text, where the exhortation to patience and courage is sharpened by a warning not to impede the process: 'This journey towards the necessary and sufficient unity, in the communion of the one church willed by Christ continues to require patient and courageous efforts. In this process, *one must not impose any burden beyond that which is strictly necessary'* (par 78; emphasis added).

is idolatry to be fled, whereas those who would identify with Christ must be open to the insistent movement of faith in the power of Christ who draws the faithful in all their diversity into one communion:

> The cup of blessing that we bless, is it not a sharing in the cup of Christ? The bread that we break, is it not a sharing in the body of Christ? Because there is one bread, we who are many are one body, for we all partake of the one bread (1 Cor 10:16-17).

One remembers here the prayer preceding communion in the Roman Catholic liturgy, where the whole congregation prays, 'Lord, I am not worthy to receive you, but only say the word and I shall be healed.' Any tendency should be severely checked which allows the mystery of the eucharist to be functionalised along the lines of confessional boundary-keeping around the 'already said' of doctrinal absoluteness. One wishes for at least as much attentiveness to the more open spirit of this prayer, towards the 'not yet said', to the prayer that asks the Lord to say but the word that would heal our unworthiness.[37]

Enda McDonagh posits the dilemma in terms of how to relate without consuming the other.[38] His insights throw light on a range of contested areas – ecological, ecumenical, or in relationship to ethnicity and gender. He connects the challenge to the interchurch and intercultural relationships in Ireland, asserting that through the stance of 'communion', Christians and churches can relate without the drive to consume one another or the creation of which we are all a part.

---

37. One still looks for some stronger recognition from the Roman Catholic Church, and indeed from other churches in Ireland, of what has been already said in ecumenical discourse. Thus the Faith and Order statement from the Santiago conference should be underlined: 'We suggest that the churches, while respecting the eucharistic doctrine, practice and discipline of one another, encourage frequent attendance at each other's eucharistic worship. Thus we will all experience the measure of communion we already share and witness to the pain of continued separation', *On the Way to Fuller Koinonia: Official Report of the Fifth world Conference on Faith and Order*, ed. Thomas F. Best and Günther Gassmann, WCC, Geneva, 1994, 248.

38. Enda McDonagh, *The Gracing of Society*, Gill & Macmillan, Dublin, 1989, 38-40. See also, Timothy Radcliffe's, 'Jurassic Park and the Last Supper', in *idem*, *Sing a New Song: the Christian Vocation*, Dominican Publications, Dublin, 1999, 13-28.

Identity and Communion on the Ecumenical Journey
Ecumenism as a social movement, and in its formal ecclesial expressions, has contributed to the endeavour of inter-community and interchurch understanding, making an impact ethically and ecclesiologically. Communities like Corrymeela in Ballycastle, Currach (wedged on the peaceline of Shankill and Falls) with their witness and praxis of community dialogue and reconciliation come to mind. But there are others. Some towns have moved to establish their own churches' forum, with fruitful co-operation between local churches being encouraged by civic authorities, with bodies like the Irish School of Ecumenics providing safe spaces for conversation and study, facilitating the contribution and participation of local congregations and drawing in local clergy where possible.

At a formal level there are visible expressions of dialogue and exchange through official (though still quasi-parallel) bodies, viz. the Irish Inter-Church Meeting and the Irish Council of Churches.The leaders of the four larger churches on the island have for many years met regularly and have made some significant statements towards the easing of political tensions, holding violence in check, and more recently in the direction of peacebuilding. In some places, few though they be, encounters of local clergy, where these have persevered, are beginning to co-operate on common projects (one thinks of creative joint endeavours of the Anglican St Anne's and St Peter's Roman Catholic Cathedrals in inner-city Belfast), or some innovative developments on peer mediation in a group of North Belfast Schools, sponsored by a few clergy and teachers. But the pace is slow and the extent inadequate to the need. In terms of ecumenism, whether in its theological or pastoral witness, the churches are still missing the mark.

In his recent study of communion in relation to Christian origins and contemporary ecumenism, Nicholas Sagovsky comments on the vital mutual necessity in Christian life between diversity and unity. Adducing the best insights of early church tradition, especially in the fourth century, he points to the experience of Augustine as disclosing the paradoxical nexus of identity and communion:

> It was the fragility of human communion that wakened in Augustine the quest for communion that could not be broken. What the Christian tradition asserts … is that no break-

> down of *koinonia* is ever finally irretrievable, that 'within every human meeting there is an implicit hope of unbroken *koinonia* ... as memory, as hope, and perhaps, for a moment in time, as experience, but never as unbroken and unbreakable possession.[39]

One can but concur with Sagovsky as he draws out further implications for the dynamics of interaction for individuals or churches. He might have had the churches in Ireland in mind, in describing *koinonia* as, 'a process that involves conflict, reconciliation and risk.' Churches are not innocent of these dynamics, but they are 'set against an eschatological horizon of unbreakable communion.' Sagovsky rightly insists that it is the churches' common life which will shape common understanding and not the other way round. Practice shapes doctrine. It is through liturgical celebration that discord can be forgotten and conflicts suspended. If only for that brief space, *koinonia* is shared and reaches out in eschatological hope, depending not on our efforts, though demanding our dedication and trust in the Spirit:

> What makes such risk-taking possible is the presence of the Spirit, for the substance of relation is the substance of the Spirit, and it is the presence of the Spirit in each human encounter, whether between individuals or communities, whether for a moment or miraculously sustained, whether in agreement or disagreement, which makes each encounter a moment of new creation and a fresh occasion of hope. It is the activity of the Spirit that generates the common life.[40]

Today as in the early church, we are summoned to reconcile and be reconciled (2 Cor 5). Authentic reconciliation calls churches to more than polite co-existence, more than civil indifference, more than the careless ignorance that presumes identity (or communion) to be closed to conversion. In the struggle to overcome violence, churches face the responsibility that divided churches cost lives, and the challenge together to generate new ways of confessing their faith in Christ, and invoking with one voice the Spirit that gives utterance to each.

The capacity for reconciliation in the north of Ireland is fragile and overwrought. In their character of pilgrim people, churches need to set aside the baggage of bitterness and blame,

39. Nicholas Sagovsky, *Ecumenism, Christian Origins and the Practice of Communion*, Cambridge University Press, Cambridge, 2000, 206.
40. Nicholas Sagovsky, *Ecumenism*, 208.

to exchange trust rather than seek for guarantees. It invites churches to the kind of reconciliation that is rooted in inter-church 'recognition' and 'resonance' within a living ethos and identity of Christian discipleship.[41] But there is also a need to study and learn. In the words of Simone Sinn they must come to regard 'the development of Christian identity as dialogical competence between tradition and situation [as] a vital hermeneutical and ethical task.'[42]

In this context, ecumenism *is* a dangerous activity – and a delicate one. But its threat is to identities already outgrown and pinching. Its invitation is to allow churches to be transformed through the grace of exchange and shared life. The churches' way of ecumenical reconciliation is a journey into truth still unguessed, a journey into compassion for the others' suffering, and into a willingness for shared witness to the dangerous memory of the Easter message. As Ireland enters into a new era alongside people of other ideologies, cultures and faiths, the church's integrity is at stake in respect of the ecumenical imperative to ward off the old temptation to identity-based religion, and to find new ways of witnessing to the divine *pleroma* that is revealed in every act of listening to those beyond our Pale.

And so, to Drumcree as the starting point of this chapter and a concrete location of the theological reflection on identity and reconciliation. 'The symbol gives rise to thought', as Ricoeur reminds us.[43] Seamus Heaney, likewise, demonstrates the under-

41. It is worth drawing attention here to the section in Konrad Raiser's, 'The Report of the General Secretary', at the Harare Assembly, where he describes the *oikoumene* as 'an 'energy field' of mutual 'recognition' and 'resonance' generated by the Holy Spirit'. Within this field exist different levels and ways of ecclesial discipleship by which respective groups 'recognise' that others 'have the same spirit'. Each hears the Shepherd's voice, is formed by it and responds to the Shepherd's call in *different but mutually recognisable* forms of life and witness. This metaphor of resonance and recognition within a common energy field is a potentially dynamic one for holding the tensions of the rich and complex reality of particular forms of discipleship within a holistic pattern and character of church life and witness in the world. See *Together on the Way: Official Report of the Eighth Assembly of the World Council of Churches*, ed. Diane Kessler, WCC, Geneva, 1999, par 18, 90-91(italics, mine).

42. Simone Sinn, op. cit., 70.

43. Paul Ricoeur, *The Symbolism of Evil*, Beacon Press, Boston, 1969, 347-357.

lying imaginative lifeworld that can sustain any second-order analysis of this topic. Here poet precedes theologian offering a fund of symbols and memories that underlie the understanding of identity in this contested place, as well as the imaginative possibilities of some transcending communion. Entering the stream of memories and contradictions that swirl around his own South Derry childhood, Heaney recalls his precarious moving between the houses of his grandparents in Bellaghy and Castledawson as between two cultural worlds, different, but never disconnected. He celebrates the hoard of language and history that this double existence bequeathed him, and knows himself to have been twice blessed by its contrariness and ambiguities. In this vein, Heaney teases out the fertile meanings of '*Terminus*', the God of boundaries, and the Irish correlate, '*Tearmann*' (glebe land, marked off for ecclesiastical use) suggesting that identity can be both bounded and open. He senses the double meaning in the colloquially named boundary between farms and neighbourhoods – a 'march' as in a 'march drain' or 'march hedge' – expressing how one field was distinct from, yet, lay alongside another. The word hinted ambivalence – of surface separateness and deeper solidarity,[44] and these symbols tease the reader's imagination on the human need for boundaries – though primarily as borders to be crossed – but also intimate the 'possible boundlessness of our sympathies'. Such symbols sustain a vision of identities leaning into one another, intimating '"a world of true understanding", which is always lying just beneath the surface and just beyond the *horizon* of the actual words we speak.' Of course, the 'march drain' also awakens in the poet the harsh reality of a divided community, and echoes the dissonant overtones of Northern Ireland's 'marching season'. Nevertheless, even the painful core of this symbolic heartland continues to yield up its surplus of meaning and offers the promise that

> the marching season need not *just* be the season of parades and provocation but that in the ground of the language and in the ground beneath our feet there is another march which promises far more creative conditions for the mind and soul … The encounter at the march drain represents the possibility of going out onto the stepping stone in order to remove yourself from the hardness and fastness of your home ground.

44. Seamus Heaney, 'Something to Write Home About' in his *Finders Keepers: Selected Prose*, Faber and Faber, London, 2002, 48-58, p.p. 49ff.

> The stepping stone invites you to change the terms and the *tearmann* of your understanding; it does not ask you to take your feet off the ground but it refreshes your vision by keeping you and bringing you alive to the open sky of possibility that is within you.[45]

And so the poetic imagination sustains the ethical and theological claim that has been the burden of this chapter: on the necessity of keeping identity (identities) open for communion, yet without any implication that the Christian bid to be ecumenical, in venturing beyond the march hedge of one's home ground, denies the need for a place to stand; and always conceding the other person or community's need for a place to stand their ground, and to find terms of reference within which to operate without threat or danger. The assertion that the marching season 'need not *just* be the season of parades and provocation', is a salutary caution to the tactless among ecumenists, that respect for the other's fears and hopes for their own culture, and honesty about each one's current terms, is the first meeting-place of different identities and the basis for any possible communion. The allure of the open sky of ecumenical reconciliation does not require the other community to relinquish its particular 'season of parades and provocation'. We can still seek passable stepping-stones.

Here poet and theologian tentatively come together: as people of incarnation and pilgrimage, Christian communities trust in the given grace 'that within every human meeting there is an implicit hope of unbroken *koinonia* … as memory, as hope, and perhaps, for a moment in time, as experience, but never as unbroken and unbreakable possession.'[46] It is enough.

45. Heaney, ibid, 58 (emphasis added).
46. Sagovsky, Ecumenism, note 39 above.

CHAPTER 7

Faith and the Cure of Poetry: A Response to the Crisis in the Catholic Church in Ireland

Enda McDonagh

In seeking a theme appropriate to Gabriel Daly's major contributions to Irish church, academy and society, it seemed right to connect his two great interests of faith and culture to confront the continuing crisis in the Irish church. My own interest in the poetry dimension of Irish culture helped specify the theme more exactly.

The title of this paper is not entirely original, taken in part from a book by an American literary critic, Mary Kinzie, called, *The Cure of Poetry in an Age of Prose.*[1] But having reflected on the crisis in the church in Ireland – and it is still a crisis – very many of what might be called the *conventional* responses do not connect with where the *real* problem is. So this is, in a sense, an experiment in how we might approach some of these difficulties. Let me briefly indicate some elements in the crisis.

The crisis hit centre-stage in the early nineties, and front page and headline news with the resignation of Bishop Casey. There followed a series of clerical sexual abuse cases, one of which actually brought down the government in very bizarre circumstances. While that itself was shattering for many people, it was to some extent more a symptom than a cause. It was more the coming to expression of a long-standing and developing crisis than a simple explosion, because we had been in crisis in the Irish church, I believe, at least since 1968. Some people in my generation think the world began in 1968. Some people in my generation think the world ended in 1968. But we can take 1968 as a handy kind of 'after the Council' date – the revolutionary year in Europe and elsewhere, and, internally to the Catholic Church, the year of *Humanae Vitae*. All of that was feeding into a modernisation that was taking place in Ireland anyway, for which my church was ill-prepared and with which it did not

1. Mary Kinzie, *The Cure of Poetry in an Age of Prose: Moral Essays on the Poet's Calling*, Chicago: University of Chicago Press, 1993.

begin to deal for a long time. Curiously, the visit of the Pope in 1979, a striking public success, if it did not intensify the crisis, certainly obscured it. People lapsed back into thinking that all was well with traditional Catholicism in Ireland.

Through the 80s this was clearly not so, and the two bitter referenda fought on abortion and divorce left a bitter taste, and left many people worried about where we were going as a society, and what kind of leadership the Irish church could offer in a rapidly changing society. But the rapidity of change increased greatly again in the 1990s. This was partly political, partly compounded still by the troubles in Northern Ireland, partly economic in that we had been through a certain number of upswings and some serious downswings. And then the upswing started to take over. Can the church thrive in a prosperous society? Can the Irish Catholic church handle a prosperous country in which there would be people of much more independent mind? Could it recover from the scandals? These were important questions, but I believe that there was a deeper underlying difficulty which was certainly about the church and its mediation of the gospel of good news. This was an underlying difficulty about God, about faith, a difficulty that was not being recognised by bishops, clergy or even by some theologians. And maybe that was because we might not be able to face it in ourselves. Because the faith question was too searching, we stayed with the church question. The God question, and what might be called the risk of God, was too difficult for people who were trying to keep the show on the road, keep people going to church and Catholic schools full. We did not notice a kind of darkness growing inside ourselves; a kind of opacity to the presence of God and the light of the gospel.

Of course there were many counter signals. There were many people doing remarkable things both in the Irish church and out of the Irish church; particularly remarkable in regard to poverty at home and development abroad. These things were still moving on, catching and attracting young people of considerable talent. Yet in some ways over that period, there was a closing down and a closing in. The church was busy at some level, whether it was in catechetics or in justice work or in parish councils or in liturgy development, or whatever it might be, which did not reach where the closure was occurring. We were moving into a dark, opaque stage as far as our minds and hearts were concerned in relation to God, and we did not recognise it. This of course was not only revealed in what we might call the numbers game. There was still in 1990 about 85% weekly mass attendance, although that had dropped by 1998 to something like 61%. There was an extraordinary drop in vocations, by about 90% between the early 1970s and the mid 1990s. That was part of what I mean, but in those of us who put ourselves forward as church, there was a lack of openness to the spirit of God, a kind of darkness into which we were being drawn; and maybe we needed the darkness. Maybe now we have to live with it and in it and take it fully seriously. Part of the swings and roundabouts of the last ten or fifteen years has been like the aftermath of the papal visit: you get a great upswing when something good happens, and then you get a great downswing when some other scandal emerges. But it is not here that we should be concentrating our attention or our energy.

There is in our culture and in ourselves, an increasing darkness in terms of the true meaning of our humanity, and the ultimate meaning of it that we call God. And that darkness we cannot banish by any particular tricks, even any particular eloquence or any particular pastoral strategies. And it is not peculiar to Ireland and not peculiar to the Catholic Church. It is something that is shared much more widely, if not always remarked upon; or it is remarked upon in a kind of fundamentalist, apocalyptic way, that actually misunderstands the darkness and misunderstands above all that it could be a generative darkness for us. I chose for my topic 'Faith and the Cure of Poetry' because I thought that the poets and the artists among us might have some experience of that darkness, some experience of its creativity and generativity, and that they might indeed be stumbling on some things that we need, in terms of the graciousness of reality, of its liberating quality and richness. I also selected it because there has been an enormous resurgence in the arts in Ireland in tandem, and roughly contemporaneous with the decline of the church.

Just as the decline of the church is not something homogeneous or simple, but complex, with developments as well as declines, so the resurgence of the arts is not all masterpiece. There is bound to be a lot of dross in the amount of activity that is going on in Ireland, in music, painting, sculpture and writing. But it is less important that there is a lot of dross than that there is a great deal of creative effort, and a considerable amount of creative achievement with which the church needs to make contact. Traditionally, we have thought of the great Catholic Church as being a patron of the arts. Related to that characteristic of the Catholic Church is what we call its sacramentality, that is its embodiedness. When you think about it, faith is above all a body language. It is the body language of the members of the body of Christ. It is the body language of people who entrust themselves to one another in love, which is the great faith act of our lives. It is the body language of God and his chosen people – in the incarnation, in the whole of the creation – described by Sallie McFague, as you may remember, as the body of God.[2] And that body language seemed to me important because if we are stumbling around in the dark, if we are taking our darkness seriously, we have to listen more carefully to our own bodies, we have to listen more carefully for other bodies; we have to be tactile; we have to feel our way. And that language, all language, is body language. It resonates out of our bodies, it comes through in a way beautifully described by Micheal Ó Siadhail, an Irish poet, in a remarkable article, 'Spirituality and Art.'[3] The resonance of speech as it comes through the body is so important. And this again is the embodiedness of the body language of our faith, characteristic of us as Christians and, particularly, dramatically true of Catholics.

We have, however, distorted and suppressed much of that body language. We have only to look at the drab line of people going up to communion to see how lacking the body language is for this great bodily occasion – receiving the body of Christ, as members of that body of Christ. It seemed to me that we would find something of help from those artists who, out of their bodies offer us encounters with reality, encounters with truth, whether in word or paint or music. I was drawn further to that, partly by our own tradition, partly by listening to the artists themselves, like the wonderful Irish painter, Tony O'Malley, who died recently, who used to say that the paintings happen to him. The graciousness of it, the gift of it, is received before it is achieved. That is the remarkable theme of the novel, *Gracenotes*,

2. Sallie McFague, *The Body of God: An Ecological Theology*, London: SCM, 1993.

3. Micheal Ó Siadhail, 'Spirituality and Art', *The Furrow* 48 (1997) 145-151.

by Bernard MacLaverty, a north of Ireland writer.[4] One of the astonishing elements of that book is that it is a man writing about a woman composer – and women critics say that he gets it right. But what is remarkable is its account of how the notes come and how the composition begins and how she agonises through it, all pieced in with her own agonising, the birth of her child, the abandonment by her partner, and her own painful origins back in Northern Ireland. But again it is that graciousness embodied in us which prevails, and that we have to rediscover.

In reading Mary Kinzie's *The Cure of Poetry* and a number of other critics, including Richard Kearney's *The Wake of Imagination*,[5] we see not so much that kind of attention to the resonance and the resource and the cave, as Heaney says, where these images begin, but attention to what Kearney distinguishes as the ethics and the poetics of imagination. And in his ethics of the imagination, he is concentrating on the embodied, or the facial, presence of the other, taking his cue I have no doubt from Emmanuel Lévinas among others. But it is that presence that is the call to us, and it is the inventiveness, the poetic imagination as he calls it, which allows us to devise a response appropriate to that presence, recognise it and respond to it; whether it is in conversation, in that kind of embodied language, or whether it is in writing or painting or music. And it is that kind of alertness, that attention to the other, which Kearney talks about, that instils in us, as it were, the disciplines necessary for creative response, so that the discipline and the creativity come together. This is also very much a theme of Mary Kinzie's book, as she analyses a whole range of poets, and sees poetry as a calling; and a calling must eventually be rooted in reality, in the reality of human others, in the larger reality and the responses to it. The articulation of it is a matter of receiving the grace and answering the call, but also of developing the skills, the voices, the words and so on. But it will always be an embodied response, a body language.

In pursuing that just a little further, we can see that Eavan Boland, in her book *Object Lessons*, is talking also about the ethics, that call and gift, internal to poetry itself, internal to language, but then rooted in the political – as she sees it in the place

4. Bernard MacLaverty, *Gracenotes*, London: Jonathan Cape, 1997.
5. Richard Kearney, *The Wake of Imagination*, 1988; London: Routledge, 1994.

of women in society and in the role of woman as poet.[6] All this is pushing the project of faith and poetry on, but it has to be tackled more concretely. As we stumble around in the dark, as we try to find, to recognise, to articulate, as we learn from the artist, as we develop both the ethical imagination and the poetic imagination, of which Kearney and Kinzie both write, we may begin to see where the cure element comes in. This is addressed and named directly by Seamus Heaney in his Oxford lectures, *The Redress of Poetry*, as somehow setting things right in a particular way.[7] He is thinking about it in literary and political terms, in European and Irish terms, but also in personal terms. It is not yet what you might call redemption; it is not yet explicitly Christian in that way, but he is into that mood which is beyond ethics and invention, and is about setting right, redressing. And as we move in that direction, we could pick up on Ó Siadhail's article, where he sees in the making of a poem the bringing together of reality, that there is a reconciling act at work. And that is taking another step, and in another way.

In George Steiner's *Real Presences*, the poem or the painting is a way of mediating presence – human presence – but also ultimate presence; Steiner is working again out of a tradition that is not simply his own.[8] And the best example of all, of books of recent vintage, is a reprint of a book by Elizabeth Jennings, entitled *Every Changing Shape*[9] – a study of what she calls mysticism and the making of poetry. And it is at that stage, with Jennings, that we come to understand something of the cure of poetry. But you cannot rush these stages. I have named them, but not worked through them. I have not yet found the cure. I think I know the line along which it may lic. Some examples are needed that would help us to understand that line, and enable us to take the darkness seriously, and so begin to move towards the light. To that end I have chosen a number of poems by contemporary Irish writers.

---

6. Eavan Bolan, *Object Lessons: The Life of the Woman and the Poet in our Time*, New York: W W Norton, 1995.
7. Seamus Heaney, *The Redress of Poetry: The Oxford Lectures*, London: Faber and Faber, 1995.
8. George Steiner, *Real Presences: Is there Anything in What we Say?* London: Faber and Faber, 1989.
9. Elizabeth Jennings, *Every Changing Shape*, Manchester: Carcanet Press, 1996.

I do not wish to press the poems into a false context, but what Heaney and so many other critics say is that the good poem, taken in its own meaning and on its own merits, has a transformative value. After wrestling with these good poems for some time, I think that their transformative capacityhas enabled me to see something that – perhaps – the poets did not have in mind, but which I hope will not involve a travesty of their poems. The first of these is by Derek Mahon, in some ways the most underrated poet of his generation in Ireland, and in some ways the most powerful and the most European. This poem is called 'A Disused Shed in Co Wexford'.[10] In a startling opening stanza, Mahon introduces us to the prison hours of the lost spirits of the world: 'Peruvian mines, worked out and abandoned/ … Indian compounds where the wind dances/ … And ... a disused shed in Co Wexford', which he comes upon with friends and camera and where:

Deep in the grounds of a burnt-out hotel,
Among the bathtubs and the washbasins
A thousand mushrooms crowd to a keyhole …

They have been waiting for us in a foetor
Of vegetable sweat since civil war days …

Those nearest the door grow strong –
'Elbow room! Elbow room!'

These 'Powdery prisoners of the old regime' recall the dark dungeons of so many human prisoners, past and present. They conjure the darkness which the many inhabit and which inhabits the many. Mahon's final stanza re-echoes those screams, the cries for salvation we need to hear from others and to release in ourselves, and, I would add, in our church.

They are begging us, you see, in their wordless way,
To do something, to speak on their behalf
Or at least not to close the door again.
Lost people of Treblinka and Pompeii!
'Save us, save us,' they seem to say,
'Let the god not abandon us
Who have come so far in darkness and in pain.

10. Derek Mahon, 'A Disused Shed in Co Wexford,' in Derek Mahon, *Collected Poems*, Oldcastle: Gallery Press, 1999, 89-90.

We too had our lives to live.
You with your light meter and relaxed itinerary,
Let not our naive labours have been in vain!'

The next poem at least hears the cry for help and is troubled by it. It helps us to pick up, too, what we suppressed in our own tradition, and what might have saved us from some of this darkness if we had been alert and listening. It is a poem by Eavan Boland, entitled 'The Oral Tradition'.[11] After a public reading the poet is getting ready to face the winter journey home. As she puts on her coat she hears two women talking in the shadows, capturing her attention with words like, 'Summer,' 'birth,' 'great-grandmother.'

'She could feel it coming' –
one of them was saying –
'all of the way there,
across the fields at evening
and no one there, God help her ...

... It was nearly night ...'

'... when she lay down
and gave birth to him
in an open meadow.
What a child that was
to be born without a blemish!"

The poet recalls how she had become drawn into the experience in all its sensuous vivid significance, conjoined with these women in a living oral tradition.

One moment I was standing
not seeing out,
only half-listening

staring at the night; the next
without warning
I was caught by it:
the bruised summer light ...

where she lay down
in vetch and linen

11. Eavan Boland, 'The Oral Tradition', *Selected Poems*, Manchester: Carcanet, 1989, 74-76.

and lifted up her son
to the archive they would shelter in:

the oral song
avid as superstition,
layered like an amber in
the wreck of language
and the remnants of a nation.

It is commonplace to say that the Catholic Church, and the Irish Catholic Church, have neglected the oral tradition of its women, have neglected their dignity and their need, have neglected the hints and innuendos that lie underneath the surface, and so have lost that sense, a sense 'suddenly of truth, its resonance'. It is the overhearing in the half-light that may help us through the darkness, but it will be an ambiguous darkness, ambiguous light. Going still deeper into the structure and poetic skills of the poem would be still more revealing of the healing effect of the poem.

To come back to my earlier figure, that of body language with its own enormous ambiguities: it remains central to us in the great mysteries of human loving, and in that symbol of divine human loving we call the Eucharist. The centrality, the ambiguity and the possibility of healing are wonderfully expressed in Nuala Ní Dhomhnaill's poem, based on an old Irish tale. It is called '*Féar Suaithinseach*' or 'Marvellous Grass'. I use Michael Hartnett's translation.[12] She begins by addressing her priest-lover:

Nuair a bhís i do shagart naofa
When you were a holy priest

She then relates how this priest dropped 'the blessed host' when he saw her approaching him for communion. She was ashamed, became seriously ill and nearly died. To her in bed came all the usual experts, medical and religious, but no cure. Let men go out to 'cut the bushes, clear the rubble ... the misery/ that grows on my tragic grassland'. There they will find 'a patch of marvellous grass' from which the priest will bring the lost host to her; on her tongue 'it will melt and I will sit up in the bed/ as healthy as I was when I was young.'

12. Nuala Ní Dhomhnaill, 'An Féar Suathinseach,'/ 'The Marvellous Grass,' in Nuala Ní Dhomhnaill, *Selected Poems – Rogha Dánta*, Translated by Michael Hartnett, Dublin: New Island Books, 2000, 74-76.

This poem was, of course, written long before we knew of the recent clerical scandals, but it does convey something that many of Ní Dhomhnaill's poems convey: the relationships between the marvellous, the 'marvellous grass'; the body, the sexual body; the body of the Eucharist, the mystical body; how we cannot, as it were, evade these. And while again, one has to respect the poem as it is – and it is not easy to understand the different levels – it does strike me as pushing us back again to taking seriously our physical bodies and our body language, and our body as a community.

I should like to continue this discussion not with a poem but with another image of body and its resonances. In our present situation we in our western world are seen very much as consumers. And when we look at the people in disused sheds in Uganda, or Burma, or wherever it may be, we pass by, or put our few pence in the box. We forget the screams, half-silent screams, because we are too busy consuming; a bit like the mushrooms, those at the front, crying, 'Elbow room' in Mahon's poem. But we are consumers because we are bodily beings. It is part of our glorious and gracious condition that we consume. We could not live without consuming, and our universe is in some extraordinary way a self-consuming universe. But as we are consumers we are communers. Communion is as important to us as consumption; they can be at odds. Because we consume so much, we are not in communion with very many of our fellow human beings around the world, who are deprived. In the story, the story of the good news, beginning even in Genesis and the marvellous communion between God and humanity, and Adam and Eve, there is the breach in that communion by the sin of consumption, the particular sin of consumption as the myth, and the great poem of Genesis tell us.

This breach became so characteristic of the history of humanity, that though given the fruits of the earth to enjoy that we might commune with one another, we tried to seize them, to get more than our share at the expense of others. That is the history of our relationship with God, the breach in communion because of our push to consumption; so that God had to become consumer and took flesh. And he was a consuming foetus within his mother's body and consumed at her breast and grew up knowing the difficulties of and the need of consumption – and how it had to be in the context of communion. To make that clear, he established a tradition of meals. Whether they were meals of miracle or simply meals of companionship, it was the new kind of meal that established the new communion, the new *koinonia*.

All that was too much for the powers that were, and they conspired – as they often do – to have him eliminated. As they did that, it seemed that even God's last, best throw of overcoming this enmity between consumption and communion had failed. In the story of Good Friday, as we used to read it in the old liturgy and the Vulgate, are Jesus's famous final words: *consummatum est* – it is consummated; it is finally consumed. And Jesus is finally consumed by his enemies, by death, by the earth in which he is buried, and that might seem the end of the effort to overcome the enmity between communion and consumption. But a couple of women on Sunday recognised him; and a couple of people on the way to Emmaus were joined by a stranger and persuaded him to stay to break bread; and in the breaking of bread they recognised him. They knew the meaning, because on the night before he died, he took bread and he blessed and broke and gave to them and said, 'Take and eat, this is my body – bodies again – Take and drink, this is my blood. Do this in memory of me.' It is by consuming the body and blood, the bread and wine, that Holy Communion is established. The breakthrough, whereby the body language of communion would be ultimately and irreparably the body language of consumption, and *vice versa*, had been established; established in Jesus, established for humanity, but yet to be realised in history.

It is that body language that we have to pick up again. It is in this darkness that the disciples felt when they left the supper room, or at Calvary, that we can again begin to get the sense that consuming together is communing together, and that it is a divine call for the whole world. And that the ambiguities in all our communing and consuming, mean there is still a patch of 'marvellous grass' – and we will be as well as we were when we were young. And this is what we look to, hope for, attend to.

It may be that from these and other poems, from the poems of people's own lives, from the poems that are scripture, from the poetry and drama of the Eucharist, we will begin to recover a sense of the marvellous, begin again to move out of the darkness. But we have to be prepared to start at the beginning. We have to relearn the fumbling body language. We have to trust the first encounters we make, strange and demanding as they may be. It is too much to hope that poetry will cure our ills, where all the doctors and friars and priests summoned to the bed did not. But we will at least, from these and other artists, learn to read again the body language of our world, and of our own scriptures and our own sacraments, and in that way begin to respond to the crisis that is surely ours, but which could be grace and not destruction. Perhaps the community of faith could yet be what it was meant to be, 'a patch of marvellous grass.'

CHAPTER 8

Ecumenism, Vatican II, and Christology

Dermot A. Lane

One of the many distinguishing features of the life of Gabriel Daly OSA has been his theological ability to enable Christian faith to interact creatively with history, culture, and science. It was this particular gift that prompted him to reread and reinterpret what took place during the modernist crisis in the life of the Catholic Church in the late 1890s and the early twentieth century, and this in turn resulted in the publication of *Transcendence and Immanence: A Study in Catholic Modernism and Integralism*, which is to this day regarded as a benchmark study in modernism.[1] Equally impressive has been his commitment throughout his life to the theory and praxis of ecumenism. This commitment is clearly evident in the fact that he taught part-time in the Irish School of Ecumenics from 1970 to the present. In an unpublished paper, presented to the Academic Council of the Irish School of Ecumenics Trust on 22 February 2003, he expressed some concern about the danger of inter-religious dialogue and peace studies taking over from the unfinished business of the ecumenical movement: 'I would wish to argue strongly against allowing interfaith and peace studies to eclipse interchurch studies.' The purpose of this chapter, in honour of the outstanding contribution of Gabriel Daly to theology and ecumenism, is to take up this concern and review the state of ecumenism in the light of recent set backs.

It is well known that the ecumenical movement, after a lot of progress since the Second Vatican Council, has in the last number of years run into serious conflict and crisis. One expression of this crisis is the ordination of women in the Anglican Communion and the negative effect this has had on relations between Catholics and Anglicans. Another sign of the crisis can be found in the worsening relationships between the World Council of Churches and the Orthodox Church during a series

1. Gabriel Daly, *Transcendence and Immanence: A Study in Catholic Modernism and Integralism*, Oxford: Clarendon Press, 1980.

of meetings in Geneva in 2000, as well as ongoing tensions between the Orthodox and Catholic churches at a meeting of the 8th plenary session in Emmitsburg, Maryland, US, also in 2000. A more recent and better known expression of this crisis in ecumenism is to be found in the mixed reactions to the publication of *Dominus Iesus: On the Unicity and Salvific Universality of Jesus Christ and the Church* published by the Congregation for the Doctrine of the Faith on 5 September 2000. Chapter five of this document, entitled the 'Unicity and Unity of the Church', provoked a negative response not only from the churches originating in the Reformation but also from many within the Catholic Church from above and from below. The tone and content of *Dominus Iesus* has seriously damaged relationships between the Catholic Church and other Christian Churches.[2]

The language used in many of the reactions to the document tells its own tale: a watering down of progress, a dash of cold water, a neglect of twenty-five years of dialogue, a cooling-off in relations, a turning back of the clock, lost in a fog, an 'unchurching' of Christian denominations, and 'deep disappointments which troubled our hearts and diminished our expectations.'[3] In a time of crisis it is often necessary to go back in order to move forward. In this chapter I propose to go back first of all to the teaching of the Second Vatican Council on ecumenism and then to go back further to the person of Jesus Christ as the centre point of ecumenism, and finally in the light of this going back I will seek to go forward through the power of imagination and memory.

I THE SECOND VATICAN COUNCIL ON ECUMENISM

It is quite remarkable how the memory of the Second Vatican Council on ecumenism has been allowed to fade. One eyewitness to the event observes: 'Ruthless time is dispossessing us of council participants who in their tellings could still re-present the event.'[4] Indeed it needs to be recalled that Pope John XXIII in

2. For a sample of reactions see *Sic et Non: Encountering Dominus Iesus*, ed. by Steven J. Pope and Charles Heffling, New York: Orbis Books, 2002.
3. Bishop Walter Kasper, 'Week of Prayer for Christian Unity, 2001: I am the Way, and the Truth, and the Life', *Bulletin-Centro Pro Unione*, N. 59, Spring 2001:30.
4. Thomas Stransky, 'The Observers at Vatican Two: An Unique Experience of Dialogue', *Bulletin-Centro Pro Unione*, N. 63, Spring 2003: 8-14, 8.

his opening speech to the Council reminded his audience that the main reason for convening the Council was to redouble the efforts of the Catholic Church to work for the unity of all Christians.[5] Because of this purpose some 80 representatives from other churches were invited as observers to the council (by the end of the Council 167 observers had attended) and their positive influence on the work of the Council should not be underestimated. Further, it should be noted, it was in the opening speech of John XXIII that the distinction between the substance of the faith and the way in which it is expressed first appeared – a distinction that was to have a profound influence on subsequent ecumenical discussions. According to one commentator it was this particular distinction that broke open the conceptual monism that had characterised Catholic theology up to the Second Vatican Council.[6]

One of the highlights of the Council was the publication of the *Decree on Ecumenism*, November 1964 (*Unitatis redintegratio*) which outlined new principles on ecumenism for the Catholic church and crystallised the thinking of the Council on ecumenism. It should be remembered, however, that other important perspectives on ecumenism were also articulated in other documents of the Council. These include the teaching of a single source of revelation given in the person of Jesus Christ available in scripture and tradition together;[7] that the one church of Christ subsists in the Catholic Church as distinct from being identical with the Catholic Church, which had been the teaching prior to the Council;[8] that the search for truth must be carried out with respect for human dignity;[9] that the guiding idea of the council, especially for understanding the church is that of communion/ *communio/koinonia*;[10] that the church though sanctified is always in need of purification;[11] that a distinction exists between the

5. John XXIII, 'Opening Speech' 11 October, 1962, *Documents of Vatican II*, ed. by Walter Abbott and John Gallagher, New York: America Press, 1966, 717.

6. Thomas G. Guarino, *Revelation and Truth: Unity and Plurality in Contemporary Theology*, London and Toronto: Associated University Presses, 1993, 29.

7. See *Dei Verbum*, 1965, a. 7-10.

8. *Dogmatic Constitution on the Church*, 1964, a. 8.

9. *Declaration on Religious Freedom*, 1965, a. 3.

10. See especially the *Dogmatic Constitution on the Church*.

11. *Dogmatic Constitution on the Church*, a. 8.

content of faith and the expression of faith;[12] and that a guiding principle in dialogue should be the ancient axiom going back to Augustine, and ultimately to the Acts of the Apostles (15:28): 'Let there be unity in what is necessary, freedom in what is unsettled, and charity in everything else.'[13]

It is, however, in the *Decree on Ecumenism* that we find ecumenical principles which have been allowed to fade from memory and need to be more to the fore in the ecumenical praxis of the Catholic Church. These principles are worth recalling at this time of crisis within the ecumenical movement because they serve as a check on the way the church has conducted itself in the search for unity among Christians.

The *Decree on Ecumenism* begins by reminding us that the 'restoration of unity' is one of the principal concerns of the Second Vatican Council and describes the ecumenical movement as the work of the Spirit (a. 1). This objective of the Council, now forty years old, has produced real progress but it is a matter of regret that some of this progress seems to have been undone in the last few years.

The decree acknowledges that the present division among Christians 'openly contradicts the will of Christ, scandalises the world and damages ... the preaching of the gospel' (a. 1) and then goes on to say there is blame 'on both sides' for these divisions (a. 3). Acknowledgement of blame is of course a good point of departure in ecumenical dialogue and needs continually to be to the fore among all participants in the search for unity.

The decree points out that 'some, even very many, of the most significant elements and endowments which together go to build up and give life to the church , can exist outside the visible boundaries of the church: the Word of God ; the life of grace; faith, hope and charity, with the other interior gifts of the Holy Spirit, as well as visible elements' (a. 3). This teaching of Vatican II has assumed particular importance because of statements in *Dominus Iesus* (2000) 'that the Church of Christ ... continues to exist fully only in the Catholic Church'(a. 16) and that 'ecclesial communities which have not preserved valid episcopate ... and the integral substance of the Eucharist are not churches in the proper sense'(a. 17). These claims have caused misunderstanding and offence to the churches of the Reformation. The secre-

12. *Pastoral constitution on the Church in the Modern World,* a. 62.
13. *Pastoral Constitution on the Church in the Modern World,* a. 92.

tary of the Pontifical Council for Christian Unity captured the mood of many Catholics when he pointed out: '... the text is not exclusively decisive and needs to be understood in the context and the perspectives of other texts, especially ... the more binding documents of the Council and of the encyclical *Ut unum sint*.'[14] The *Decree on Ecumenism* just quoted (a. 3) claims that the church of Christ can exist outside the visible boundaries of the Catholic Church and this understanding of the decree is confirmed in the *Acta* of the Council.[15] Further it is noted that John Paul II repeats this positive understanding of ecclesial communities at Vatican II in his encyclical: 'Indeed, elements of sanctification and truth present in other Christian communities ... constitute the objective basis of communion, albeit imperfect, which exists between them and the Catholic Church. To the extent that these elements are found in other Christian Churches, the one church of Christ is effectively present in them'(a. 10) and he then goes on to make the point: 'It is not the case that beyond the boundaries of the Catholic community there is an ecclesial vacuum'(a. 13).[16] These clarifications, it is hoped, may reduce some of the misunderstanding created by *Dominus Iesus*.

On more than one occasion the decree of the Council stresses the important role that the laity, not just clergy or bishops, but 'clergy and laity' have to play in the work of ecumenism (a. 4). At present there is evidence of a growing gap between laity and the teaching authority of the church in the ways each reads the quest for Christian unity. This gap can be seen in strong reactions from below toward the document *One Bread, One Body* (1998) of the Bishops of England and Wales, Scotland and Ireland and the publication of *Dominus Iesus* in 2000. Part of the problem is the failure of the church to communicate its teaching

14. Walter Kasper, 'The Nature and Purpose of Ecumenical Dialogue', *Harvard Divinity Bulletin*, Winter 2001-2002, 19-23, 22.
15. See *Acta Synodiali Concilii Vaticani*, III/2,335 which says: 'In these (ecclesial) communities the one church of Christ is present, albeit imperfectly in a way that is somewhat like its presence in particular churches, and by means of their ecclesiastical elements the church of Christ is in some way operative in them.'
16. An elaboration of these points can be found in Jared Wicks, 'The significance of the "Ecclesial communities" of the Reformation', *Ecumenical Trends*, December 2001:10-13; Francis A. Sullivan, 'Introduction and Ecclesiological Issues', *Sic et Non: Encountering Dominus Iesus*, 47-56.

in an understandable language and part of the problem is the way the contents of these two documents were reported in the mass media.

The *Decree on Ecumenism* encourages 'every effort to avoid expressions, judgments and actions which do not represent the conditions of our separated brethren with truth and fairness' (a. 4). In this context the decree says in the same article: 'In all things let charity prevail'(a. 4).

The decree also points out that 'if, in various times and circumstances, there have been deficiencies in moral conduct or in church discipline or even in the way that church teaching has been formulated ... these should be set right at opportune moments and in proper ways' (a. 5). This demand of the Council was implemented in a service of repentance by John Paul II on the first Sunday of Lent in the Jubilee Year 2000. The requirement of repentance is spelt out in the claim 'there can be no ecumenism worthy of the name without interior conversion' (a. 7). The call to Christian unity among all the churches is ultimately a call to conversion.

On the difficult, painful and controversial issue of Eucharistic sharing, the Council says:

> Worship in common is not to be considered as a means to be used indiscriminately for the restoration of unity ... There are two main principles on which the practice of such common worship depends: first, that of the unity of the church which ought to be expressed; and second, that of sharing in the means of grace. Expression of unity generally forbids common worship. Grace to be obtained sometimes commends it (a. 8).

The decree goes on to note that the course of action to be adopted is a matter for decision by the local Episcopal authority. One wonders how these two principles in the decree have been taken into joint consideration. Clearly, if unity between the churches does not exist it cannot be expressed in the Eucharist; equally, indiscriminate inter-communion could be unwittingly counterproductive by having the effect of reducing the urgency of the renewal and reform required of all the churches in the journey toward unity. Is it conceivable, however, on special occasions that Eucharistic hospitality might be reconsidered on a limited scale on the basis of the second principle as expressed in this decree? The publication of *One Bread, One Body* by the Bishops of

England and Wales, Scotland and Ireland, though controversial at the time, did try to extend the exceptions permitting inter-communion – but these exceptions have been rarely enough taken up in pastoral practice.

The Council decree proposes that the Catholic Church should approach other churches in dialogue 'on an equal footing' (a. 9). In this way there will be a more open and honest exchange and a better understanding of the differences that exist between the partners in dialogue.

The decree advises that 'when comparing doctrines with one another, they (theologians) should remember that there exists an order or 'hierarchy of truths' since they vary in their relation to the foundations of the Christian faith'(a. 11). This new principle for ecumenism was well received at the time of the Council and was described by Oscar Cullmann, an invited guest, as 'the most revolutionary' statement of the Council and by the Catholic historian Joseph Lortz as 'possibly (the) most fruitful thought of the council;'[17] yet it does not appear to have been a determining influence in contemporary ecumenical exchanges.

In discussing relations with other churches and ecclesial communities, the decree says that our 'thoughts are concerned first of all with those Christians who openly confess Jesus Christ as God and Lord and as the only Mediator between God and man for the glory of the one God, the Father, the Son, and the Holy Spirit' (a. 20). This same article concludes by saying 'we rejoice that our separated brothers look to Christ as the source and centre of ecclesiastical communion' (a. 20).

It should be remembered that the *Decree on Ecumenism* and the *Dogmatic Constitution on the Church* were promulgated on the same day, 21 November 1964. In the speech that Paul VI gave on that occasion, he said, addressing himself to the non-Catholic observers, that the doctrine on the church 'in the *Dogmatic Constitution on the Church* was to be interpreted in the light of explanations given in the decree on ecumenism'.[18]

Finally, it is worth recalling that on the second last day of the

17. William Henn, 'The Hierarchy of Truths and Christian Unity', *Ephemirdes Theologicae Lovanienses*, Tomus LXVI (1990), 111-142, 118 n 21.

18. See A.A.S. 56, 1964,1012-3 and Francis A. Sullivan 'The Significance of Vatican II's decision to say of the Church of Christ not that it 'is' but that 'it subsists' in the Roman Catholic church', *Bulletin – Centro Pro Unione*, 29 - Spring 1986.

Council, 6 December 1965, Pope Paul VI and Patriarch Athenagoras I agreed to remove and lift from history the mutual sentences of excommunication issued by the Roman Catholic Church and the Orthodox Church of Constantinople in 1054 against each other.

II THE CENTRALITY OF CHRIST TO ECUMENISM

As already noted toward the end of the *Decree of Ecumenism* the Second Vatican Council emphasised, almost in passing in a short paragraph, that the person of Jesus Christ is 'the source and centre of Christian Unity' (a. 20). Looking back over the last forty years of ecumenical dialogue among the churches, it is remarkable and puzzling that few agreed statements have been made by the churches on the primacy of Christ for Christian unity. There are notable exceptions to this generalisation and we will deal with them presently.

Why is it that the churches have not come together to discuss the centrality of Christ in the quest for Christian unity? In defence of the churches, it could be pointed out that the Final Reports of *ARCIC-I* (1981) and *ARCIC-II* (1999), *BEM* (1982), and the *Joint Declaration on the Doctrine of Justification* (1999) by Catholics and Lutherans have christologies implicit in their statements, and that the person of Jesus Christ is assumed to be the key to unity for the churches. However, what is only implicit and/or taken for granted is often most vulnerable to questioning. Further, what is assumed and simply repeated without going through the process of historical retrieval and theological reinterpretation is in danger of becoming an empty formula.

At present a serious gap exists within the ecumenical movement among the many multilateral and bilateral statements on the church, Eucharist, ministry and authority on the one hand and christology on the other hand. This gap is all the more striking when one takes account of the renaissance in christology in the second half of the twentieth century. The christological renewal of the last fifty years has been informed by extensive biblical, patristic, theological, and historical studies on the person and work of Jesus Christ. These studies have brought many benefits to a deeper appreciation of the mystery of Jesus as the Christ: a rediscovery of the humanity of Jesus, a recovery of the importance of the historical life and ministry of Jesus, a better understanding of the Reign of God in the preaching and *praxis* of

Jesus, a new emphasis on the unity of the paschal mystery of the death and resurrection of Jesus, and a richer theology of the incarnation. One of the most striking features of the renewal in christology is how much basic agreement there is across denominational lines among biblical scholars in their approach to the study of the bible.[19]

In the light of this renaissance in christology, John P. Galvin talks about 'a paradigm shift in Catholic Christology' in the last 25 years.[20] William P. Loewe describes this shift in terms of a movement from an ahistorical, metaphysical approach to a more historical account of christology.[21] Elizabeth E. Johnson claims that historical research into the gospels is 'changing the traditional Christian imagination regarding the dynamic of Jesus' life and destiny'.[22] It needs to be said that these developments go well beyond what George Tyrrell describes as Harnack's account of 'nineteen centuries of Catholic darkness' and the 'liberal Protestant face seen at the bottom of a deep well' at the beginning of the twentieth century study of the gospels.[23] It is no longer simply 'faith alone' or 'history alone' but rather 'history and faith' working together in a mutually critical and correcting relationship within contemporary experience. The study of Jesus and the gospels has clearly moved beyond historical positivism and theological fundamentalism.

And yet this rich harvest in christology, inspired by cross-denominational collaboration in the study of the New Testament, has had only an indirect impact on the ecumenical search for unity 'in Christ'. In brief, these biblical and theological insights into the historical life of Jesus, the crucified and risen Christ,

19. See Raymond F. Collins, 'What has Happened to the Study of the New Testament in the Last Forty Years?' *Catholic Theology Facing the Future: Historical Perspectives*, edited by Dermot A. Lane, Dublin: Columba Press, 2003, 46-61

20. John P. Galvin, 'From the Humanity of Christ to the Jesus of History: A Paradigm Shift in Catholic Christology,' *Theological Studies* 55 (1994), 256.

21. W. P. Loewe, 'From the Humanity of Christ to the Historical Jesus', *Theological Studies* (2000), 314-331, 331.

22. Elizabeth A Johnson, 'The Word made flesh and dwelt among us: Jesus research and Christian Faith', *Jesus, A Colloquium in the Holy Land*, ed. by Doris Donnelly, New York, Continuum Books, 2001, 146 –166, 150.

23. George Tyrrell, *Christianity at the Cross-Roads*, London, 1909, 44.

confessed as Lord and proclaimed as the Word made flesh, are of outstanding significance for the way Christian churches should configure themselves. As disciples of Christ, charged with a mission and ministry rooted in Jesus' preaching and *praxis* of the Reign of God, all of the churches are called by the same Spirit to announce the good news of resurrection to the world and to build up the Body of Christ into an ordered communion of communions 'in Christ'.

This call to the christological centre of Christian unity is all the more urgent when, paradoxically, there is on the one hand a decline in institutionalised Christianity across denominations, at least in Europe and North America, and on the other hand there is an extraordinary fascination by the secular world with the reality of the historical Jesus.[24] To be sure, Christianity is more than Jesus – but the historical Jesus of the gospels is a good point of departure for understanding the church's proclamation of Jesus as the Risen Christ who is the Son of God made flesh, the source of the living Spirit of God, and the centre of unity among all Christians.

Moreover, this call to a christological centre is now more pressing than ever for all of the Christian churches in the light of the growing interest in inter-religious dialogue. This new dialogue is raising searching questions about the uniqueness of Jesus, about the role of Jesus as the one Mediator between God and humanity, about the universality of salvation in Christ, about the relationship of the eternal Word made flesh in Jesus to other expressions of the presence of the Word of God in history and in the world, and about the particular activity of the Spirit of Christ in the churches and the universal action of the Spirit in other religions. This, I take it, is part of the point that Gabriel Daly was intimating in his talk to the Irish School of Ecumenics in 2003 when he called for closer attention to be given to ecumenical theology.

As stated, there are some notable exceptions to the general statement that christology has not been prominent in ecumenical conversations between Anglicans, Protestants and Catholics.

---

24. See for example *Time* magazine with the cover story devoted to 'The Search for Jesus', 8 April, 1996 and again *Time* magazine with a cover story 'Jesus at 2000' 6 December, 1999 and E. P. Sanders on 'In Quest of the Historical Jesus', *The New York Review of Books*, 15 November, 2001, 33-36.

The first significant exception to our general thesis about the neglect of christology in ecumenism is to be found in an agreed statement between the Uniting Church and the Lutheran Church in Australia in 1990 entitled 'One Christ in Church and World'.[25] This statement sets out to answer the question 'Who is Jesus Christ for us today?' and has the great merit of highlighting that for Luther, faith in Christ as 'both God's Son and the Virgin's Son in one person, though of two natures', is ultimately what is necessary for salvation, and that for Calvin placing 'Christ at the centre' is of paramount importance.

Two other exceptions are dialogues between the Catholic Church and the Oriental Orthodox churches, and the Catholic Church and the Assyrian Church of the East. The Oriental Orthodox churches (Coptic, Syrian, Armenian, Ethiopian, and Malankara) rejected some of the teaching of the Council of Chalcedon in 451 and became known subsequently as 'Monophysites'. In 1988 they signed in Vienna a Christological Formula with the Catholic Church which affirms the central claim of Chalcedon namely Jesus as true God and true man while avoiding some of the technical language of Chalcedon.

In a similar move, the Assyrian Church of the East, which goes back to the Persian Empire which existed where Iran and Iraq are today, sometimes though improperly called the 'Nestorian Church', in 1994 agreed upon a Common Christological Declaration with the Catholic Church.[26] This *Common Christological Declaration,* signed by Pope John Paul II and Catholicos-Patriarch Mar Dinkha IV of the Assyrian Church of the East, brought to an end disputes that had separated these two churches since 431. In that document, the Catholic and Assyrian churches go behind the complex language of the council of Ephesus, 431, reaffirming the full divinity of Jesus while recognising at the same time the legitimacy of praying to Mary as the Mother of Christ our God and Saviour within the

25. Available in R. Williamson (ed.), *Stages on the Way: Documents of the Bilateral Conversations between Churches in Australia,* Melbourne: Joint Board of Christian Education, 1994, 236-242.
26. This *Common Christological Declaration* is available in *The Heythrop Journal* xxxvii (1996), 389-390 with a commentary by Gerald O'Collins and Daniel Kendal entitled 'Overcoming Christological Difference', 382-389.

Assyrian Church and praying to Mary as the Mother of God within the Catholic tradition.

These two christological statements transcend the technical language of Chalcedon and Ephesus in order to reaffirm the underlying content of these councils. These two agreed statements on christology are significant for the ecumenical movement in general and in particular for dialogue among Christian churches in the West for at least three reasons. First of all, they alert us to the fact it was over christology that early divisions began to take place within the Body of Christ. Second, these agreed christological statements highlight that a significant degree of pluralism is possible when it comes to expressing the identity of Jesus Christ. Third, these statements indicate how it is possible to go behind some of the most dogmatic statements within the Catholic tradition to recover their underlying truth within another formulation.[27]

A fourth notable exception to the above generalisation about the neglect of christology in ecumenism is of course the *Joint Declaration on the Doctrine of Justification* signed by Catholics and Lutherans in Augsburg, 1999. While the declaration deals specifically with justification, it is premised on agreements between Catholics and Lutherans that are explicitly christological: 'Our Lord, Jesus Christ: Only Mediator between God and humankind', 'Christ, Mediator and Reconciler', and 'Word of Christ Reveals He is the Son within the Trinity'. It was these clear christological confessions of faith that paved the way for agreement between Lutherans and Catholics on the very specific though basic doctrine of justification. While there may be some discussion among other Reformation churches as to how central the doctrine of justification is as an organising principle and criterion for articulating the gospel,[28] there is surely no disagreement about the primacy of Christ as the source, ground and goal of unity among all Christians. The great lesson to be learned from the *Joint Declaration* for the ecumenical movement is that when there is agreement on the full mystery of Jesus Christ, then agreement on other doctrinal issues is not far behind.

27. See Leo D. Lefebure, 'Christology in Ecumenical Dialogue: Expressing the Identity of Jesus Christ' *Chicago Studies*, 39 (1999), 154-164, 164.

28. See Alan D. Falconer, 'The Joint Declaration: Faith and Order Perspective', *Journal of Ecumenical Studies*, Winter, 2001, 5-16.

A feature common to these exceptions is their relative innocence of the various 'Quests' of the historical Jesus throughout the twentieth century. Some will see this as a strength of these christological statements, while others will see it as a weakness. There is surely a middle position to be adopted here. It is clear, of course, that some of the quests of the historical Jesus, especially as found in the US 'Jesus Seminar' from the middle 1980s onward, with the publication of sensational findings, have been unhelpful and seem for some to have driven a wedge between historical research and christology. A middle position, however, should be able to avoid a fideism which neglects history and an historicism which ignores faith in approaching the gospels. Christian faith does not depend on the changing results of historical research into the gospels and is not therefore grounded simply in the findings of history alone. On the other hand, Christian faith is a historical faith and this faith is mediated by the historical narratives of Jesus as given in the New Testament, especially in the four gospels. Christology must make room for the historical Jesus of the gospels, because a christology divorced from Jesus is in danger of becoming a 'myth', of being overly inflated in its doctrinal claims, and of losing contact with the full humanity of Jesus of Nazareth.

A further exception, this time not in terms of agreed statements between churches, to the general neglect of christology in ecumenism can be found in the work of Walter Kasper, theologian, bishop and currently Cardinal Prefect of the Pontifical Council for Promoting Christian Unity. Kasper the theologian has written extensively in the area of christology.[29] As far back as 1976 he noted:

> The unresolved questions of ecclesiology can be answered only with a renewed christology and only a renewed christology can enable the church to regain its universality and catholicity (in the original sense of that term) without denying the foolishness of the cross and surrendering the unique provocation of Christianity.[30]

Kasper puts his finger on a neuralgic issue in contemporary Catholic theology, namely the relationship between christology and ecclesiology. He is clear in his own theology that 'the church

29. See for example Walter Kasper, *Jesus, the Christ*, London: Burns and Oates, 1976 and *The God of Jesus Christ*, London: SCM Press, 1984.
30. Walter Kasper, *Jesus, the Christ*, 16.

must always be on its way towards Jesus Christ' and that the church 'has continually to reconsider its origins. It has to think back to Jesus Christ, to his word and deeds, to his life and destiny.'[31] Kasper, the bishop, on the occasion of being made an honorary professor of the University of Tübingen, pointed out in a public lecture that 'faith in Jesus Christ as one, unique, and universal Mediator of salvation … is the basic presupposition of all ecumenism.'[32] The way forward to unity 'is not individual conversion to the Catholic Church but the conversion of everyone to Jesus Christ'.[33] In brief, it is the person of Jesus Christ who is 'the measure of ecumenical movement'.[34]

This recovery of the centrality of Christ to ecumenism points to the way forward for all Christians in the twenty-first century. It reminds us forcefully that Christianity is not about a book we call the bible, is not about a code of morality called the commandments, is not about a set of ideas called dogmas; instead it is about a relationship with a living person called Jesus, recognised as the Christ, who is the eternal Son of God made flesh, actively present as Spirit in the community of his Body called the church. The role of the bible, and of morality, and of the dogmas are important insofar as they mediate the empowering presence of Christ crucified, risen and alive as Spirit in the church and in the world. The primary role of the church is to be the face of Christ to the world. This is the task of the churches in the twenty-first century and there can be little doubt that this could be done more credibly, more effectively, and more imaginatively if they spoke united as one around the person of Jesus Christ.

Living in a world marked by a strong sense of historical consciousness, it is impossible to see how the churches as many or as one 'in Christ' can proclaim the good news without some reference to historical research into the life of Jesus of Nazareth as contained in the four gospels. It was the churches of the Reformation that led the way in the twentieth century in applying the science of historical research to the bible. The Catholic Church, it could be said, caught up through the publication and

31. *Jesus, the Christ*, 28

32. Walter Kasper, 'The Future of Ecumenism', *Theology Digest* 49:3 (Fall 2002), 204

33. Ibid., 205

34. Walter Kasper, 'Week of Prayer for Christian Unity 2001', Homily, *Bulletin - Centro Pro Unione*, N. 59, Spring 2001, 30.

application of *Divino Afflante Spiritu* (1943), the 1964 Instruction 'On the historical truth of the gospels', the *Dogmatic Constitution on Divine Revelation* at Vatican II in 1965, and the 1993 Biblical Commission document on 'The Interpretation of the Bible in the Church'. These documents have brought about a significant degree of ecumenical collaboration in the study of the bible. When historical, literary, social, and redactional criticism are brought to bear on the gospel from within a community of faith, then new perspectives are opened up on the life of Jesus that are important to the proclamation of the good news and the quest for unity. The historical narrative of the life of Jesus in the gospels aided by research provides an ever-fresh understanding about the Reign of God in the prophetic preaching and *praxis* of Jesus, about the privileged place of the poor and marginalised in the life of Jesus, about the new table fellowship initiated by Jesus, about the person of Jesus as a teacher of wisdom, about the temptation to legalism in our relationship with God and our neighbour, about the way authority is to be exercised among all the followers of Jesus, and about justice as a prerequisite to worship. This narrative of the life of Jesus in the gospel has important theological significance for ecclesial faith and *praxis* – not to mention the centrality of the kenotic Jesus on the cross, the glorified Christ sitting at the right hand of God the Father, sending his Spirit in the service of truth and reconciliation in the world.

In making this plea for a return to Jesus Christ as the centre of the ecumenical movement, it needs to be said at the same time that the christology being proposed should not be understood as a call to christomonism. To the contrary: the reason why christology is emphasised as a core issue in the search for unity among the churches is that it is the person of Jesus Christ who reveals the full mystery of God. The christology being suggested and merely outlined here is a christology that is theocentric, that is, a christology that enables the churches to encounter the living presence of God and discover the Christian God as a unified communion of Father, Son and Holy Spirit. It is this trinitarian christology that provides the basis for an ecclesiology of communion. Equally, it is important to stress, if only in passing, the theocentric and trinitarian character of christology, because some Protestant churches stress more than others the sovereignty of God's action with God's People as mediated through Christ.

One further point about christology as the basis of unity for the churches concerns the relationship between christology and eschatology. Anyone reading the New Testament will sense quickly the eschatological tension that exists between being 'in Christ' and becoming 'in Christ', between that which has already been realised in Christ and that which is yet to come, between the First Coming of Christ and the Second Coming of Christ. This tension is explicitly evident in the symbol of the cross and the enduring presence of an apocalyptic outlook in the gospels. The Christian unity sought by the churches must realistically recognise this eschatological tension in the New Testament. Even if the churches were to be united tomorrow, they would only be able to prefigure, quite inadequately – though more effectively than at present as divided – the fullness of God's plan to unite all things in heaven and on earth in Christ.

III. MOVING FORWARD THROUGH THE POWER OF IMAGINATION AND MEMORY

In the light of going back to the teaching of the church at Vatican II and to the gospel of Jesus Christ, it is now time to move forward through the power of imagination and memory. In doing so, we need to recognise that the context of the ecumenical movement has been changing under the impact of pluralism, globalisation and interfaith dialogue. The movement towards Christian unity from 1910 (Edinburgh) through 1948 (World Council of Churches) to 1962-1965 (Vatican II) was premised on a perception of unity that has changed over the years. It is difficult to chart that change because it has included shifts from an ecumenism of return and restorationism, to an ecumenism that recognises the need for conversion by all churches as the primary way forward to a visible unity, or a reconciled diversity, or a communion of communions 'in Christ'.

The growing presence of pluralism within theology is now recognised as something to be valued and treasured within the unity of Christian faith. Pluralism is increasingly accepted not as a threat but a gift provided it has a coherent centre of unity. The unity sought in the ecumenical movement is no longer one of uniformity but a unity-within-diversity, no longer a call to conformity but a summons to a shared communion 'in Christ'.

Second, the globalisation of life brought about by the new information technologies highlights the multicultural character of the whole of existence and how, therefore, one and the same

Christian faith can and does exist in a great variety of cultural forms. This diversity is perceived as something that can be enriching for both faith and culture alike.

Third, there is an ever-increasing demand for interfaith dialogue. This wider ecumenism *ad extra* calls for a new level of dialogue with the other religions of the world – no longer as an optional extra but as something intrinsic to the dynamism of Christian faith. The encounter between Christianity and the other living faiths is exerting a new pressure on all Christian churches to move towards a unity of Christian faith so that with one voice they can fruitfully engage in this process of interreligious dialogue.

Looking at ecumenism *ad intra* it is important to remember the prayer of Jesus: 'that they may be one … As you, Father, are in me and I am in you, may they also be in us, so that the world may believe that you have sent me.'[35] The goal of Christian unity, therefore, is not unity for the sake of unity, but that the world may believe and have faith in the one true God. Anyone who believes in the historical revelation of God in the person of Jesus Christ can only become impatient with the institutional reluctance of all Christian churches to promote a more imaginative search for the unity of Christian faith and *praxis*. This impatience at times turns to suspicion when Christian churches refuse to let go of what are often less than strict theological differences, especially in the light of so much agreement now reached by the different Christian churches over the last thirty-five years of bilateral and multilateral agreed statements: *ARCIC-I* (1981), *BEM* (1982), *ARCIC-II* (1999), and *JDDJ* (1999).

There is growing disillusionment among many Christians today when tightly controlled institutional expressions of faith become an end in themselves – almost as if Christian unity could come about by some kind of conceptual hegemony. The priority given to orthodoxy over *orthopraxis* is also experienced by many as something that goes against the grain of the gospel, which is understood primarily as a way of living in the world. Further, there is a question mark around the capacity of the divided churches to mediate and incarnate the living presence of the crucified and risen Christ as the primary symbol of unity. It is the face of Jesus welcoming the stranger and embracing the other, the face of the disfigured Jesus on the cross forgiving his

35. John 17:21.

executioners, the face of glorified Christ, present in the Spirit, that the world seeks in this time of extraordinary exclusions, excessive brokenness and bewildering fragmentation.

In the light of these developments, what is most needed within the ecumenical movement is a new imagination that can come up creatively with an alternative understanding of Christian unity. The failure of the churches to arrive at unity is at base a failure of the imagination. The ingredients for the unity of faith in Christ Jesus among the churches are already given in terms of the scriptures, the early creeds and the twentieth century agreed statements. What is lacking is an exercise of the creative imagination in the construction of a new model of unity-within-diversity.

Imagination as a faculty has suffered in the past by an unfortunate association with personal projection, the merely fanciful, and the unreal. However, something of a rehabilitation of the centrality of the imagination within human understanding and interpretation has been taking place in recent times.[36] This recovery of the role of the imagination needs to be applied in particular to the quest for Christian unity among the divided churches. Imagination is the unique capacity of the human spirit that is able to unite what is divided, to heal what is wounded, and to gather what is scattered. Imagination enables the heart to go beyond the merely mundane aspects of human experience to begin to discover the invisible finality of life itself, to add what is missing within human experiences, and to complete what is partial in the perceptions of life. At present there is too much that is unfinished, too much that is unfulfilled, too much that is broken within the Body of Christ. To this extent imagination has an important role to play in ecumenism in the search for new models of unity-within-diversity and the quest for a new communion 'in Christ' among the communions.

The dynamism of the human imagination under the influence of the gospel of Jesus Christ has the capacity to go beyond the endless analyses of agreed statements by the churches to embrace the unity implicit in these statements and to hold together in new and creative ways that which initially appears as divisive. These impulses of the imagination towards Christian unity

36. See for example Richard Kearney, *Poetics of Imagining: Modern to Postmodern*, Edinburgh: Edinburgh University Press, 1998; Mary Warnock, *Imagination*, London: Faber, 1976 and James P. Mackey (ed.), *Religious Imagination*, Edinburgh: Edinburgh University Press, 1986.

are best evaluated by a shared *praxis* of faith and not by reason alone, just as the truth of Christian faith is something that is ultimately only available within the *praxis* of self-surrender to the grace of God revealed in Jesus Christ.

There is already present within the history of Christianity a strong tradition that evokes imagination. Examples of this can be found in the apophatic imagination of the East, the analogical imagination of Aquinas in the West, and the dialectical imagination emanating from Luther's theology of the cross. This use of imagination within the Christian tradition has been able to hold in unity a rich diversity of Christianity for over a thousand years. This exercise of the imagination is now something that should be applied to the ecclesial quest for unity 'in Christ' so that what appear to be mutually exclusive doctrinal positions of the churches can in fact be united as one within a new imaginative framework.

Equally, it is through the power of imagination that the gospel is able to hold together in dynamic unity the scandal of particularity alongside the universal claims for the Christ-event. That is to say, the oneness of the historical life of Jesus exists alongside claims about the ultimacy of Jesus as the crucified and Risen Christ. It is, in effect, the power of the imagination that enables Christians to proclaim Jesus as the 'concrete universal' to the world. In this way the Christian imagination has the capacity to reconfigure in a creative unity different ecclesial positions which at first may appear incompatible or opposite to each other.

In seeking to arrive at a fundamental unity-within-diversity it is important to recognise that there already exists a considerable degree of plurality within and among the different ecclesial communities and that, therefore, in fostering unity for example between Anglicans and Catholics one must not seek a unity that exceeds the already existing plurality *within* either denomination. In other words we must not expect a unity with other churches which is not demanded or does not already exist within particular Christian denominations. There are often deeper divisions between 'liberals' and 'conservatives' within a particular denomination than there are between one denomination and another at the formal level.

Further, all of the churches should remember (as already noted above) that the Christianity of the New Testament is a thoroughly eschatological religion and that, therefore, a certain eschatological proviso must accompany all models of Christian unity.

If the path to Christian unity hinted at here through the exercise of a new ecumenical imagination is to succeed, then it will also be necessary at the same time to initiate a process of healing in relation to ecclesial memories. One of the most promising signs of progress within the ecumenical movement at present is the growing awareness among many Christian churches of the need to heal our respective historical memories.

All too often memory has been reduced to nostalgia and sentimentality. There is, however, a richer meaning to memory within Judaism and early Christianity. Further, memory is closely connected to the composition of human and religious identity and so a loss of memory diminishes identity, whereas a recovery of memory can often renew identity and create communion. On the other hand, memory is frequently fragile and fallible. Historical memories can often be the bearers of distortion, misunderstanding and misrepresentation. Consequently it will be necessary to revisit history in order to reopen memories so that there can be a healing of the distortions and hurts within history with a view to recovering a lost unity.

It is important, therefore, to stress that memory is more than just a psychological recall; it is also something that is constitutive of human identity and Christian self-understanding. Further, memory has the power to disrupt the tyranny of misunderstandings in the present in a way that enables people to realise that the way we are, for example divided as Christians, is not the way we have to be. Above all it is memory that has the capacity to heal misunderstandings, overcome differences, and transform divisions into a new unity.

The language of 'healing of memories' has begun to appear in recent ecumenical exchanges. For example the healing of historical memories has been to the fore in the documents of the French *Groupe des Dombes* from the early 1980s onwards. This ecumenical group claims that without what it calls a 'converted rereading' of history, our ecumenical study of the scriptures will continue to be selective:

> In our judgment, without this necessary passage (through history), the recourse to scripture threatened to hide our respective presuppositions in a selective reading and a skewed

> interpretation. Our task is rather to re-read history with a conscience that is as alert as possible to what is at stake, in order to gather up the whole of what it teaches us, while respecting its richness and the complementarity of its diverse data.[37]

A similar example of the importance of the healing of memories can be found in the complex relationship between the Orthodox and Catholic churches. In spite of many agreed doctrinal statements, insufficient attention has been given to the different accounts and conflicting narratives of history underlining the divisions between Catholics and the Orthodox:

> We can change the future but we cannot change the past, and it is the bitter heritage of this past that is blocking all ecumenical progress today. The hostilities created by that dolorous past are deep-rooted in the psyche of Eastern Christians, both Orthodox and Catholic, so deep-rooted that the average Westerner finds them perplexing, at times even infantile and ridiculous. All of which provides stark confirmation of the need for 'the healing or purification of memory'.[38]

A third example can be found at a meeting between John Paul II and leaders of the Swiss Evangelical Church Federation in 1984 celebrating the 500th birthday of Ulrich Zwingli and the 475th anniversary of the birth of John Calvin, where he pointed out:

> The cleansing of our memories is an element of capital importance in ecumenical progress. It implies the frank acknowledgement of reciprocal wrongs and errors committed in a way of reacting to each other when indeed each one wanted to make the church more faithful to the will of the Lord.[39]

Similarly in 1990, in a report entitled *Towards a Common Understanding of Church* between the World Alliance of Reformed Churches and the Roman Catholic Church, there is a

---

37. Groupe des Dombes, *Le ministère de Communion dans l'Eglise Universelle*, Paris: Centurion, 1986, 16. I owe this reference to Catherine E. Clifford, 'Dialogue and Method: Learning From the Groupe des Dombes' *One in Christ*, Vol. 38, No. 2, April 2003, 43-57, 49-50.

38. Robert Taft, 'Anamnesis not Amnesia: The 'healing of memories' and the problem of 'uniatism'', Lecture at Saint Michael's College, Toronto, 1 December 2000. Available at http://www.utoronto.ca/saintmikes/theology/taft/kelly2000.htm

39. John-Paul II, 'To the Swiss Evangelical Church Union', *Kerhrastz*, June 14, 1984 *Information service* 55 (1984) 8-47.

section entitled 'Toward the Reconciliation of Memories' which refers to myths and misunderstandings about each other and then suggests 'we must go on from here ... to a reconciliation of memories in which we will begin to share one sense of the past rather than two.'[40]

Again, this language of the healing of memories is also found in the encyclical of John Paul II, *Ut Unum Sint*, that talks about 'the necessary purification of past memories.'[41]

To help develop this idea of the healing of memories, I wish to draw a little on the work of Paul Ricoeur, especially from an essay by him on how to effect European unification.[42] There are some striking parallels between the search for European integration and quest for unity among Christian churches.

Human beings, as individuals and members of communities, live out of their memory of a particular narrative and it is this narrative that gives shape to human identity. It is increasingly clear that if we are to know who we are, we need to be able to draw upon a narrative. In reality, the self is accessible only in and through narrative. Ricoeur outlines three important principles about human identity in this regard.

According to the first principle: 'narrative identity is not that of an immutable substance or fixed structure.'[43] Instead, a certain mobility of human identity is necessary when account is taken of the surrounding events within history when we listen to the same narrative as told by others.

A second principle proposed by Ricoeur is that every human 'identity is mingled with that of others in such a way as to engender second order stories; ... the story of my life is a segment of the story of your life ... we are literally "entangled in stories".'[44]

A third principle recommended by Ricoeur is that the exchange of memories relating to identity is often inhibited by 'the influence exercised over the collective memory by what we term

40. 'Towards a Common Understanding of Church: Reformed/Roman Catholic International Dialogue, second phase (1984-1990)', *Information Service* 74 (1990) 15 -16.

41. John-Paul II, *Ut unum sint*, a. 2, 1995.

42. Paul Ricoeur, 'Reflections on a new Ethos for Europe', Paul Ricoeur, *The Hermeneutics of Action*, ed. Richard Kearney, London: Sage Publications, 1996, 3-13.

43. Ibid. 6.

44. Ibid.6.

"founding events" ... which tend to freeze the history of each cultural group.'[45] This particular principle endorses earlier comments about how important it is to be able to go back to the founding events of the history of christology.

If we apply these principles to the narrative of our different ecclesial identities, we can begin to see that a particular church identity and self understanding need not remain fixed and in fact does not remain fixed. For example, the identity of the Catholic Church at Vatican II was significantly different without being contradictory to the identity and self-understanding of the church at Vatican I. As noted earlier, the presence of so many non-Catholic observers at Vatican II had a constructive influence at how the church expressed its identity at the Second Vatican Council. By retelling our respective stories in the company of each other we can begin to heal misunderstandings, correct misrepresentations and change perceptions within our respective traditions. A healing of historical memories can alter, even transform, the way we describe our particular ecclesial identities. This will happen when we discover that we are far more bound up with each other's narratives than we care to admit and that often these historical narratives are feeding off misrepresentations and misunderstandings of each other. This has certainly happened in the past in regard to the way we have told the stories of the split between East and West in the eleventh century and the stories of the Reformation in the sixteenth century that have resulted in deep ecclesial divisions.

Of course, within the healing of historical memories among the different churches there comes an important moment when forgiveness must be offered for the misunderstandings and sufferings inflicted on each other. Such forgiveness must not be confused with forgetfulness because forgiveness, which forgets, is merely 'a product of shallowness and indifference'.[46] Instead, 'the work of forgiveness must be grafted onto the work of memory and the language of narration'.[47] What is ultimately important is that the healing of memories has the power to shatter 'the law of the irreversibility of time by changing the past, not as a record of all that has happened but in terms of its meaning for us

45. Ibid. 7.
46. Ibid. 11.
47. Ibid.11.

today.'[48] In a very important sense, it can be said, as others like Walter Benjamin have suggested, the past is not necessarily closed and fixed and final. Rather, through the power of memory the past can be revisited, reopened and changed in the present, especially in its significance for the present through the healing power of memory and the offer of forgiveness. This does not mean that the events of the past can be changed – but it does suggest their meaning in the present can be reconfigured, especially in the way we map narrative identities in the present.

In the light of so many agreed statements between the different Christian churches over the last thirty-five years, the time now seems ripe for the initiation of a formal process of healing the historical memories among divided Christian denominations. Such a healing could be addressed to the rift between East and West as well as the division between the churches emerging out of the Reformation in continental Europe and later in England. If this process of healing is to be effective, then it should be embodied in distinctive acts of forgiveness and these acts of forgiveness in turn ought to be dramatised in ritual forms which refuse to forget the pain of past divisions and the damage done to the proclamation of the Word of God and the Body of Christ. In this way there is at least the hope that this pain will not be repeated in the future.

In brief and to conclude, all of the Christian churches, by going back to their historical roots in the person of Jesus Christ and by exercising the power of memory and imagination in the light of the Christ-event and tradition, can begin to move forward towards a new unity 'in Christ' as the gift of the Spirit in this time of crisis.

48. Ibid, 10.

CHAPTER 9

Christian Ethics and Culture

Maureen Junker-Kenny

The themes with which Gabriel Daly's name is connected, faith and culture, the modernist crisis, science and religion, the distinctive forms Christianity has taken in the Catholic and Protestant churches, give Christian witness through the liberating work of the intellect. Thinking for oneself in institutions, renewing the present expression of faith by actualising the resources of the Christian tradition in a hermeneutical analysis of their settings, shows the strength of an immanent critique. I want to apply Gabriel Daly's critical mediation of the Christian testimony with modernity to the question of what role Christian ethics should play in a pluralist society which still owes many of its values to the cultural event of Christianity.

But is it possible to speak of 'Christianity' *tout court*? We know already that 'the Christian faith' is not such a clear-cut entity. Gabriel Daly questions the metaphor of husk and kernel that Adolf von Harnack used to describe the changing appearance of a Christianity whose essence he thought remained unchanged. But even if one shares Daly's doubts whether this image captures the relationship well, it is still true, as Johann Baptist Metz insists, that there never has been and never can be a 'naked Christianity'. It will always be clothed in the garb of its time and region, in specific images, concepts, and modes of life. The human question for salvation takes on a different expression in each paradigm. What do we need to be liberated from, what does it take to make us 'whole,' redeemed, reconciled? The history of theology shows in how many different ways the human brokenness that needs to be healed has been identified: as a dualism between matter and spirit, body and soul, nature and mind, or as a conflict within the mind to seek fulfilment in finite objects over against the infinite. It is the task of Christian ethics to investigate what is the basic form of 'sin,' which major temptations come with the distinct possibilities of each period, what shape the quest for salvation and the vision of the good life take today. Only in response to these questions can the relationship of the Christian faith to contemporary culture be assessed.

I shall proceed in three steps by investigating, first, a position that identifies Christian faith and modern culture, second, that radically opposes them, and third, that claims the ongoing need for democracy to be founded on the Christian faith. The first view, of Christianity reaching its summit in the modern culture of free individualism, is supported by the observation that secular culture has come about as a result of the desacralisation of the world effected by the Jewish and Christian traditions with their belief in a divine good creator and their ranking of the human person as a partner with God. Modernity has absorbed basic tenets of these traditions. The Jewish and Christian convictions of the equality of all the children of God, their trust that each person's name is inscribed on God's hand, the call to love one's neighbour, the sense of self-worth conveyed by the Christian belief that God became human in Christ, live on in the determination of the Declarations of Human Rights from the eighteenth century onwards to respect the incalculable value of each person by not allowing the basic rights of individuals to be sacrificed for the needs of the collectivity. In view of these links of Christianity with the best elements of a democratic culture, can we not describe a participative and just society as Christianity realised? How do philosophers and theologians regard the proposition that modern culture is the fulfilment of Christianity?

In my second step, the concept of Christianity is put into question. Especially in Kierkegaard's scathing critique of 'Christendom,' the ambiguity of this term has been highlighted. 'Christendom' signifies the established, staid system of Christian religion which admires in self-satisfaction the cultural expressions – cathedrals, oratorios, *Summas* and *Institutes* – it has brought forth. Is it cultural or radical Christianity that we are comparing to secular culture, and would a culture of Christendom be really worth defending? I shall compare in this second section the diverging viewpoints of the nineteenth-century thinkers of religion Søren Kierkegaard and Friedrich Schleiermacher, whose dogmatics takes on the challenge of modernity's turn to human autonomy and explains the Christian faith on its basis.

Finally, what recent views exist on the kind of impact the Christian religion should have on secular culture? The German

Protestant systematic theologian Wolfhart Pannenberg puts forth a view that many may share in Ireland. The law should protect the religious foundations of the state. But does this position respect the autonomy of culture, the validity of the state which has been accepted at least by liberal Protestant theology and by Catholic theology since the Second Vatican Council? On what grounds should Christian theologians argue in the ethical controversies of our time? Should they presume that everyone ought to have a religious outlook, or do they need to recognise the legitimacy of a plurality of worldviews and ethical convictions? If so, can they argue for anything but the lowest common denominator of all moral judgments from different backgrounds? What route is open to them then for contributing their specific insights and demands to contemporary public debate?

I MODERN CULTURE AS CHRISTIANITY REALISED?

One does not have to go back as far as Hegel to find the position that Christianity has fulfilled its task in helping to bring about the present state of reason. Now that the self-confidence of modernity has come so much under attack, it may seem difficult to imagine in what positive light modern culture was seen even in the 1970s. Theologians were hailing equality, enlightenment and emancipation as the definitive yardsticks by which Christian contributions to culture were to be measured. Since then, these correct, but moralistic goals have been differentiated and relativised by the discovery of different spheres of justice and of the need to combine deontology with an ethics of flourishing. A different expression of the alignment of Christianity and culture can be found in present theories of Practical Theology. They describe the threefold shape of modern Christianity: the official or explicit form, i.e. the churches; the individual or private form; and, what they call the general form, i.e. the vestiges of the former Christian worldview persisting in the principles of the Constitution, in the justice principles of the welfare state, in the customs, music and literature of the people.[1] Thus, a legally constituted, democratic society comes to be the 'general form of Christianity' which needs the official form – the churches – to be reminded of its roots but still deserves this title.

1. See Dietrich Rössler's approach of founding Practical Theology as a discipline, *Grundkurs der Praktischen Theologie*, Berlin-New York: de Gruyter, 2nd ed. 1994.

In this view, a participative, justice-orientated society cannot be substantially post-Christian. Its main elements are the very realisation of Christian impulses. How does this theory stand up to scrutiny?

On the one hand, it is true that modern secular culture cannot be called pagan in the same sense as the polytheistic cultures of antiquity that surrounded the early church, precisely because contemporary society belongs to the history of effects of Christianity; yet, on the other hand, an unreserved confession to modernity comes close to a triumphalism that not only the post-moderns but also the more reflective defenders of the history of freedom do not share. Critics within this tradition set out to explain which course the modern principles of freedom, self-consciousness and reason have taken.

In the *Dialectic of Enlightenment*, written jointly in their Californian exile from Nazi Germany in 1944, the Jewish philosophers Max Horkheimer and Theodor W. Adorno try to understand why 'mankind, instead of entering into a truly human condition, is sinking into a new kind of barbarism.'[2] Combining insights from psychoanalysis, from Marx's theories of the division of labour and exploitation of the working class, and from Hegel's master/slave analysis, they use Homer's epic *The Odyssey* to illuminate the lure of nature against which the modern subject had to differentiate himself. They interpret Odysseus's proverbial 'cunning' as the ruse of the modern subject to defy the forces of nature which fascinate but threaten his consciousness. For them, the denial of nature in man is the root cause of the subsequent dominations of outer nature and fellow-humans. Instrumental reason has brought forth the consciousness we excel in. But at what price for the human subject, intersubjectivity, and nature!

In the chapter, 'Odysseus or Myth and Enlightenment', they drive home the extent of the struggle that marked the dawning of human self-consciousness. To them, Homer, living 700 years before Christ, has written 'the basic text of European civilisation' (46). The 'hero of the adventures shows himself to be a prototype of the bourgeois individual' (43) whose 'title of hero is only

2. M. Horkheimer, Th. W. Adorno, *Dialectic of Enlightenment*, New York: Continuum, 1989, xi. Subsequent page numbers are included in the text.

gained at the price of the abasement and mortification of his instinct for complete, universal, and undivided happiness.' (57)

In their interpretation, 'modern' culture (which starts with the Greek epics), is built on 'a denial of nature in man for the sake of domination over non-human nature and over other men.' (54). They analyse: 'As soon as man discards the awareness that he himself is nature, all the aims for which he keeps himself alive – social progress, the intensification of all his material and spiritual powers, even consciousness itself – are nullified, and the enthronement of the means as an end, which under late capitalism is tantamount to open insanity, is already perceptible in the prehistory of subjectivity. Man's domination over himself, which grounds his selfhood, is almost always the destruction of the subject in whose service it is undertaken.'

One episode in *The Odyss*ey is chosen to illuminate the domination of self, others, nature, and its price: the encounter with the Sirens. Odysseus orders his men to tie him to the mast of their ship and to plug their ears with wax. Horkheimer's and Adorno's interpretation of this scene is itself classical: 'It is impossible to hear the Sirens and not succumb to them; therefore he does not try to defy their power ... Odysseus recognises the archaic superior power of the song even when, as a technically enlightened man, he has himself bound ... The bound listener wants to hear the sirens as any other man would, but he has hit upon the arrangement by which he as a subject need not be subjected by them. Despite all the power of his desire, which reflects the power of the demi-goddesses themselves, he cannot pass over to them, for his rowers with wax-stopped ears are deaf not only to the demi-goddesses, but also to the desperate cries of their commander. The Sirens have their own quality, but in primitive bourgeois history it is neutralised to become merely the wistful longing of the passer-by.' (58)

They add, 'Since Odysseus' successful-unsuccessful encounter with the Sirens all songs have been affected, and Western music as a whole suffers from the contradiction of song in civilisation – song which nevertheless proclaims the emotional power of all art music.' (58-60)

One may wonder how Gretel Adorno and Rose Maidon Horkheimer, to whom all these pages were dictated, might have felt: the 'archaic superior power' of the Sirens, their 'promise of undivided happiness,' 'the wistful longing of the passer-by'...? It is a very male account of the so-called 'introversion of sacrifice,' the change from vitality to consciousness. Max and Theodor do refer to Penelope and her cunning in undoing her weaving every night to delay the advances of her male suitors. Her virtue is to renounce adventures, her husband's glory is to survive them. A feminist reading of the introversion of sacrifice at the beginning of civilisation might come to different conclusions. But even if one agrees to yet another criticism, namely that Horkheimer and Adorno put forward a naïve, pure, and unmediated concept of nature, their main point of the strain to dominate oneself in order to be able to dominate others[3] is insightful and well expressed.

Fifty years earlier, before the excesses of suffering of two world wars and the Holocaust, the liberal Protestant theologian Ernst Troeltsch also put his finger on a specific type of rationalisation that has produced modern capitalist culture, by cutting individualism off from its religious sources: The 'imposing but also terrible expansion of modern capitalism, with its calculating coldness and soullessness, its unscrupulous greed and pitilessness, its turning to gain for gain's sake, to fierce and ruthless competition, its agonising lust of victory, its blatant satisfaction in the tyrannical power of the merchant class, has entirely loosed it from its former ethical foundations; and it has become a power directly opposed to genuine Calvinism and Protestantism. When it no longer practices asceticism for the honour of God, but for the gaining of power, to the honour of man, it has no longer anything in common with Protestantism except its strongly individualistic spirit now no longer held in check by the social and religious spirit of early Calvinism.'[4]

These are accounts of the history of freedom that admit its degeneration into domination and competition once it casts off its former ethical and religious foundations. Reason turns into instrumental reason; the freedom that once found fulfilment in

3. Cf Helmut Peukert, 'Enlightenment and Theology as Unfinished Projects' in Don S. Browning, Francis Schüssler Fiorenza (eds.), *Habermas, Modernity, and Public Theology,* New York: Crossroad, 1992, 43-66, 47-48.

4. E. Troeltsch, *Protestantism and Progress: The Significance of Protestantism for the Rise of the Modern World* (1906), Philadelphia: Fortress, 1986, 74-75. He affirms Max Weber's critique of an asceticism divorced from its religious roots in Weber's *Ethic of Protestantism and the Spirit of Capitalism* (1904/05).

recognising the equal freedom of the other is superseded by the will to power. Modernity has the seeds of both possibilities within itself:

- a market freedom that binds itself to finite objects and seeks satisfaction in augmenting them, whatever the price for fellow-subjects;
- a freedom which shows its unconditional character in respecting the other as an end in herself and is committed to the infinite in the other and in God.

Does autonomous freedom need God to realise its own potential? Should secular culture be returned into the lap of God? These questions will be explored in section three. But first, it has to be asked: Is it only the secular world that can show the ambiguity of the two courses that human freedom may take? I shall investigate the views of one of the greatest critics within the Christian tradition, Søren Kierkegaard, and compare the theological decisions behind his evaluation with those of the 'father' of cultural Protestantism, Friedrich Schleiermacher.

II CULTURAL CHRISTIANITY OR RADICAL CHRISTIANITY?

The two nineteenth-century religious thinkers Kierkegaard and Schleiermacher are not just two classical authors for a modern theology committed to the 'turn to the subject', without whom one cannot understand the approaches taken in the twentieth century, e.g., by Barth, Bultmann, and Rahner. Both are also being reclaimed as contemporaries. This is not surprising when one looks at their critique of the Enlightenment and of Hegel's idealism which is so close to our own: against an abstract notion of reason Schleiermacher reclaimed 'feeling or immediate self-consciousness'; against a rationalistically impoverished understanding of culture the Romantics explored the diversity of languages, the power of myths and fairy tales; against Hegel's objective reconciliation of gaping antitheses in the mere concept of reason, Kierkegaard insisted on the subjective experience of painful paradoxes and the existential validation of any intellectual solutions. Schleiermacher, Romantic preacher, author of riddles and aphorisms, and witty conversationalist in the Berlin 'Salon' of Henriette Herz – whose Jewish house was a meeting point for poets, philosophers and reform-minded ministers at the turn of the nineteenth century, whose husband Marcus Herz had received from Immanuel Kant the famous birth letter of the

'Critique of Pure Reason' – this multi-disciplinary theologian defended religion 'against its cultured despisers' as the 'intuition of the universe,' as the 'sense and taste for the infinite.' Two hundred years later, the appeal of this concept of a free-floating religiosity or 'spirituality' besides the institutionalised forms of religion seems to be even more compelling than in 1799. His rewriting of the Ten Commandments for Women could serve as the motto for many a feminist critique of culture: 'You shall not bear false witness toward men; you shall not conceal their barbarism through word or deed.'

But even more than Schleiermacher's attempt to reconcile Christian faith with the sense of history and the discovery of human subjectivity in his day, the reflections of the Danish religious writer Kierkegaard fifty years later seem to resonate with our own late modern experiences. *Therapy*, one of the most recent books of David Lodge – former professor of English literature whose campus novels portray the power plays, relationships and modes of life in university corridors and Common Rooms and on international conference grounds – contains an intensive study of Kierkegaard's writings. Tubby, the hero and narrator of the story, a well-known TV series writer and hypochondriac, plagued by discontent, and user of aromatherapy, physiotherapy, cognitive behaviour therapy, acupuncture, psychotherapy, and tennis, finds the key to the crisis of his life in titles such as *Either/Or, Fear and Trembling,* and *The Sickness unto Death.* Therapy is sought also through a visit to Kierkegaard's native city, Copenhagen. His categories elucidate modern lifestyles, among them the cultural phenomenon that the pilgrimage to Santiago de Compostela has become in a post-Christian Europe. Kierkegaard's three stages of existence are used to classify different types of pilgrims, the aesthetic, the ethical and the religious: 'The aesthetic type was mainly concerned with having a good time, enjoying the picturesque and cultural pleasures of the Camino. The ethical type saw the pilgrimage essentially as a test of stamina and self-discipline. He (or she) had a strict notion of what was correct pilgrim behaviour (no staying in hotels, for instance) and was very competitive with others on the road. The true pilgrim was the religious pilgrim ... the whole point was that you chose to believe without rational compulsion – you made a leap into the void and in the process chose yourself. Walking a thousand miles to the shrine of Santiago was such a leap. The aesthetic pilgrim didn't pretend to be a true pilgrim. The ethical pilgrim was always worrying whether he was a true pilgrim. The true pilgrim just did it.'[5]

On the question of Christianity's relationship to culture, Schleiermacher and Kierkegaard take opposite stances.[6] For the Danish writer, one of the worst aspects of contemporary church and culture is a 'public' marked by conformity and superficiality. Jostein Gaarder's bestseller, *Sophie's World*, summarises his critique of the crowd mentality with 'all their non-committal 'talk'' in the memorable line from fifteen-year-old Sophie: 'It's one thing to collect Barbie dolls. But it's worse to be one.'[7] Against this mass conformity emerging in a more and more urbanised society, Kierkegaard sets up his ideal concept of the Christian church. Three quotations may illustrate its characteristics:[8]

(1) 'The definition of "Church" found in the Augsburg Confession, that it is the communion of saints where the word is rightly taught and the sacraments rightly administered, this quite correctly (that is, not correctly) grasped only the two

---

5. D. Lodge, *Therapy*, London: Secker & Warburg, 1995, 304-05.

6. For the points of comparison and an evaluation of Schleiermacher's and Kierkegaard's ecclesiologies from their basic theological presuppositions, see Thomas Pröpper, *Erlösungsglaube und Freiheitsgeschichte. Eine Skizze zur Soteriologie*, München: Kösel, 2nd ed. 1988, 115, Fn. 213: 'The suggested critique of the 'lack of history' (*Geschichtslosigkeit*) of Kierkegaard's solution refers above all to his almost exclusive determination of the form of revelation as "Incognito", which barely pays attention to Jesus's life as inviting sign of the love of God ... It also refers to the lack of significance (resp. the diminution of significance as a merely claimed memory) of the historical mediation of faith in the concept of "contemporaneity" and "eternal history"... The idea of "choice" which is the real focus of Kierkegaard's determination of the "scandal" (*Ärgernis'*) of Christ is by no means neglected if one understands the history of Jesus as the revealing reality of the love of God. The offer of this love in effect always includes the call to conversion and thus the call for decision.'

7. J. Gaarder, *Sophie's World*, London: Phoenix, 1994, 317.

8. For insightful quotations from Kierkegaard's Journals to illuminate his ecclesiology, I am indebted to Charles L. Creegan/Nicola Hoggard Creegan, 'Schleiermacher and Kierkegaard: Dialogue on Ecclesiology' in: Terrence Tice et al. (eds.) AAR Schleiermacher Seminar Washington 1993: *Schleiermacher at the Growing Edge of Theology Today*, 40-70. References for the quotations are included in the text: *Journals and Papers*, 7 vols., ed. and trans. by Howard H. Hong and Edna Hong, Bloomington/Indianapolis: Indiana University Press, 1967-78.

points about doctrine and sacraments and has overlooked the first, the communion of saints (in which there is the qualification in the direction of the existential). Thus the church is made into a communion of indifferent existences (or where the existential is a matter of indifference) – but the 'doctrine' is correct and the sacraments are rightly administered. This is really paganism.' (*Journals and Papers*, # 600 (X4A 246 [1851]) The deficiency of conventional ecclesiology consists in neglecting the inner moment of irreplaceable commitment of the individual believers. Proclamation and sacramental worship are evaluated as a purely exterior matter. Being a Christian is qualified as existential discipleship.

(2) Against the presumption that the sheer number of members already grants its truth, he reminds us: '"Community" is certainly more than a sum, but yet it is truly a sum of ones; the public is nonsense – a sum of negative ones, of ones which are not ones, who becomes ones through the sum instead of the sum becoming a sum of the ones.' (*Journals and Papers*, § 2952 [1850]).

For Kierkegaard, it is inconceivable to attain one's self by borrowing from a larger entity: the church, the nation, a subculture, a sports club ... A church assembled in this way is a 'sum of zeros'. The guiding idea of his ecclesiology is the irreplaceable commitment of the individual to his faith.

(3) As little as the number of adherents does the long history of reception guarantee the truth of Christianity. 'The first generation was right. It handed over to the next: We have believed. But from then on we come to the generation which delivers to the next generation – not the testimony that we have believed, but that the preceding generation had believed, that we believe, that the preceding generation had believed!' (*Journals and Papers*, # 1648 (X4A 505 [1852])

In comparison with the apostles who believed themselves, what we have is not even a second-hand, but an eightieth-hand faith. This radical devalorisation of the principle of tradition is counterbalanced by the category of contemporaneity which defines the individual believer's relationship to Jesus. He is contemporaneous to every age. As promising as this appraisal of our bond with Jesus may sound, the category of contemporaneity is problematic. It does not show how the believer and he become contemporaneous. It is an actualistic concept which blends out the historical mediatedness of faith. The history of Christianity only counts as a manifestation of unfaithfulness to the witness of Christ. The faith-constituting role of tradition, to which the individual responds in a commitment to Christ, is suppressed.

Kierkegaard criticises the established church for wasting its energy in exterior rituals, for sacrificing the principle of discipleship to the organised superficiality of religious praxis and for trying to please everyone in a search for a harmony which forgets about the truth. While these are questions against which pastoral practice should be interested in checking itself, what is underrated in this type of insistence on practical discipleship is the *symbolic structure of faith* itself which points beyond ethical-religious praxis.[9] If, moreover, tradition is conceived of as unequivocal decline, then the mediating effort which first makes faith accessible to us is not adequately portrayed. The 'corrective,' as which he intended his critique, needs to be corrected itself by the counter-balance of a more comprehensive framework.

Schleiermacher's construction of church provides a counter-model to Kierkegaard's radically Christian approach. Thirty years before this attack on the middle-of-the-century Danish established church, the Reformed theologian – teaching in Berlin at the Humboldt University which he co-founded, along with Hegel whose system he critiqued no less than Kierkegaard – gives an anthropological foundation of church in the communicative and community-building character of piety.

§6 of *The Christian Faith* states: 'The religious self-consciousness, like every essential element in human nature, leads necessarily in its development to fellowship or communion; a communion which, on the one hand, is variable and fluid, and, on the other hand, has definite limits, i.e. is a church.'[10] (26) . From the Romantic Age to Postmodernity, the expressive and community-seeking nature of piety ranges from a vagrant, shifting,

9. An equally radical theologian who cannot be suspected of offering 'cheap grace,' Dietrich Bonhoeffer, sees practical discipleship as founded in the prior initiative of God. Against Kierkegaard's dismissal of infant baptism he can therefore say, 'What church is in its essence, can be seen most clearly in infant baptism.' *Gesammelte Schriften*, ed. E. Bethge, vol. V, München 1972, 255.

10. F. Schleiermacher, *The Christian Faith*, Edinburgh: T & T Clark, 1986, 26. The revised second German edition which was translated into English dates from 1830, the first from 1821-22.

and unstable religiosity to the organisational form of the church, the cradle of institutions in European history.[11] The concept of church is rooted in the human constitution. It is specified in the Christian realm as the corporate life issuing from Jesus whose God-consciousness it mediates. The strength of this approach is to combine an anthropological with a christological foundation by which church is further defined as the process of witnessing and mediating faith in the person of Jesus. More convincing than Kierkegaard's undervaluation of the faith-inviting appeal of Jesus's proclamation, emphasising instead the 'infinite qualitative difference' between God and the human person as well as the 'Incognito' of Christ, is Schleiermacher's recognition of the impression that Christ made on his believers. Who would not be inspired in their own God-consciousness by the certitude of his God-relatedness! This christological point, however, also highlights the major weakness of Schleiermacher's construction: What is mediated, is only the 'constant potency' of a God-consciousness (§ 94, ET 385) the seeds of which every human being already has in her nature.[12]

In Schleiermacher's determination of the essence of Christianity, the content of redemption is ultimately only the actualisation of a possibility of human nature. But then, the lasting significance of the person of the Mediator cannot be grounded. If this is true, there is also no criterion that protects the reflection of

11. What is clear for the origin of the universities from monastic schools, can be extended to other forms of institutionalisation. This is a point P. Ricoeur brings to bear on the secularisation debate in *Critique and Conviction: Conversations with F. Azouvi and Marc de Launay*, trans. K. Blamey, London: Polity Press, 1998, 136: Religion 'had not only the function of educating individuals but also the function of institutionalisation. I am in complete agreement with Marcel Gauchet on this point in saying that the religious produced the institutional even outside of the ecclesiastical. The history of the Middle Ages shows perfectly that most of the great institutions were generated after the ecclesiastical model, whether it be the university, municipal government, markets or intellectual societies. As a consequence, it is not possible to imagine an extreme situation in which the religious would have been totally eliminated from the self-understanding of cultures and from the modern nation-state. It is an integral part of their formation, of their *Bildung*.' One could say it is a result of *Bildung* to recognise: 'All the European peoples are ... Latinised and Christianised barbarians.'

12. This critique is developed in my study, *Das Urbild des Gottesbewusstseins*, Berlin/New York: de Gruyter, 1990.

faith from drifting into a theology of culture and the content of Christianity from absorption into the spirit of reason. The church then becomes the servant of the advance of this spirit. The question of whether this would be the Spirit of Jesus can hardly be posed anymore.

In his effort to distinguish true Christianity from the superficially pious habits of Christendom, Kierkegaard dismisses totally the efforts of the believers who went before us. But is it true that all the generations after the first disciples have only succeeded in twisting, denying, and betraying the Christian faith? Schleiermacher is not thinking in categories of decay when he emphasises the need for handing on and at the same time transforming the Christian tradition. Kierkegaard proposes a Christian contrast society; Schleiermacher's view is closer to the image of leavening which the Christian faith could provide for secular society. 150 years later, the principal adversary of Christianity is not the crowd mentality. It is instrumental, strategic, manipulative reason, or the will to power. Without the resources of the Christian faith, the project of the Enlightenment might degenerate into pragmatism at best, or domination and barbarism at worst.[13]

Having investigated ambiguities both within culture and Christianity in modernity, I shall examine a contemporary theological position that claims a foundational role for religion in a democratic society. The questions arising from Wolfhart Pannenberg's programmatic analysis will then be related to the current debate whether the Christian God should appear in the European Constitution (III).

III THE CHRISTIAN PERSPECTIVE IN PUBLIC DEBATES – FORCE OF LAW OR THE POWER OF THE BEST ARGUMENT?

Pannenberg's argumentation in *Anthropology in Theological Perspective* proceeds in three steps:

1. Religion is a fundamental constitutive element of human nature.

2. The decay of public institutions in modernity is due to their having cut their links with their religious foundations.

13. The danger of descent into self-interested pragmatism can also be shown at the level of social philosophical theories such as John Rawls's Theory of Justice. See, e.g., P. Ricoeur, 'Love and Justice,' in *Figuring the Sacred*, trans. D. Pellauer, ed. M. Wallace, Minneapolis: Fortress Press, 1995, 315-329.

3. The Christian perspective should be protected by law in order to restore institutions to viability. I shall illustrate each step by quotations and analyse them.

1 Religion as necessary for the constitution of the human subject

'(R)eligion is not a collection of transmitted or newly proliferating superstitions, but a constant factor in human existence from the very beginning and a specifically human trait ... the constitution of the human being as a subject, as well as the constitution of the social group as a collective unit, seems from the beginning to have been the work of religion.'[14]

Here, Pannenberg is not only endorsing Schleiermacher's position that religion is an irreducible feature of human subjectivity but claiming that it 'constitutes' the subject. The reason for this need for a religious foundation lies in the fact of our 'exocentricity': 'Human exocentricity compels men and women to find outside themselves a centre that will give unity and identity to their lives.' (480) In Pannenberg's religious reading, the basic premise of 'exocentricity,' taken over from the philosophical anthropology of Helmuth Plessner, seems to deny the possibility for unity and identity based on the autonomous freedom of the human subject. The need for 'unity' as an integrative framework for reality is also at the basis of the following conclusion: 'Because religions are concerned with the unity of all reality, it is possible and necessary to seek and find in religion the ultimate frame of reference for the order of human life in society.' (474)

No doubt it is possible to 'find in religion the ultimate frame of reference for the order of human life in society.' But is it 'necessary'? What follows if it is seen to be that? It seems difficult to state as much for the foundations of society, without having to embrace as a consequence, a return to the old Roman view that atheists are public enemies.

2. Legitimation crisis and decay of institutions as a result of the decline of religion

'(R)ecent years have seen a new awareness that the secular state in all its forms suffers from a chronic defect of legitimacy. We are therefore justified in asking whether modern secular society can exist indefinitely without a religiously based legitimation.'

14. W. Pannenberg, *Anthropology in Theological Perspective,* trans. M. O'Connell, Philadelphia: Westminster, 1985, 482-83, and Fn. 234.

(474) A similar pattern as in the previous step emerges; of restating a widely shared perception, such as the legitimation crisis of the State, analysed in 1976 by Jürgen Habermas, and then extrapolating from it the need for a religious solution. While the justification of political power is an ongoing issue, different levels have to be distinguished from wider participation in public debate and initiatives in civil society, reflections on their effects on governmental decision-taking, to the philosophical and theological question of the origin of power. The problems of motivation, horizon of meaning, and values nourishing the commitment to norms of justice are equally posed in a way that suggests their only answer lies in 'religion': 'As public culture and social institutions have come to be increasingly emptied of meaning, the process of detachment from the sources of religion has imperiled the continuous existence of secular society itself. This society must recollect itself and reflect on its religious sources if it is not to be destroyed by the collapse of all binding norms and the antagonisms produced by unfettered selfish interests.' (482)[15]

It would be more accurate and less alarmist to acknowledge that there are several ways of analysing and acting against the crisis of values, which is evident, e.g., in the market imperatives pushing the application of genetic research, and look for allies in civil society to defend the legitimate interests of those with no public voice. Pannenberg's line of reasoning, however, rises to a more abstract level, when the two tasks of creating 'unity,' for the individual and for the political community, are related to each other: Since 'political rule has for its task the unification

15. While it is right to emphasise the historical importance of the Christian contribution to the development of the concept of human dignity (as a 'universally binding basis for a public culture') and its current heuristic and motivational significance in questions of application, it is problematic to claim a 'religious foundation' for these Western ideas in the sense that they would not be valid without it. It shows already the denial of autonomous freedom as the basis of obligation towards the other: 'Disillusionment (as to the ability of philosophy and science to create or bring to light a universally binding basis for a public culture and thus give legitimacy to political rule) is one factor ... in the decline of the modern state's legitimacy. We may expect the decline to continue as long as the needed reflection on the religious foundation of the Western ideas that are normative for political life and the political order is avoided or deferred.' (478)

and ongoing integration of society, it must derive its legitimacy from the religious foundations that make reality intelligible as an ordered and meaningful whole. It may therefore be claimed that there is no longer any legitimacy for the secular state of the modern age, since it is no longer related to any religious foundation.' (474)

3. The revitalisation of the Christian foundations of the social system

The third step after the unidirectional interpretation of critical symptoms in political life is to suggest a degree of legal protection for the religious perspective in order to revitalise 'the Christian foundations of the social system': 'Once the true place of religion is grasped, it will claim the universal and public attention and place that belongs to the fundamental things of human existence.' (483)

What does this sentence signify: that religion is too fundamental to 'be left to individual preference'? Should it be mandatory for citizens to believe in the Christian Trinity?[16]

Clearly, for Pannenberg, the autonomy of culture does not rank highly. It is a perilous self-misunderstanding of secular culture to think it could prevail without religious foundations.[17] The project of a public theology that wants to engage in the competition of ideas only with the convincing power of well-reflected arguments instead of the help of the legal system seems

16. 'A society, however, that understood itself to manifest the divine will to law (*Rechtswillen*, ET: justice), that is, a Trinitarian self-commitment of divine omnipotence to the legal order (*Selbstbindung an das Recht*, ET: justice), would also be capable of developing a lifestyle that transcends while at the same time incorporates pragmatic needs.' (484) (The modifications of the English translation are mine).

17. Pannenberg's tendency to underestimate the ability of secular culture to stand on its own feet is rooted in his corresponding dismissal of autonomous freedom: 'The legitimacy crisis of the secular state … has deeper roots in the loss of the religious foundation for moral obligation and the authority of the law.' (472). He does not distinguish, as Kant did, between the level of moral obligation which is rooted in the unconditional character of autonomous freedom, and the level of the realisation of morality on which the question of meaning arises from the antinomy of practical reason. For a critique of Pannenberg from the position of a Christian theology of freedom, cf. Th. Pröpper, 'Das Faktum der Sünde und die Konstitution menschlicher Identität. Ein Beitrag zur kritischen Aneignung der Anthropologie Wolfhart Pannenbergs' in *Theologische Quartalschrift* 170 (1990) 267-289, 288-89.

dismissed. How would Kierkegaard and Schleiermacher view this proposal?

Schleiermacher shares Pannenberg's assumption that religion or even God-consciousness is a natural part of the human constitution. But nowhere does he draw the conclusion that views coming from a religious perspective should be more protected than others. And just imagine how Kierkegaard would have reacted to this temptation to let the State take over what should be the genuine and unalienable right and responsibility of each believer: to bear witness to her faith's convictions! It is the one thing that should not be replaced by institutional privileges for the churches.

Pannenberg's overemphasis on the protection of the State for religious and more specifically, Christian, convictions also seems to suggest that by and large the institutionalised churches have successfully mediated the content of the gospel. Yet, a great number of rights – such as the right to due process, to religious freedom, many women's rights – whose origins, as Pannenberg has rightly insisted, can be attributed to the change in human self-perception that arose from Christian belief in the incarnation of God in our human brother Jesus[18] – had to be vindicated against the institutional churches. Secular sciences such as psychoanalysis may not only be questioned from the perspective of Christian anthropology, e.g., with regard to the transcendent dimension; they also have something to teach theology about repression, systemic self-alienation, and the infantilisation of adults in total institutions. It is a two-way process of interrogation, as David Tracy's revised model of a reciprocal correlation proposes, each party putting questions and giving answers, not a unilateral correlation of humanity's question and Christianity's response. One can even conceive of a relationship between secular and religiously inspired positions in which each edges the other towards its greatest potential: the importance of equivalence in secular justice orientations to check the 'hyper-ethical' religious demand to love one's enemy with a resistance that demands him to change, and the need for justice to be rescued from a self-serving *do ut des* calculation by the religious motivation towards *agape*. The downward spiral towards the

18. See Pannenberg's debate with Hans Blumenberg in *Gottesgedanke und menschliche Freiheit*, Göttingen: Vandenhoeck & Ruprecht, 1972, 114-128.

lowest common denominator[19] is replaced by the upward spiral of exchanging one's best arguments for the best possible solution.[20]

IV CHRISTIANITY IN THE SELF-CONCEPTION OF EUROPE

But if that is so, if neither secular culture nor the Christian faith have ready answers, if one cannot privilege the Christian voice through legal measures above the other convictions held by citizens in a pluralistic society, how should it partake in contemporary debates? Is its only contribution at the level of public deliberation, which would be impoverished without it, or is there a rightful place for it in legal frameworks and constitutions? The recent controversy at the Convention on the Future of Europe on whether to include reference to Christianity into the draft Constitution of Europe, finalised in June 2003 in Thessaloniki, is a telling example for the embarrassment of a great number of public representatives about the Christian roots of Europe. The process, its handling in the media, and its outcome hold an unwelcome warning against naïve and sanguine expectations about bringing different convictions to bear on concrete matters of policy.

While the major issue from a legal point of view may be that reference is made to Art. 11 of the Amsterdam Treaty safeguarding the current legal positions of the churches in different countries, the self-description of Europe in its intellectual and ethical heritage is as significant from a historical, cultural and ethical perspective. A first indication of the vein in which Christianity's role for the conception of a united Europe was to be discussed is given in the heading for newspaper articles and letters to the Editor, 'God in Europe's Constitution.' This title is clearly mis-

19. This is how the Christian ethicist Dietmar Mieth characterises the effect of an 'overlapping consensus' under the overarching interest in social stability. D. Mieth, 'Common Values in Europe – towards a European Constitutional Society' and 'Reply', in *Biomedical Ethics* 5 (2000) 79-84, 88, 88.

20. This is where P. Ricoeur's model beats those of Rawls's overlapping consensus and Habermas's consensus through discourse, suspended to the future for its validation. See my 'Capabilities, Convictions, and Public Theology,' in M. Junker-Kenny (ed.), *Memory, Narrativity, Self, and the Challenge to Think God: The Reception within Theology of Paul Ricoeur's Recent Work*, Münster: LIT-Verlag, 2003 (forthcoming).

leading since it would suggest that an acclamation of God had been proposed, as, e.g., in the Preamble of the German *Grundgesetz* or in the Irish Constitution.

What turned out to be controversial in formulating the self-understanding of Europe was the question of the historical contribution of Christianity to its cultural identity and political unity. As far as the Draft Constitution was concerned, there was a straight line from Greek and Roman antiquity to the Enlightenment; any religious influences could be safely ignored.[21] The compromise terms first suggested to bridge the gap, 'spirit-

21. The intellectual and ethical heritage of Europe was encompassed in references to 'the civilisations of Greece and Rome and the 18th century European Enlightenment. They have anchored in the life of society the perception of the central role of the human person, of its inviolable and inalienable rights and also respect for the law'' (*The Irish Times*, May 29, 2003, p 13). Two points are relevant in our context, one concerning the development of the idea of the human person as an end in herself (a), the other, the status of law (b): a) If the 'civilisations of Greece and Rome' in all their ambivalences (e.g., the exclusion of women and slaves from Greek 'demo'cracy, *Pax Romana*) resulted in 'the perception of the central role of the human person', then this was made possible through the mediation of Christianity. Without Jewish and Christian religious roots, the following turns in human self-understanding could not be explained: the values of justice and compassion, the equality of man and woman acknowledged in both being made in the image of God and able to be baptised, the turn from the Greek ideal of a contemplative life of *theoria* to the *vita activa* of Christianity, the breaking of the power of the forces of the cosmos by the belief in one God who calls the human person into a partnership of responsibility for the future of creation, the cultivation of a relational subjectivity in the practice of prayer, Augustine's discovery of 'interiority' leading to a philosophy of self-reflection, the unique value of each individual whose name is inscribed in God's hand, and who can hope for resurrection. On the 'reversal of contemplation and action', see Hannah Arendt, *The Human Condition* (1958), Chicago: University of Chicago Press, 1998, 289-294. On 'inwardness', see Charles Taylor, *Sources of the Self. The Making of Modern Identity*, Cambridge: CUP, 1989, 111-207. b) 'Respect for the law': Contemporary sociologists and philosophers (e.g., Hans Joas, Charles Taylor, Jürgen Habermas, Paul Ricoeur) point out the significance of religious sources for creating values and for sustaining the motivation to aim for an inclusive, just and solidaric world. A society that can only shore up its co-operative practices by law, but lacks the interior motivation to abide by them, should accept its need for sources of renewal and hope, and respect people's faith in a transcendent God.

ual' and 'religious', but not 'Christian,' throw a light on the processes of negotiation. Its outcome illustrates not even an 'I give, so that you give' exchange attitude but a 'you take, so I take' resignation, ending in a complete spiral of silence. Now all the sources of Europe's cultural identity are kept under lids in the same box where they may talk to each other but not to the present citizens, nor to other cultures: Instead of naming Antiquity, Christianity, and the Enlightenment as the formative intellectual traditions, vague reference is made to 'humanistic' and 'religious' sources. What is left after this intellectual sell-out is the culture of mercantile interests. Even if Pannenberg's analysis and conclusions have to be resisted in the name of autonomy (as self-obligation, not as choice) and of the recognition of diversity, it may be true, after all, that institutions decay and culture shrinks when the role of religion cannot be acknowledged.[22]

---

22. This is true on three levels: the recognition of historical facts, personal identities, and the ability to understand one's own culture. First, a Constitution cannot engage loyalty and achieve its unifying function if it is allowed to be an ideological battleground, failing to recognise the historical reality of the plurality of religious and secular traditions that made a geographical entity divided by many different languages into the project of political co-operation and unification. Secondly, institutions cannot afford to ignore the deep convictions held in their constituencies. To deny the ongoing significance of Christianity for the personal identity of many of its members, risks alienating a majority of citizens who are Christian (Catholic, Protestant, and Orthodox) believers. Thirdly, it takes education to understand one's own culture. It is remarkable in the context of acknowledging Christianity's role in Europe that France, which has now been a laicist country for almost a hundred years, has reintroduced the study of the bible into its secular schools. Having lost knowledge of the bible, its young citizens lack the cultural background to understand the masterpieces of their own French history of art and architecture, literature, philosophy, and music. Excluding the biblical heritage thus results in ignorance and an inability to connect to defining monuments and moments of French and European history, such as the cathedral of Chartres, the writings of Pascal and Kant, and its music from madrigals to Bach and Messiaen. Paul Ricoeur has deplored the 'incredible amputation of culture' that happens when the religious sources of European culture are ignored. See his 'Education and Secularism' in *Critique and Conviction*, 127-138, 129-130.

CHAPTER 10

In Memory of the Other's Suffering: Theological Reflections on the Future of Faith and Culture[1]

Johann Baptist Metz

I *MEMORIA PASSIONIS* AS A BRIDGING CATEGORY BETWEEN FAITH AND CULTURE

Christian talk about God is joined to a very specific kind of memory. I would like to characterise it as a *memoria passionis*. What does this mean? It is evident that the biblical traditions' way of talking about God is distinguised by a sensitivity to suffering. It is a God-talk that is constitutively 'broken' by the theodicy question which remains as unanswerable as it is unforgettable. This God-talk does not have one answer too many, but one question too many for all our answers. It is a way of speaking about God in which history is not simply the history of the victors but above all a history of suffering. It is therefore historically focused on the *memoria passionis* without which the Christian *memoria resurrectionis* would also develop into a pure myth from the side of the victors.

Admittedly, again and again Christian speaking about God took on the trappings of a monotheism marked by the politics of power. This is why it is still under suspicion today as being a source of legitimation for a pre-democratic concept of sovereignty and the source of inspiration for fundamentalisms that are hostile to pluralism. But talk about the God of Abraham, Isaac and Jacob – who is also the God of Jesus – is in its core a God-talk that is sensitive to suffering. It is not the expression of just any kind of monotheism but, as one might say, of a monotheism of empathy.

Certainly, this empathic monotheism is also a kind of universalism. For this monotheism, God is either a theme for all humanity or it is not a theme at all. This God cannot be 'my' God

1. I have further developed the thoughts put forward in this text in Lothar Kuld, Johann Baptist Metz and Adolf Weisbrod, *Compassion: Weltprogramm des Christentums*, Freiburg: Herder, 2000.

if God cannot also at the same time be 'your' God. God cannot be 'ours' if God cannot also be the God of others, indeed, of all the others. Thus we Christians would turn out, in a certain sense, to be the last universalists in the era of the postmodern fragmentations. This is why we shall not give up the 'great' themes (about morality and the good, about peace and justice, about religion ...). But we shall try to speak about them in new ways, with new categories which may sound 'weak' or 'fragile' in comparison with the familiar ones.

We are living in a world of unfathomable plurality. What is called for, it is said, is tolerance and dialogue or discourse. Is this the answer? Is it enough? Are there not also limits to tolerance and criteria for dialogue? As always, pluralism is not simply the answer, but first of all the question and the problem. To resolve this problem does not mean to dissolve pluralism, but to develop a form of responding to it that is accessible and reasonable to all. In this we seek to avoid a cultural relativism without, however, relativising the cultures themselves. Yet what then would be this 'universal' link – the 'universal good' that is mostly denied or at least found missing today, what could be generally accessible and acceptable, that does not relativise cultures, but helps constitute them? The taking into memory of alien, foreign suffering, the suffering of the other. How can what we call tolerance avoid cultural relativism? Where are the limits of tolerance? Who defines them and who guarantees them? There is only the resistance of a category that is 'weak' in itself, the category of *memoria passionis*.

The biblical traditions to which Christian talk of God is committed know this special form of universal responsibility. One must realise, however, that the universalism of this responsibility is not orientated primarily to the universalism of sin and failure, but to the universalism of suffering in the world. Jesus' first glance was not upon the sin of others, but upon their suffering. For him, sin was, above all, the refusal of compassion for the suffering of others, the refusal to think beyond the horizon of one's own history of suffering. Sin was for him what Augustine later called the 'heart's curving back on itself', the abandoning of oneself to the secret narcissism of the creature. Thus, Christianity began as a community of memory and narrative committed to the discipleship of Jesus whose first glance embraced the suffering of others.

There are parables of Jesus in which through their telling he entered the memory of humanity in a special way. One of them is the parable of the 'Good Samaritan' which he relates as an answer to the question: 'Who is my neighbour?' In our context the question is: For whom am I responsible? To whom am I accountable? One insight emerges crystal clear from this parable told in the images of a provincial society of ancient times: this realm of responsibility, this area of accountability cannot be unambiguously outlined and defined by us in advance.

The 'neighbour' and thereby the partner to our responsibility is never only the person whom we imagine and accept as such. The range of our responsibility is in principle unlimited. The criterion for its measure and extent is – and remains – the suffering of the other, just like the man in Jesus's parable, who fell among thieves and whom the priest and the levite pass by for the sake of a 'worthier cause'. Whoever is looking for 'God' in the sense that Jesus describes, does not know of any 'worthier cause' that would excuse him or her. A person who speaks of 'God' in the sense that Jesus does accepts the risk that the misfortune of outsiders may damage his or her own preconceived certainties. Thus, to talk about this God means that one simply must find expression for the suffering of the stranger. A theology learned in Jesus's school about God is one full of empathy.

The taking of suffering into memory becomes thereby the basis of a universal responsibility by always taking into account the suffering of the others, the suffering of the foreigner and – what is genuinely biblical – even the suffering of the enemy. And this other's suffering is then not forgotten when one considers one's own history of suffering. (I always had the suspicion that when Jesus was talking about loving one's neighbour, he was thinking primarily of the love of one's enemies.) This memory of the other's suffering is not only the moral basis for the synchronic understanding between human beings; it reaches deep into the diachronic political landscape of our world. For this there are examples, examples of a 'war of memories' as well as examples for a 'peace of memories'.

In the former Yugoslavia, the memories of suffering became the burial shroud for a whole nation and the gallows for any attempt at understanding between ethnic groups. Here the individual peoples remembered only their own histories of suffering, and thus this purely self-referential *memoria passionis* did not grow into a source of dialogue and peace, but became a source of enmity, of hate and of violence. The fact that Christian denominations also participated in this staged production of memories of suffering makes the process worse and more painful. We can but hope that the present situation between Israel and Palestine will be different. One scene remains for me unforgettable: when the Israeli Izaak Rabin and the Palestinian Yassar Arafat took each other's hand and mutually pledged that they would not only consider their own suffering, but that they were ready to remember and take into account also the suffering of the others, the suffering of the former enemies. This is essentially politics of peace from a biblical *memoria passionis*! I know that the movement toward understanding on this basis is extremely fragile, that it has already cost great sacrifices and will cost more. But is there an alternative? And is there one for Ireland?

II THE AUTHORITY OF THE SUFFERING

In the present debates about a 'global ethos' or a 'world culture' there is often mentioned an ethical universalism which is to grow on the basis of a minimal consensus laboriously added together, or perhaps simply cleverly concocted. Yet this ethical universalism can develop, if at all, only on the basis of a fundamental consensus between peoples and cultures that has to be continually regained and that is constantly being threatened. There is, indeed, one authority that is recognised in all great cultures and religions and that has not been superseded by any critique of authority: the authority of those who are suffering.

This authority cannot first be prepared for hermeneutically nor can it be secured through discursive argument. With regard to this authority, obedience comes before understanding – and, indeed, unconditionally, at the price of being moral at all. This authority does not have to be further justified; towards it, there is for moral reasoning no possibility of a refusal to obey its command, perhaps by invoking the concept of 'autonomy'. In this sense the encounter with the suffering of the other is a kind of 'state of emergency', something not based on general rules which one could then use to hide behind. For me, as a Christian theologian, this authority is the only authority in which the authority of the judging God is manifested in the world for all peoples. Through obedience to it, moral conscience is formed;

what we call the voice of conscience is our reaction to accepting the presence among us of this alien suffering. It is well-known that Jesus, in his parable of the Last Judgment in Matthew 25 (again one of those stories with which he entered into people's hearts), submitted the entire history of humanity to this criterion: 'Whatever you did to the least of my brothers and sisters you did to me ... whatever you failed to do for one of the least of these, you failed to do for me.'

To respect alien suffering is the condition of all great culture (even if there is no culture, as Walter Benjamin rightly supposed, that does not contain within it a certain element of barbarism). And the bringing of the suffering of others to expression is the presupposition of all universalist claims, including and especially those of Christianity. Thus it could be that the 'weak' category of *memoria passionis* succeeds in going beyond the kind of Christian thinking in terms of identity in which only the circular self-understanding of a specific culture, namely the Western-European civilisation, is mirrored and reaffirmed. This Western culture, despite its universalistic orientation, has always found it difficult, and still finds it so today, to perceive adequately the worlds of experience and discourse of other cultures. The 'weak' taking into memory of alien suffering, and the narratives formed by this memory, could prove a powerful force enabling communication between religions and cultures, and with this become aware of the great number of the histories of suffering in the world – for example in the encounter with the ethics of compassion of the great Asian religions, especially of Buddhism (which is, granted, quite diverse in itself). In recognising the authority of those suffering, the monotheistic religions could, I think, find a meeting point with Eastern religions and cultures.

It is true that the biblical traditions do not speak primarily about a morality, but about a hope. Their speaking about God does not culminate in an ethics, but in an eschatology. Yet it is precisely in this orientation, despite the supposed or the actual powerlessness and lack of vision, that one finds the strength not simply to abandon or arbitrarily to minimise the standards of responsibility. I know that it is difficult to rescue this kind of universal responsibility from the suspicion of overblown abstraction. And without continually refocusing the priorities of our commitment, one cannot move ahead. Yet, it is precisely the desperate situation of the choices that we face that confirms the premise that our scope of responsibility is not shrinking and being reduced to smaller, more local situations, as is often suggested by a postmodern outlook, but rather, that it is continuing to expand. The promise, for instance, that Europe will be a blossoming rather than a burning multicultural landscape, a landscape of peace and not a landscape of imploding violence and escalating civil wars, also has its moral price. The payment has yet to be made.

III AN ERA OF CULTURAL AMNESIA?

Friedrich Nietzsche tried to write the epitaph for Christianity: 'All the possibilities of Christian life, the most intense and the most relaxed, the most harmless and thoughtless, and the most reflected upon have been thoroughly tried; it is time to invent something new …' And he linked his 'new way of living' to the triumph of cultural amnesia, which increasingly molds our 'postmodern' landscape and in which tradition orientated religions and worldviews are ever more threatened with disappearance. 'Yet in the smallest and in the greatest happiness there is always one thing that makes happiness be happiness … Whoever is not able to sit down on the threshold of the moment, forgetting all the pasts, whoever cannot stand on one spot like a goddess of victory without dizziness and fear, will never know what happiness is …'[2] The archetype of happiness would thus be the amnesia of the victor; its precondition, the merciless forgetting of the victims. This is indeed totally contrary to the biblical mindset of covenant and the anamnestic solidarity demanded by this covenant. It is completely opposed to the significance of '*memoria*', especially of the *memoria passionis* which is woven into the Christian understanding of peace and happiness. The vision of God of the biblical traditions stands opposed to the attempt to fix the happiness of the human family at the price of its amnesia.

The contemporary triumph of amnesia supports itself on various pillars. One of them, in my opinion, is theology itself. In constructing its notion of history, has it not always used much too 'strong' categories which gloss over far too quickly all the violent interruptions in history, all the gaping wounds, all the disasters and catastrophes. And then, has it not 'protected' its

2. Friedrich Nietzsche, *Thoughts Out of Season*, Vol II, 1, cf *On the Use and Abuse of History for Life*, 1873.

talk about God from the pain of memory? Should not at least a catastrophe such as that of Auschwitz operate as an ultimatum against an all too pliable theological treatment of history? At least now, should not the question arise about the standing and the significance of this horror in the midst of the *Logos* of theology? Should not, at the very least, theology now be convinced that it cannot itself heal all wounds? That it is simply no longer possible for it to conceptualise the identity of Christianity – once again – similar to Plato's ideas or – in a fashionable turn from history to psychology – only as a gnostic myth of redemption divorced from history?

To be sure, even modern science and scholarship do not simply break the spell of the cultural amnesia here referred to. In our civilisation, science is the essence of normality, and in this sense it can be said of it, too, that it heals all wounds and does not know the pain of remembering. Especially with regard to the academic discipline of history, I would like to make a comment: if I am right, since the so-called German *Historikerstreif*, (the controversy among historians on whether the atrocities committed under the reign of National Socialism are just one more instance of the violation of human rights, or whether this programme of mass annihilation of the European Jews needs to be evaluated as unique and outstanding in the history of humankind), the standpoint of 'historicising' National Socialism and its crimes has more or less won the day. Certainly, this catastrophe cannot simply be taken out of history, it cannot be allowed to be stylised into a kind of negative myth, into a tragedy beyond history. To do this would then simply amount to losing the standpoint of responsibility, of shame and radical change. Yet, in view of Auschwitz, for me the question remains how a horror that threatens – again and again – to evade being historically conceived, can nonetheless be kept in memory. This can succeed only with a way of writing history which is itself supported by an anamnestic culture, a culture of remembering, a historiography which is also aware of the kind of forgetting that reigns in every historicising objectification.

'*Wissenschaft* heals all wounds': Is not this belief also true for large and prominent sections of contemporary philosophy? 'Israel or Athens: Where does Anamnestic Reason Belong?': this is the title of a text with which the German social philosopher Jürgen Habermas tried to prove to me that the anamnestic spirit of the biblical concept of time has long since been taken up by the concept of reasoning in European philosophy.[3] In this way, it would seem that at least with the defences of professional European philosophy, the dangers of cultural amnesia can be resisted. But then why does, e.g., the catastrophe of Auschwitz appear in Habermas's work only in his 'Small political Writings' – and there, as is well known, it does appear in a both decisive and influential way – but not, not even with one word, in his great philosophical writings on communicative reason? Does not communicative theory also heal all wounds? But how is it possible then to speak in a generalisable way of what remains as evil (*Unheil*), of what cannot be healed, of what should not be allowed to disappear behind the shield of cultural amnesia, of what cannot be contained within seamless normality? How can one speak of something that, if at all, needs another kind of forgiving than the forgiving that time produces when it is said to heal all wounds, or the forgiveness imparted by a theory which covers them over?

What remains when it appears that all the wounds have been closed is difficult to describe. There is a peculiar sense of something missing, a sense that resists having the pain of remembering being totally alleviated, be it in a 'purely theoretical' way, be it in a psychological or aesthetical way, be it in a commemorative service or even in a 'religious' way. In the present age, this experience of missing something can hardly be understood if one, as usually happens, turns it into a typical condition of the older generation. Yet even more, this experience of something missing manifests itself with the younger generation; it nourishes the scepticism of the young, their indifference, sometimes also their anger with regard to what the older generations have to offer them as *the* experience, *the* view of things, *the* lesson from history which is then elevated to the canon of normality. What strikes me in the contemporary discussion about Daniel Goldhagen and his book about 'the ordinary Germans and the Holocaust' is that the almost unanimous criticism of the experts (which according to the criteria of professional historiography seems justified) was not able to put to rest the worries of many, especially young people, about the extent of this history of guilt.

The *memoria passionis* as remembering alien suffering re-

3. Jürgen Habermas, *The Liberating Power of Symbols: Philosophical Essays*, Cambridge: Polity, 2001, 78-89.

mains a fragile category in a time in which people believe they can finally protect themselves only with the weapon of forgetting, with the shield of amnesia against the histories of suffering and evil deeds which continue to pour in: yesterday Auschwitz, today Bosnia and Rwanda, and tomorrow ... ? But even this forgetting is not without consequences. Something that has always deeply affected and disturbed me in the situation 'after Auschwitz' was the unhappiness and desperation of those who survived this catastrophe. So much unspeakable unhappiness, so many suicides! Here, clearly, human beings have collapsed under the despair about what human beings are 'capable' of doing to other human beings. Thus Auschwitz has greatly lowered among human beings the metaphysical and moral boundary below which one still feels shame. Only the forgetful have overlooked something like this. Or those who supposedly have been successful in forgetting that there is something they have forgotten. But they do not remain untouched. The wound has not closed. One cannot, not even in the name of humanity, sin whenever and wherever. Not only the individual human person, but also the 'idea' of the human person and of humanity, is vulnerable; indeed it can be destroyed. Only a few connect the present crises of humanity, the so-called 'decline in values' – the increasing degree of deafness against 'great' claims, the crisis of solidarity, an extreme modesty about one's own ability (a modesty cleverly adapted to each situation) and so forth – few connect these traits of contemporary culture with the crisis that Auschwitz signifies as well as with the more recent catastrophes which also have fallen victim to cultural amnesia.

There is not only a superficial history of the human species, there is also a deeper history, and it is indeed vulnerable. Do not the orgies of rape and violence in our time acquire something like the normative power of the factual? Do they not – behind the shield of amnesia – corrode the 'basic trust of civilisation', those moral and cultural reserves in which the humanity of human beings is rooted? How much of these resources are still available? How far have they already been exhausted? Does what is happening here amount to bidding farewell to a concept of the human person as it has been familiar to us in history? Could it be that not only has God become lost to men and women under the spell of this cultural amnesia, but that the human person herself is going missing more and more, by losing what up to now has been called emphatically her 'humanity'? What remains after we have once again successfully closed all the wounds? When cultural amnesia has been completed? The human person? Which human person? Man as computerised intelligence who is not able to remember anything because – just like a computerised robot – he is also not able to forget anything, thus, an intelligence without history, without the ability to suffer and without morality?

In his book, *The Clash of Civilizations?*, the American writer Samuel Huntington envisages that the global conflicts of tomorrow will not only be defined by political blocks of power, but by the conflict of civilisations or cultures. For many, his thesis is controversial; the question contained within it, however, remains explosive. The conflict of Western culture with other cultures, for example, and especially with the culture of Islam, can indeed be described as the conflict between one cultural world that is guided by remembrance and another, 'modern' world, that is to a great degree guided by discourse. It becomes evident that cultures guided by remembrance have distinctive disadvantages against those led by discourse. They contain obstacles to modernity of a special kind; they paralyse curiosity, are suspicious of experiments, ritualise their lifeworld and are too much orientated towards mere repetition; they become trapped in fundamentalisms all too easily.

But what type of cultures would there be without any kind of a uniting, binding memory, cultures which then are exclusively discourse-oriented, cultures whose memory is ruled by discourse, but whose memory cannot guide discourse? Will human beings in them end up being anything more than an unlimited experiment upon themselves, humans who are threatened more and more with going under in the technological whirlpools that they have set in motion? How will the European West, if it is based on a cultural amnesia, be able to weather the oncoming challenges and conflicts? The future of European modernity, as well as the recognition of the dignity of other cultural worlds, rests upon the rescue of a cultural memory, itself guided by the taking into memory of the suffering of others.

Translated by Peter P. Kenny

CHAPTER 11

Faith and the Culture of Experience

Andrew Pierce

Christian theology has always operated with some form of appeal to experience. This appeal is usually – or ideally – characterised by deft dialectical footwork in order to prevent the mystery that is named as God from being domesticated into one strand in the tapestry of human experience. Appeals to experience – *our* appeals to *our* experience – require, therefore, constant, critical monitoring, particularly concerning the concept of experience presupposed in any given appeal.

This chapter reflects on the emergence of one, highly influential, form of appeal to experience in twentieth-century theology, that of William James in his Gifford Lectures, *The Varieties of Religious Experience.*[1] Despite its enormous significance, James' account of 'religious' experience is by no means the only contemporary contender as a way of appealing to experience. George Tyrrell, of whose life and thought Gabriel Daly is a distinguished interpreter, offers an account of experience which, though not without its own shortcomings, avoids some of the evident difficulties in the Jamesian tradition.

As a constant concern of Christian theology, therefore, experience merits attention. This is compounded, however, by our current cultural climate; ours, according to Michael Paul Gallagher, is a 'culture of experience rather than of tradition'.[2] We stand in a hermeneutical minefield: distrust of tradition has fuelled a particular form of the turn to experience, in which tradition and experience – now defined into a relationship of sheer opposition – have become simply stereotypes. One of the major casualties of this dichotomised culture is our capacity to integrate experience with criticism: critique-fatigue fuels new forms

1. William James, *The Varieties of Religious Experience: A Study in Human Nature,* With an Introduction by Arthur Darby Nock. Twelfth impression. Glasgow: Collins, 1985.
2. Michael Paul Gallagher SJ, 'New Forms of Cultural Unbelief,' in Padraig Hogan and Kevin Williams, eds., *The Future of Religion in Irish Education,* Dublin: Veritas, 1997, 19-31; 22.

of fideism, often in sophisticated garb. The English theorist of culture, Fred Inglis, has noted that one of the hallmarks of great thinkers in the human sciences has been their ability to keep 'experience intransigently alive in their theory.'[3] In looking to a figure like George Tyrrell, it is important to note that, despite his emphasis on affection and volition, he remained convinced of the need to keep theory intransigently alive in all talk of experience. Experience – however it is understood – is not a new 'gap' in which God may seek temporary asylum.

I EXPERIENCE CONFINED TO THE BIZARRE

In 1987, a Gallup Poll in Britain found that 48% of those surveyed claimed to have 'had' a religious experience. What, according to Gallup, is a religious experience? The poll revealed a wide range of experiences that were accepted as 'religious,' including the oneness of reality, a pattern detected in events, answers to prayer, and a variety of felt presences – of the dead, the sacred in nature, of God, of something that was not God. For almost half of the population surveyed, these kinds of experiences were considered to be religious.

This poll was one of a number commissioned, and partly conducted by the Alister Hardy Research Centre, currently based at Westminster College in Oxford. The Centre was established in 1966 by the marine biologist – and Gifford Lecturer – Sir Alister Hardy, who considered that religious experience merited scientific investigation. Just as marine biologists attend to a certain range of 'facts,' so too, Hardy believed, there is another range of 'facts' – religious experiences – which ought to receive attention from scientists of religion. In order to gain some idea of what Hardy had in mind by 'religious experience,' it is instructive to consider the letter that he had written in 1925, to the General Press Cutting Association in London, when he began to collect religious experiences. He requested:

> … all the cuttings – news or articles – dealing with or referring even remotely to:
> Religion
> God
> Faith
> Prayer

3. Fred Inglis, *Cultural Studies*, Oxford and Cambridge, Massachusetts: Blackwell, 1993, 6.

> Relations or antagonism of Religion and Science
> Anything in fact of a religious or spiritual nature,
> *provided that they are not*
> Ecclesiastical or church notices or news, reports of services or sermons (unless arousing public interest or controversy), obituary or other notes on the lives of ministers of any denomination, or dealing with psychic research, spiritualism and kindred subjects (unless in a religious connection).[4]

The impact of Hardy's positivistic pursuit of religious facts perdures in a work by a former director of the Hardy Centre, David Hay. Despite the book's reassuringly empiricist title – *Religious Experience Today: Studying the Facts* – it is worth considering what sort of 'facts' are involved in this appeal to experience. Going by this book, finding facts is an uncomplicated business: with apologies to E. M. Foster, students of religious experience need 'only collect'. Hay distinguishes between what he calls 'direct experience' (i.e., the raw 'fact'), and subsequent interpretation of that direct experience (which is added to the fact later on, notably by language). Fact-finding is straightforward; Hay is willing '... to accept at face value what people have to say about their experience ... Temperamentally, I am averse to the hermeneutics of suspicion.'[5] The hermeneutics of suspicion is, however, concerned with more than matters of temperament.

The hermeneutical focus of much recent systematic theology has reminded us forcefully – *pace* Albrect Ritschl and the remarkably persistent neo-Pascalian and neo-Kantian theological temperament – that judgements of fact and judgements of value remain inseparable, however vital it may be to distinguish between these two orders of judgement. The attribution of facthood is a value judgement. Hay, however, regards disputes between 'facts' and 'interpretation of facts' as a philosophical, and not a scientific, matter. Moreover, the interpretation of facts occurs only after the facts have been collected – it does not impact on how facthood is defined. Second order discourse is thus confined to being chronologically second place discourse and is esteemed as second rate discourse only.

This way of appealing to experiential facts evidences a number of problems. The approach taken by Hay and Hardy has,

4. Cited by David Hay, *Religious Experience Today: Studying the Facts*, London: Mowbray, 1990, 20.
5. Ibid., 39 n. 4.

however, a distinguished and influential precursor in William James, whose *Varieties of Religious Experience* is one of the classic texts of twentieth century theology, and whose account of religious experience has become widely accepted in contemporary culture. It is important, therefore, to look more closely at the argument advanced by James.

The definition of religion with which James operated is well-known; religion is:

> ... the feelings, acts and experiences of individual men in their solitude, so far as they apprehend themselves to stand in relation to whatever they may consider the divine.[6]

James' divinity remained vague throughout his lectures, but in his conclusion he ventured some thoughts on what his individual man in his solitude might be encountering:

> He [i.e., the individual man] becomes conscious that this higher part [of himself] is coterminous and continuous with a MORE of the same quality which is operative in the universe outside of him, and which he can keep in working touch with, and in a fashion get on board of and keep himself when all his lower being has gone to pieces in the wreck.[7]

This supports an elitist account of religious experience, in which 'real' religion is confined to a mystical minority – the founders of religious traditions – whose followers must live 'at second hand upon tradition.'[8] Relying on Francis Newman's distinction between once-born and twice-born religious temperaments, James opts for the twice-born as being the more religious of the two.

The kinds of experiences that James had in mind when writing about religious experience are not as varied as one might have expected, and certain assumptions about both religion and experience remain constant. A Jamesian religious experience is necessarily an individual's experience – real religion is personal, according to James, defining personal as the opposite of institutional. Real religious experience bypasses tradition, and consists of what he calls 'direct personal communion with the divine'.[9] Real religious experience, finally, is characterised by its lack of 'ecclesiastical theological complications'.[10]

---

6. James, *Varieties*, 50.
7. Ibid., 484.
8. Ibid., 49.
9. Ibid., 49.
10. Ibid., 445.

James was the first author actively to promote an understanding of religious experience principally as a discrete and unusual kind of experience, and his influence has proved remarkably tenacious. It is, however, an account of experience that is open to question on a number of fronts – for example, in its striking individualism, its inattention to the context within which experience occurs and through which experience is shaped, and its reliance on a confessional paradigm found largely in narratives of revivalist conversion. If religious experience is to be treated with greater emphasis on its variety, then the Jamesian positivism of experience requires correction.

II RESISTING EXPERIENTIAL POSITIVISM

Those who have read James and his critics with close attention are likely to agree with the warning, issued by Sallie McFague, to anyone preparing to reflect theologically on the theme of experience:

> 'Experience' is a word so fraught with misunderstanding, bad press, and dissension that introducing it without at least two chapters of qualifications and critiques by Kantians, Hegelians, deconstructionists, feminists and womanists, as well as Whiteheadians and empiricists, may be the height of folly.[11]

'Experience,' therefore, a term that often suggests spontaneity, immediacy and theory-unladen facts, may, on closer inspection, prove deceptive. Holding the reality of experience together with critical distance is a considerable challenge. To borrow Fred Inglis' terminology, can theologians acknowledge the rightful claims – or 'intransigence' – of both experience and theory?

The philosopher of religion Wayne Proudfoot has distinguished between two forms of reductionism – descriptive and explanatory – and has applied these to the study of religious experience.[12] Descriptive reductionism, according to Proudfoot, involves a failure to respect the way in which experience was experienced by a subject. Thus, a student of religious experience can commit no greater sin than to adjust the account rendered of an experience with a view to making that experience more ex-

11. Sallie McFague, *The Body of God: An Ecological Theology*, London: SCM, 1993, 85-86.

12. Wayne Proudfoot, *Religious Experience*, Berkeley, Los Angeles and London: University of California Press, 1985, 196-198.

plicable. Explanatory reductionism, on the other hand, is a virtue. Having faithfully described the subject's experience, the student of religious experience must then proceed to explain it. Those who 'describe' religious experience as finally ineffable, semantically elusive and occasionally paradoxical in character, are, according to Proudfoot, in fact prescribing approaches to the topic of religious experience in order to safeguard its irreducibility, *a priori*. Theologians from Friedrich Schleiermacher to Ninian Smart are guilty, according to Proudfoot, of constructing what he calls 'protective strategies' to prevent religious experience from being explained in non-religiously apologetical ways. Perhaps not surprisingly, therefore, Proudfoot praises William James and Jonathan Edwards for their descriptive approaches to the particularities of religious experience, and praises Emile Durkheim for explaining religious experience without cutting descriptive corners.

Unlike Hay's aversion to the hermeneutics of suspicion, Proudfoot's approach is characterised by an equally positivistic distrust of approaches to experience informed by a hermeneutics of reception. Both 'religion' and 'religious experience' are products of a particular – and recent – period of western intellectual history, and each concept has been defined within a context in which religious explanations for experiences have been increasingly supplanted by explanations drawn from the natural sciences. Attempts to minimise – or to deny – explanatory commitments embedded in appeals to religious experience, seek 'to limit all inquiry and reflection on Christian faith, or religious experience and belief, to internal elucidation and analysis.'[13] The drawback of this approach is that it presupposes too strong a contrast between description and explanation, and once again we catch an echo of an excessively rigid contrast between facts and values.[14]

How then are we to hold together criticism and experience? In a helpful article, George Schner has surveyed and evaluated a number of the ways in which theologians have appealed to experience.[15] His conclusion takes the form of a number of 'rules'

13. Ibid., 236.

14. For a discussion of Proudfoot's approach see Thomas M. Kelly, *Theology at the Void: The Retrieval of Experience*, Notre Dame, Indiana: University of Notre Dame Press, 2002, 51-70.

15. George P Schner SJ, 'The Appeal to Experience,' in *Theological Studies* 53 (1992) 40-59.

to be borne in mind by those interpreting the – potentially deceptive – theme of experience. First, experience is a construct; it is not, therefore, characterised by immediacy. Second, experience is intentional; it is not, therefore, private experience that takes place in the solitary confinement of human subjectivity. Third, experience is derivative – a person's experience is never so uniquely hers or his that it can be rendered immune from the criticism of others. The fourth and final rule is that experience is dialectical; experience is an inherently unstable concept, and appeals to experience will involve dialectical tensions between, say self *and* others, or between past, present *and* projected future.

These 'rules' evidence a sea-change in theological attitudes to experience in the century since William James delivered his Gifford Lectures. The privileging of the individual man in his solitude has been challenged by an acknowledgement that the human self does not exist – and therefore does not experience – in gender-unspecific, disembodied Cartesian isolation (whether splendid or nervous). The experiencing self, moreover, exercises agency in experiencing: experience is not simply something that befalls us and in the face of which we are passive. Experience is something that we do. An emphasis on agency is especially noticeable in the growing acknowledgement of the role of interpretation as a constituent element of experience. Interpretations are not stiched into experience *a posteriori*: the cultural and linguistic shaping of our social selves is not switched off in experience; rather it makes possible that experience. This indicates the importance of seeking an alternative to the pervasive positivism that often characterises theological appeals to experience – as evidenced in the approaches of Hay *et al* and of Proudfoot – in which religious experience is presented either as irreducible, or else as thoroughly explicable. It also makes plain that the theological appeal to experience is not necessarily – or even ideally – an appeal to a specific type of experience (usually unusual), but rather it is concerned with a certain way of interpreting experience.

III EXPERIENCE AND INTERPRETATION IN DIALECTICAL TENSION

Schner observes that in the period since 1902, theology has been characterised by a 'turn' to experience, but this dating links the turn to experience too strongly with the work of James, whose work presupposes such a turn. A far more significant turn had, in fact, taken place in the last decades of the eighteenth century, with the emergence of Immanuel Kant's critical philosophy, which had tried to coax an uncritically empiricist culture away from the rocks of scepticism by making plain the *a priori* conditions of experience. Provoked by Kant's Copernican turn in epistemology, many nineteenth-century Liberal Protestant theologians attended closely to the form of their appeal to experience (evidenced by, e.g., pervasive reference to 'religious consciousness'), in contrast to James whose interest lay more with content, i.e., experiences. Attempts to answer Kant – or even to ignore him proactively – dominated theological agendas during the nineteenth century, and played a key role in setting the stage for the modernist crisis in the Roman Catholic Church in the early twentieth century.

In 1907, Pope Pius X's encyclical *Pascendi Dominici Gregis* described and proscribed 'Modernism' as the 'synthesis of all heresies.'[16] *Pascendi*'s exposition of modernist doctrine – drafted by Joseph Lemius OMI – is an intriguing example of the neo-scholastic imagination seeking to grasp the rationale behind antipathy to the neo-scholastic project, which had been inaugurated in Leo XIII's encyclical *Aeterni Patris* in 1879. After *Pascendi* appeared, George Tyrrell wrote to *The Times*, observing that whilst the encyclical 'tries to show the Modernist that he is no Catholic, it mostly succeeds only in showing him that he is no scholastic.'[17] Unfortunately for Tyrrell, the ascendant integralism of the day did not permit such a distinction to be made with impunity.

Theological treatments of the modernist crisis tend to restrict it to the attention of historical theologians and church historians. Often it appears as an episode of intellectual history in which the work of Tyrrell, Blondel, Loisy, Merry del Val, Lemius *et al* – 'modernists' and anti-modernists alike – can be treated purely with reference to their impact on this particular crisis. The fascinating tragedy that is the modernist crisis – however interesting in its own right – can be confined to the past only on the assumption that it has nothing further to say. Such a belief expresses a

16. Official translation, *Encyclical Letter ('Pascendi Gregis') of our most Holy Lord Pius X By Divine Providence Pope on the Doctrine of the Modernists*, London: Burns and Oates, 1907, 48.
17. M. D. Petre, *Autobiography and Life of George Tyrrell*, London: Edward Arnold, 1912, Vol II, 337.

Pascendi-like confidence that a complex and disparate collection of historians and philosophers may be confined and dismissed with little difficulty. The tendency to treat modernists as modernists – and nothing more – has been resisted with insistence by Gabriel Daly, particularly in his appeal to Tyrrell's theodicy in *Creation and Redemption*.[18] For the purposes of this chapter, however, a key point is made by Daly in his conclusion to *Transcendence and Immanence*:

> Credible Christian theology can no longer take its stand upon a rigid dichotomy between transcendence and immanence. Events, however, have committed it to a search for transcendence within total human experience just at the moment when that experience is revealing further, unsuspected, and bewildering depths.[19]

The turn to experience, however problematised and particularised by post-modernity, remains a key feature of the theological agenda. Clearly there are discontinuities between the early twentieth and early twenty-first centuries, and one cannot adopt the theology of someone like George Tyrrell without taking hermeneutical precautions. As Charles Davis has noted, nineteenth century theological liberalism in general responded to post-Enlightenment criticism by shifting 'the locus of religious experience to the innermost depths of the subject.'[20] The Modernist crisis presupposed a culture of experience similar to our own. Several philosophical 'turns' later – notably the turn to language – is there a way in which the theology of a 'modernist' like Tyrrell can be received by our current theological agenda?

In April 1909, less than three months before his death, Tyrrell was invited to speak to students of King's College London, as a guest of the Warden, G. E. Newsom. The lecture – 'Revelation as Experience' – presents together the philosophical and religious questions that had assumed existential urgency for Tyrrell in the light of his encounter with contemporary 'higher criticism'.[21] In

18. Gabriel Daly, OSA, *Creation and Redemption*, Dublin: Gill and Macmillan, 1988, 35-40.

19. Gabriel Daly, OSA, *Transcendence and Immanence: A Study in Catholic Modernism and Integralism*, Oxford: Clarendon, 1980, 231.

20. Charles Davis, *Religion and the Making of Society: Essays in Social Theology*, Cambridge Studies in Ideology and Religion, Cambridge: CUP, 1994, 56.

21. Thomas M Loome (ed.), '"Revelation as Experience:" An Unpublished Lecture of George Tyrrell,' *Heythrop Journal* 12 (1971) 117-149.

his last years, some of Tyrrell's finest work was written to answer his critics, particularly those who had – in his opinion – taken the trouble to understand him. Tyrrell used the occasion of this lecture to answer the criticisms aimed at his work *Through Scylla and Charybdis* by Hakluyt Egerton (*nom de plume* of Arthur Boutwood).

The beginning of Tyrrell's struggle with the theme of experience can be dated with some precision to an essay first published in 1899, 'The Relation of Theology to Devotion.' Over the next decade, two of the points made in that essay remained central to Tyrrell's thinking: first, a sharp distinction between revelation and theology; second, an insistence on 'experience' as the best term available to denote the nature of revelation (note, however, the *via negativa* at work here: in Tyrrell's theology of revelation, 'experience' is defined as the opposite of 'statement'). He coined the term 'theologism' to describe a theological system in which theology and revelation were not distinguished, and in which the revealed 'deposit' of faith provided the basis from which further dogmatic teaching could be developed by deduction.[22]

'Revelation as Experience' is characterised by insistence as much as by argument, but this does not reduce the essay's significance – positivism is notoriously difficult to argue against. The difference between himself and Egerton, according to Tyrrell, concerns the nature of divine revelation:

> Does it [revelation] consist in certain divine statements; or in certain spiritual experiences about which man makes statements that may be inspired by those divine experiences, yet are not divine but human statements?[23]

There is, therefore, an inextricable link between statement and experience – between, to use Tyrrell's terminology, prophetic language and the total experience – but the link underlines the distinction: experience and statement are not to be identified. To identify statement with experience, is the positivistic position of the philosophically naïve 'plain-man,' on whose views Tyrrell comments: 'His God is always man writ large – very large perhaps, but still man.'[24] Tyrrell's familiarity with mystical writers

---

22. See Daly, *Transcendence and Immanence*, 140-164.
23. Tyrrell, 'Revelation as Experience' 130.
24. Ibid., 133.

had made him sensitive to the apophatic imperative when dealing with 'statement.'

For Tyrrell, Otherness can be named only by presupposing that it can arouse a response within human experience. Creeds, scripture and dogma are more than the debris of past experience, they remain part of the interpretative framework of present experience, through which we anticipate future experience. Hence Tyrrell's blunt statement 'Experience is revelational.'[25] And if that is so, then 'revelation is as common as sunshine.'[26] The multifaceted deposit of revelation (the 'total experience'[27]) is addressed to actively experiencing subjects; talk of transcendent Otherness presupposes immanent experience.

IV CONCLUSION

At a century's distance, George Tyrrell and William James exhibit certain similarities as well as differences: both were skilled writers of prose, both saw the production of saints as the 'purpose' of religion, yet each related the mystery of God to human experience in significantly different ways. What makes a comparison of these authors interesting is that James and Tyrrell were active participants in a culture of experience, similar in some ways to our own.

Despite its popularity, the approach taken by James, and continued by Hardy, Hay and others, is problematic. This should not mean, however, that our culture of experience has nothing to learn from what has been handed down by other such cultures. Experience without tradition is a concept of straw. Other contemporary theological appeals to experience, such as Tyrrell's, provide an alternative resource for understanding the complexity of experience, and indeed for emphasising the complexity of experience. And, at the risk of anachronism, it is worth noting the level of consonance between Schner's 'rules' and Tyrrell's theology of experience. This is not, perhaps, surprising. A figure who described himself as pleasing no one, belonging to no school and as not being an original thinker, might well find the condition of post-modernism both ironic and – in some ways – congenial.

25. Ibid., 144.
26. Ibid., 136.
27. See, e.g., George Tyrrell, *Through Scylla and Charybdis: Or, The Old Theology and the New*, London: Longmans, Green and Co., 1907, 287.

CHAPTER 12

Retrieving Imagination in Theology

Michael Paul Gallagher SJ

> You may not consider it blasphemy, I hope, that belief in God depends on the direction of our imagination. You will know that imagination is the highest and most original element in us.
>
> *Friedrich Schleiermacher*

Thomas Aquinas tackles a surprising topic in the introduction to his commentary on the *Sentences,* inquiring whether the method of theology should be *artificialis*. Putting it in modern language, he asks whether theology needs an artistic dimension and he answers in the affirmative. As always it is intriguing to read his objections, in order to appreciate the contrary view that he is about to undermine. For instance, he argues (against his position) that since poetry works by means of metaphoric expression, theology as a science must necessarily avoid such wavelengths. In this context he cites the key text for modern fundamental theology (from 1 Peter 3:15) about giving reasons for our hope, and hence arguments are needed. But then he turns the tables and, almost in the manner of David Tracy, speaks of different publics for theology. When it is a question of overcoming error, then clear arguments are needed, but this is not the whole of theology. It also involves the 'contemplation of truth' and here, he suggests, that we will in addition need a 'symbolic theology' (*symbolica theologia*) that is not simply argumentative. In this context he lists the four levels of meaning in scripture (historical, moral, allegorical and analogical). However, the novel core of his argument comes when he insists that faith is based on 'a narrative of signs' and that hence 'metaphorical, symbolical and parabolical' approaches are not only acceptable but necessary. He pushes this further in his answer to the objection that poetry suffers from a defect of rational truth and therefore is not a proper model for theology. On the contrary, he concludes, since theology also seeks to explore beyond reason, a 'symbolic method is common to both' (*modus symbolicus utrique communis est*).[1]

Rescuing a forgotten dimension

The openness to the imagination present in this text of Aquinas is an aspect of theology that has been retrieved in many ways in recent decades. Under the shadow of the modernist crisis such explorations were often taboo, but gradually since the sixties many theologians, of various schools and tendencies, have given new attention to the role of symbolic and aesthetic consciousness in theology. Clearly it connects up with the positive tendency of post-modern thinking to retrieve aspects of humanity that were despised or ignored by the more narrow forms of modernity. Imagination is certainly one of these dimensions, often identified with the danger of illusion or false fantasy. For generations a mixture of rationalism and suspicion held sway in the fields of serious thought. They seemed like the ugly sisters of the fairytale, acting as bossy dictators of the house, whereas their imagination remained a poor Cinderella in the basement kitchen. Down there she could be visited by poets and other eccentrics, but she had no right of citizenship in the high debates of the ground floor.

Even in arid times, imagination had her serious visitors and faithful friends. They appreciated her as a form of creative intelligence in a pre-conceptual rather than an explicitly rational mode. Kant and Coleridge (as the former's literary interpreter in England) both saw imagination as an active power that unifies experiences, allowing a synthesis of the fragments of life, and therefore healing the dualism of self and world. The Scottish religious thinker, George MacDonald, was a nineteenth-century pioneer in recognising a central theological role for imagination. His 1867 essay, 'The Imagination, its functions and its culture' (now more easily available on the Internet than in libraries) remains an exceptional exploration of imagination as giving form to thought and of the 'embodying' and 'prophetic' forms of imagination as searching out the imagination of God. Another pioneer in the same period was John Henry Newman and much has been written in recent decades about the centrality of imagination in his description of the road to faith.[2] Suffice it to say that the manuscripts of *The Grammar of Assent* show that Newman's

1. S. Tommaso d'Aquino, *Commento alle Sentenze di Pietro Lombardo* [Prologus q.1, a.5] Vol I, Bologna, 2001, 150-155.
2. See my article 'Newman on Faith and Imagination', *Milltown Studies* (No 49) Summer 2002, 84-101.

original and preferred phrase for 'real assent' was 'imaginative assent'. In the course of the sixties he had gradually overcome his inherited fears of imagination in religion and had come to see this human wavelength as an essential source of personal or existential reality in spirituality and faith.

In the twentieth century, scientists were quicker off the mark than theologians in recognising the special potential role of imagination. Einstein is credited with the claim that imagination is more important than knowledge, and Max Planck has praised imagination as offering scientists a capacity for breaking new ground and entering new paradigms of explanation. In recent decades, however, theology has joined other disciplines in a new respect for this rich human wavelength. We have become aware of metaphoric and narrative theology, of analogical imagination, or of fresh thinking concerning God and creative imagination.[3] From a pastoral point of view there is little doubt about the crucial importance of speaking in modern parables. More ambitiously, poetry can challenge theology to emerge from its doctrinaire fixations of vocabulary. As Oliver Davies has argued in his impressive recent book, *A Theology of Compassion*, there is a new excitement about 'wanting to link fundamental theology with aesthetics and modern art in general'.[4] Pierangelo Sequeri, one of the most distinguished of contemporary Italian theologians, has devoted much attention to the spiritual role of music in particular and of aesthetic affectivity in general. In his words, 'aesthetic experience is the recurring place for the question that consciousness rarely formulates with any worthy seriousness: is this really the best of possible worlds?'[5]

A trio of witnesses

This whole theme is one that strangely unites some of the solo giants of the last century (solo in the sense that they worked independently of one another and often with some degree of suspicion of what the others were stressing). It is fascinating, for instance, to find a strong convergence on this point in Rahner, von Balthasar and Lonergan.

Rahner, in typical fashion, treated the theme of poetry in sev-

3. These expressions deliberately echo titles of books by Sallie McFague, David Tracy and Paul Avis.

4. *A Theology of Compassion: Metaphysics of Difference and the Renewal of Tradition*, London, 2001, 176.

5. *L'Estro di Dio: saggi di estetica*, Milan, 2000, 14 (my translation).

eral essays, nearly always with an emphasis on its mystagogical capacity to open doors to pre-conceptual human depth, and hence rescue the listening sensibility of a person for the Word of God. He viewed poetry as representing a wavelength of pastoral relevance. Poets 'speak primordial words in powerful concentration' and priests also need something of this ability to awaken people to mystery.[6] Rahner also tended to stress the tragic honesty of great literature, whether written by unbelievers or believers: it can confront people with their vulnerability and ultimately with their need of salvation. Unfortunately, in his view, theology had lost contact with the poetic and with the importance of the symbolic as the least inadequate language we have to do some justice to mystery. In this spirit, in one of his last lectures, Rahner praised the arts in general for being able to liberate us from a merely 'rationalistic theory' in theology and instead to protect our 'capacity for the incomprehensible'. More ambitiously still, he proposed 'the thesis that theology cannot be complete until it appropriates these arts as an integral moment of itself and its own life, until the arts become an intrinsic moment of theology itself'. Agreeing with von Balthasar, he voiced the need to go beyond a 'verbal theology' towards a 'poetic theology'.[7]

Lonergan is possibly less known for his emphasis on the imaginative dimension and yet it is a strong if secondary concern in his writings. In *Insight* he devotes pages to the aesthetic pattern of experience as a pre-conceptual zone of 'wonder in its elemental sweep' and as offering a form of liberation for 'spontaneous self-justifying joy'. Probably his most detailed treatment of these themes comes in his 1959 lectures on education where he devotes a whole session to art, stressing again the privileged horizon of free exploration of feeling that it can offer. He sees life as in danger of becoming unlivable unless we find ways of recreating our more fundamental potentials of freedom. We live too often in a merely utilitarian and ready-made world which art can transform so that it 'heads on to God'.[8] In a way that prepares his stronger emphasis on religious experience in *Method in Theology*, he claims that 'in fact the life we are living is a product

6. 'Priest and Poet', *Theological Investigations*, III, London, 1973, 301.
7. 'Theology and the Arts', *Thought* 57 (1982), 20-21, 24-25.
8. *Collected Works of Bernard Lonergan: Topics in Education*, ed. R. Doran and F. Crowe, Toronto, 1993, 225.

of artistic creation' and it is on the artistic, symbolic level that we live our full range of humanity, discovering that we can become 'emergent, ecstatic, standing out ... originating freedom'.[9] Although there are many passages in *Method in Theology* that deal with the role of images and with art as a carrier of meaning, the main line of Lonergan's thought in this area was already established in the two previous books. One important addition comes from the linking of affective development with symbols and his new insistence that religious conversion, which he now puts as foundational in the operations of theology, is a form of affective self-transcendence where feelings and imagination are crucial.[10] In an untypical slogan-like phrase, Lonergan sums up the centrality of the imaginative dimension: 'With Giambattista Vico, then, we hold for the priority of poetry.'[11]

It hardly needs saying that more than any other major figure of the last century the name of Hans Urs von Balthasar is associated with a renewed centrality for the aesthetic wavelength within theology. Distancing himself from the tradition of subjective aesthetics, he gives priority to the beauty and radiance of form that we can perceive in the figure of Christ. If both Rahner and Lonergan tend to highlight the imaginative as a liberation towards the threshold of faith, for Balthasar it is the uniqueness of revealed Christian glory that becomes the objective and prime analogy. Hence 'Christianity becomes *the* aesthetic religion *par excellence*'.[12] Less well known are some of von Balthasar's explorations of human imagination, which he puts at the centre of both anthropology and spirituality. In line with the medieval tradition, he insists that every kind of expression of spiritual vision relies on imagination. Images, in his view, can create inner space and point beyond themselves towards mysteries that they both reveal and conceal. An authentically human intuition is possible only through the mediation of imagination. Equally, prayer requires that the eyes of the imagination enter into a zone of repose that becomes contemplative receptivity.[13]

Special versus Ordinary

9. Ibid., 217.

10. *Method in Theology*, London, 1972, 289.

11. Ibid., 73.

12. *The Glory of the Lord: A Theological Aesthetics*, Vol. I, Edinburgh, 1982, 216.

13. These points appear in an essay in *Homo Creatus Est* on the visual faculty of Christians. Other relevant passages on images occur in

Even from these brief indications, the convergence between these three major theologians is striking. They were all rebelling against a decadent narrowness in theology, and even if they differ greatly between themselves in their approaches, on this issue of imagination or the aesthetic they share a surprising degree of common ground. That common ground, however, tends to be high ground. All three theologians gravitate naturally to imagination as special, as inviting us in a privileged artistic way towards heights and depths that daily life can smother. But is there not perhaps a danger of elitism lurking here? Can the daily and the ordinary not also be a theatre of imagination, an equally important one for faith and theology? In this respect I would want to retrieve the often neglected explorations of William Lynch (1908-1987), an American contemporary of those three famous theologians.[14] He resists the Coleridgean tradition of thinking of the prime analogy of imagination in terms of high creativity. Instead he sees it as our ordinary human filter for coping with the finite drama of life: 'the task of imagination is to imagine the real'.[15] In his view a non-aesthetic model of imagination is our human gift for dealing with the concrete world inside and outside of ourselves, coping with it, shaping it and ultimately transforming it. Imagination becomes therefore a form of thought, indeed the natural and central vehicle of cognition for most people most of the time. On this basis it is hardly surprising that Lynch goes on to see a specifically Christian role for imagination. In his words, 'faith is a form of imagining and experiencing the world'.[16] Christ is 'the creator and the actuality behind a new imagination'[17] and through him we are invited 'literally to imagine things with God'.[18]

If Lynch highlights the ordinary journey of imagination as a

Chapter III of Volume I of *Theo-Logic*. I have consulted both these texts in the Italian version and hence do not offer page references here.

14. There is one book devoted to his work: Gerald J. Bednar, *Faith as Imagination: the contribution of William F. Lynch, S.J.*, Kansas, 1996, and Francesca Aran Murphy devotes a chapter to him in her *Christ the Form of Beauty*, Edinburgh, 1995.

15. William F. Lynch, *Images of Faith: An Exploration of the Ironic Imagination*, Notre, Dame, 1973, 63.

16. Ibid., 5.

17. Lynch, *Christ and Apollo: The Dimensions of the Literary Imagination*, New York, 1960, xiv.

18. Lynch, *Christ and Prometheus: A New Image of the Secular*, Notre Dame, 1970, 23.

daily march through the finite towards the infinite, he is equally aware of imagination as a battleground. The Christian imagination 'has subverted the whole order of the old imagination' but the old self-enclosed fixations find easy food. As against the avalanche of fantasy images, promoted most notoriously through advertising, Lynch sees the crucial cultural struggle of our time as the nourishing of a genuinely human and religious imagination. Behind much of popular culture (and even some tendencies in T. S. Eliot), Lynch diagnoses new forms of gnosticism or what Maritain terms the 'angelic' imagination. These cultural tendencies involve a flight from the definite and hence an infidelity to the incarnation. But in a genuinely 'analogical' imagination lies the key to our transformation under grace, through the everyday drama of living with love in the ordinary.

To ground these largely theoretical jottings let us visit a recent example of imagination, both artistic and incarnational. The Irish writer Niall Williams has soared into the bestseller lists with three extraordinary novels in the space of a few years. His style is ambitiously lyrical and has been described as a Celtic version of the 'magic realism' associated with such figures as Gabriel García Marquez. I would argue that his vision is profoundly (but not conventionally) religious, and that the rhetoric of his fiction is what Rahner would call 'mystagogy', leading readers towards glimpses of mystery and of grace. Often in these novels God is asked for a sign and no obvious sign comes. Yet a deep slow healing is the secret core of the action. In the words of the latest novel, *The Fall of Light*, 'the world itself could be repaired [and] no breakage was beyond remedy'. In this story of family fragmentation and pain, starting in the famine times in Ireland, ultimately 'imagination in some way redeemed the absence and loss'.[19]

Clearly theology can encounter such fiction as a source of thematic reflection but there is a temptation here to be acknowledged and avoided. I say this as someone who has spent many more years of my life teaching literature than teaching theology. The tendency of theologians is to zoom in on the religious content of literature as the expense of the aesthetic experience. The theological relevance of the reader's encounter with a Niall Williams novel does not lie in the occasional spiritual language, such as just quoted. Rather it lies in the whole process of being

19. Niall Williams, *The Fall of Light*, London , 2001, 128-129, 368.

invited by the flow of words and events into a different wavelength of awareness. Theology needs to approach art and literature more as experience than as message or meaning. The wavelength shared by theology and imagination lies in the whole adventure and joy of self-transcendence in its many forms. In this spirit let us close with an eloquent evocation of this adventure from Wallace Stevens:[20]

We come
To knowledge when we come to life.
Yet always there is another life,
A life beyond this present knowing,
A life lighter than this present splendour …
Not an attainment of the will
But something illogically received,
A divination, a letting down
From loftiness, misgivings dazzlingly
Resolved in dazzling discovery.

20. From 'Not Ideas about the Thing but the Thing Itself' in Wallace Stevens, *Palm at the End of the Mind: Selected Poems and a Play*, ed. H. Stevens, New York, 1972, 390.

CHAPTER 13

Simone Weil and the Impossible: A Radical View of Religion and Culture

David Tracy

I INTRODUCTION: SIMONE WEIL AS MYSTICAL-POLITICAL

Is there a unity to Simone Weil's religious thought? I do not see that there is. Her thought was so multiple – on topics, on sources, on various fragmentary attempts – that it is difficult if not impossible to propose a single unity for a thinker who wrote so much on such varied topics and in such largely fragmentary forms in so brief a life. That Weil was one of the major religious thinkers of the twentieth century is surely true. If I were forced to try to claim a unity to her thought, I would choose political-mystical philosophy. Indeed, she was the foremost predecessor of all the recent attempts – in political and liberation theologies and more recently in many other new forms of Christian thought – that attempt to reunite the mystical and prophetic strands of the Christian tradition into a coherent mystical-prophetic philosophy and theology. Of course, her thought cannot be reduced to her life. But her life itself, so multiple and united only by her tenacious sensibility, does provide some signal clues at times to her remarkable flashes of pure thought. Consider, for example, her three famous mystical experiences. Here we find clues to some tenuous unity to her thought and life and to their uncanny power to lure us like a magnet into her extraordinary presence and demands. In her first mystical experience, while hearing some Portuguese fishermen and their wives sing their songs of sorrow and joy, Weil sees the heart of Christianity: it is the religion of slaves and cannot live except by that insight. For Weil, this is Christianity's most distinctive trait: what will later be called its 'preferential option for the poor' in the midst of a radical egalitarianism ('God rains on the just and the unjust' as she loved to quote from the Bible).

In her second mystical experience, at the church of St Francesco at Assisi, yet another element of her thought showed itself: the light of the Good in the poverty and purity of God's fool, Francis, and the light of the Good radiant in the necessity disclosed to intelligence by the beauty disclosed in the play of geometric shapes and light in Giotto's frescoes on Francis at Assisi.

In her third mystical experience, at the singing of Gregorian chant at Solesmes and in reading George Herbert's classic metaphysical-theological poem 'Love', she experienced even more intensely in mystical terms her central vision, at once Platonic and Christian; first, as with Giotto, the play of light and mathematical geometric forms yielding the harmony and proportion heard in the West – from Pythagoras through Plato through Gregorian Chant and Giotto to Simone Weil (whose name well deserves to be mentioned in that list). At the same time, and pervading all this light and intelligence in thought, beauty and religion for Weil was what George Herbert articulates in his great poem – the reality of the Good, Love, God as the Ultimate Reality if we could but pay attention (her favourite spiritual exercise).

These three famous visions were neither random nor arbitrary. She stated, in *Gravity and Grace*, that the meaning of life often depends on which word one uses to describe what happens to one: chance, fate or Providence. These three mystical visions of hers (perhaps like the three allotted to Plotinus if we only knew what his were) can provide some central clues not only to her exceptional life (which is from beginning to end a mystery) but also to her thought. That thought is, again from beginning to end, a search for an order of the relationship of the Good and necessity in all its forms; an order of the relationship of the Impossible order of charity to the actual order of human wretchedness; the relationship of creation and incarnation to the cross. That order of intelligence, charity and action for the poor might, if conceived and practised by others, help to heal the three great disorders of modernity: passion separated from intelligence (never in her); practice divorced from theory – a modern insult to this Platonic activist who insisted on the importance of manual labour for the purity and accuracy of thought itself; form separated from content. Indeed the union of form and content in her work is stunning from her form of 'essays' and her form of 'treatises' on oppression and the need for roots. These Weilian forms are part Descartes-like in the form of logical, rigorous meditations; part Montaigne-like in her form of essays as attempts (*essais*), forays, thought experiments. Platonic thought for Weil also needed new forms to prove adequate to its new modern content – work, history, body, i.e., matter. Indeed Weil is more materialist than any other Platonist even as she shares Plato's love for the purely intelligent forms from mathematics to dialectics to mystical thought (*The Republic*). She is often as materialist as Lucretius and as dialectically materialist as Marx and the later revisionist Marxists of Frankfurt. Walter Benjamin is her explicitly Jewish Marxist other and may prove the best modern conversational counterpart to her. Would that Weil had learned from Benjamin, as he learned from Scholem, and thus spared herself and her admirers her narrow, willful and ignorant reading of Judaism. Emmanuel Levinas, who both shared and praised the force of Weil's insistence on the Other not the self as the proper starting point (a prophetic-ethical one) for contemporary thought, was nevertheless entirely right in his anger at Weil's mistreatment and misreading of Judaism when he uttered his violent charge hurled at her like a fist 'Simone Weil, you understand everything except the Bible!'

The Montaigne-like form of Weil's essays and Descartes-like form of her treatises in her studies of work, body and politics – made it possible for Weil to find new non-Marxist forms for leftist thought and actions of the radical left in the period between the wars. Her other preferred form, we can call *Pensées* in honour of Pascal. She shared so much with Pascal that she seemed obliged to criticise him frequently even as she rethought and critically reformulated some of his greatest insights into her own: insights on the wretchedness of the human condition; the centrality of the cross in Christianity; the centrality of suffering for understanding the cross – physical, psychological and spiritual agony – what she brilliantly renamed 'affliction'; the importance of the category of 'order'; above all, the need to acknowledge the Pascalian three orders of existence and to consider their relationships. The first order is the order of the flesh. Force and its rule for Weil is, as she argued in her essay on the *Iliad: Poem of Force*, that kingdom of the necessity of force which affects all human lives as we all must one day die. But force affects some (slaves) for their entire lives not just at death. Second, is the order of intelligence, from logic, mathematics, and science through metaphysics, where most genuine thinkers live their entire lives as much as possible. Indeed, she typically said that 'intellectuals' is an ugly word, but we deserve it. The third order for Weil, again with Pascal, is the order of charity – an order as different from the order of intelligence as the order of intelligence is from the order of the flesh; an order as difficult to sense for those only in the order of intelligence as it is for those only in the order of the flesh to understand those in the order of intelligence.

More than Pascal, but in his spirit, she showed how intertwined these three orders are, even for those in the order of charity. The order of charity is one where body – flesh – is still very much present (even for Christ) and to be made real. Her mysticism is intellectually – in spite of the perhaps true charges of anorexia against her on her own body – also a body mysticism of intelligence and body working together. Indeed that vision is the central reason why for her thinkers need manual labour. Theologically, for Weil, there is a vision of an overwhelming reality of a kenotic understanding of real bodily incarnation as well as a deeply embodied understanding of cross as crucifixion. The crucifixion, for Weil, is both bodily and spiritual humiliation. It is the personal suffering of Christ as a slave, a criminal, a reject from the body of society. Jesus's body – stripped, scourged, naked and in overwhelming pain – must suffer not merely in spirit but in body so that his soul may suffer in affliction. Jesus, for Weil, undergoes the horror of human and decisive abandonment: Jesus' cry from the cross, 'My God, my God, why have you forsaken me?' she paradoxically insists, shows the divine character of Christianity! The order of intelligence, she also insisted, must find a way to be attentive and active in the order of charity as well. She never called her own thought 'theology.' Perhaps she had good reasons for that refusal. But she did always insist on the keenest use of intelligence (logical, rigorous, demanding, speculative) in reflecting on the order of charity. And surely that is theology at its best. Recall her brilliant suggestion that John of the Cross developed a scientific account of the stages of the spiritual life. Only high intelligence participating within and yet, as intelligence critically must, distancing itself from the order of charity, could count for Weil as the right kind of theology. Recall her references to Teresa of Avila and to John of the Cross rather than to officially designated theologians. She did not admire Thomas Aquinas – he was too Aristotelian on reason, and not sufficiently mystical in spirit for her.

As any attentive reader of Simone Weil soon notes, (how rare those readers are, she writes, in her brilliant reflections on *attention* as the most necessary and nearly lost spiritual practice for true reading) Weil's prose forms – treatises, essays, *pensées* – achieve the lucidity, rigour, clarity, and elegance of the classical French tradition. She does so not only on questions of the body, on mechanical necessity, and on the structure of society, but also on the divine mysteries, understood as mysteries in the order of charity. Weil's is a prose and thought of limit even for the best thought. Hence her admiration for Kant on the limits of reason and perhaps, in Kant, tragedy and philosophy together. Simone Weil left us forms appropriate to her content, perhaps even, in one of her favorite words, necessary for that content. She left thought which never, as in the Enlightenment, divorces passion and intelligence anymore than Pascal did. She left a form of Platonism that, by its insistence on a theory of work, changed Platonism into no less an idealist position than traditionally while also becoming insistently materialist. She insisted on body, social conditions, history, matter far more than most forms of Platonism do.

Which leaves us what then? A thinker whose very forms of thinking often act like searchlights amidst our contemporary confusions. A thinker who articulated better than anyone else of her time why Christianity must be a mystical-political religion of and for the oppressed. A thinker who, in my judgement, stands with Walter Benjamin as the thinker between the wars (and like him, finally destroyed by the war) who dared to expose the self-delusions of most thinkers of that and our period. For myself, Weil and Benjamin will one day be recognised as the crucial thinkers between the wars who fragmented the ego of that age and ours just as, in post-modern thought, Nietzsche and Kierkegaard are now acknowledged as the thinkers best suited to expose and smash the self-deluding modern systems of the nineteenth century and of ours.

And yet I cannot claim that even this suggestion of a mystical-political reading does justice to the multifarious character of Weil's thought. Some other focus is also needed. Here, reflection on her as a Christian Platonist does advance the discussion of a possible (only one possible) manifold unity to her thought. For Simone Weil was clearly Christian and she always loved Plato. Therefore, it is just to call Weil a Christian Platonist as long as this title is not placed above the wider category of mystical-political and as long as we acknowledge that even Christian Platonism does not account for the full range, originality and power of Weil's thought. For what a strange Christian and odd Platonist Simone Weil actually was.

II WEIL'S CHRISTIAN PLATONISM: THE SEA-CHANGE OF TRAGEDY

Simone Weil was neither orthodox in some of her Christianity nor like most Platonists on her Platonic side. On the Christian side, she was reticent when not silent on certain central doctrines and symbols of the Christian symbol-system: especially the resurrection, perhaps because of her acute fear of any Christian triumphalism. She was also reticent on the eschatological tradition, perhaps because of her fear of how quickly any imagination – including the eschatological when literalised – can delude us by trying to fill the void with fantasies.

This double reticence on resurrection and apocalypse in the New Testament became fierce when she turned her attention to the Hebrew Bible which is also, for Christians, their scripture, i.e. their First or Old Testament. To be sure she accorded some parts of the Old Testament more attention than many Christian thinkers do to this day: above all, the Book of Job, certain Psalms (especially the Psalms of Lamentation), The Suffering Servant of Isaiah, and, more surprisingly, the creation accounts of Genesis. But it remains a puzzle why this exceptionally attentive mind and soul, so prophetic in her person and thought, would prove so deaf to the great prophets and their demand for what she most cared for — justice for the oppressed. It remains a puzzle why Weil did not read more attentively the Book of Exodus not just as another book of triumphalism by the victors over the Canaanites (although that is there). But Exodus – as oppressed peoples throughout the centuries readily sense – is, above all, a book of liberation of and for the slaves and victims of history. Even the more Hellenised wisdom literature of the Old Testament does not receive the attention one would expect from the grecophile Simone Weil.

Whatever the peculiarities of her own history – born to a highly assimilated, indeed secular Jewish family and open to Buddhism and Hinduism, Confucianism and Taoism – her closedness to and willful ignorance of the riches of the Jewish tradition, in its biblical form as well as in its later history (the only exception is that Weil may have read some readings of kabbalists) remain a mystery. That mystery is not solved, in my judgement, by deciding in prosecutorial style, that Weil was a 'self-hating Jew.' She did, like Pascal, find the 'I', the '*moi*' – her own – hateful and in constant need of decreation. But she was surprisingly (given her character) insensitive to the massive suffering of the greatest victims in Europe of her day, her fellow Jews.

Her problem here – and it is a grave problem for those of us who have learned so much from Simone Weil in her insistence that Christianity should always be on the side of the oppressed in any period – is comprised, I suspect, of psychological and historical reasons beyond our reach but not our disrespect. After all, she never allowed such excuses to others. She rightly denounced Christianity's involvement in the Crusades, the Inquisition, the treatment of her beloved Cathari, the indifference of the rich and of cultured 'Christians' of every century toward the poor in their midst. She despised Corneille on the 'grandeur' of France in the imperialist and, for her, revolting '*grand siècle*' of Louis XIV. The list of the historical figures she judged harshly could easily be expanded. Her only equal here is Nietzsche.

Weil's intellectual-spiritual problem with some versions of Jewish 'exceptionalism' or 'election' was shared by some Jewish thinkers (as she should have known) in her own day. It is even more widely shared in our day (e.g. the orthodox Jewish theologian, David Hartmann) by many Jewish thinkers who never cease fighting the problems of some triumphalist interpretations of election, including those in the bible, especially the slaying of the Canaanites. This cruel strand of the bible is for many Jewish thinkers – as she should have known – as deep and troubling as the exclusionist triumphalism and complacent sense of election and supersessionism of many Christians. Why did she fail here when she saw with such clarity that Christianity's temptation to triumphalism and totality-thinking is a betrayal of Christianity on inner-Christian terms? She always insisted that the stern reality of the cross and the clearly prophetic vocation of Christianity to privilege the oppressed, the victims of history, not the victors of what even Hegel called the 'slaughter-bench' of history: why then not her fellow Jews?

Simone Weil somehow refused to see how the same prophetic principle, the same liberationist drive for the victims of history that she found in Christianity is central to the Hebrew Bible and to the Christian reading of it as Old Testament. The Hebrew Bible is not, as she sometimes thought, a long book of Joshua. The ancient Hebrews, driven by their prophetic and legal traditions alike, were not the ancient Romans she imagined. Indeed, even some of the ancient Romans – Virgil above all – was not the vulgar triumphalist she makes him out to be. Her reading of Judaism is a sad exercise in a life and thought otherwise driven by a sense of justice and a demand for compassion.

The real Simone Weil, I continue to believe, is elsewhere than in her readings of the Hebrew Bible. The real Simone Weil is in her readings of the ancient Greeks (whose writings effectively function for her as her Old Testament) and in her partial but extraordinary readings of the New Testament. Who, except Simone Weil, could move so subtly between two profoundly different gospel accounts of the passion of Jesus: the gospel of Mark whose afflicted Jesus (as Weil never tired of reminding Christians) screams from the cross the shattering words of physical affliction and spiritual abandonment 'My God, my God, why have you forsaken me?' and the gospel of John where the very lifting up of Jesus on the cross discloses God's beauty and glory in the last words (words of necessity, not triumph) of John's Jesus, 'It is consummated.' Simone Weil affirms both gospels as she affirms how beauty in the *Iliad* is seen most clearly on the other side of intense suffering. She affirms both Mark and John as readily and as subtly as she affirms (*contra* Nietzsche) both tragedy and philosophy, both Sophocles and Plato, among the Greeks. The key to Weil's readings in both cases – Christianity and Platonism – is her unerring sense of necessity, justice, and the Good – in a word, her insistence *vis-à-vis* both Platonism and Christianity that a tragic sensibility must be maintained. Otherwise Platonism is one more totality-system (incorporating, as historically neo-Platonism did, elements not only of Plato, but of the Stoics and the Aristotelians). Otherwise Christianity is a triumphant Christendom as it so often has been – Weil insists on this over and over again – for example in the orthodox Christian triumphalist cry against the Cathari and anyone else unlucky enough to live among them: 'Kill them all; God will know his own.'

Far more clearly than Pascal, Weil understood that the true wretchedness of humanity must include not only sin (she is always clear how real and pervasive that is) but also tragedy – i.e. fate as (in her words) the necessity of suffering in life. She sometimes refers to the consequences of sin as tragedy – the curse of fate in Oedipus and even, in the way of innocent substitionary redemption, she speaks of the fate of Christ.

Simone Weil's thought is a profound Christian theological reading which affects her interpretations of all the central doctrines of Christianity. God becomes at times for her, as much as for Luther, the awe-ful Hidden God of the Void. The incarnation becomes, in the light of the cross, deeply kenotic for her, and even a cleavage as she believed is suggested by the implication of the cross and the saying in the Book of Revelation 'The Lamb is slain from the foundation of the World'. Even more, Weil's curious speculations on the inner-Trinitarian relationships of Father and Son suggest speculation such as that of Hans von Balthasar or Jürgen Moltmann. Above all, her Christian anthropology becomes one formed neither by traditional (e.g. Thomist) interpretations of nature and grace (although she too affirms our essential goodness – our natural attraction, in spite of our egoism, to the Light) nor by the traditional Reformation interpretation on sin and grace (although she affirms, as strongly as the later Augustine or Luther or Pascal) the power and reality of sin in our personal, social, and historical lives. Weil is ruled by neither the nature-grace paradigm nor the sin-grace paradigm. She is somewhere else. The wretchedness of humanity is seen by her (almost more like Racine than Pascal) as comprised of these realities: first, our greatness (our intelligence, our intrinsic drive to the light, our graced ability to love, our sense of justice); second, our tragic sensibility: the necessity of force that must eventually invade every human life, and thereby the sense of a need for justice – an equilibrium emerging from tragedy's sense of hubris, the sense of beauty as deepened by a tragic sense of fate and its curse upon us. As she insists: if this be my last day – as in the *Iliad* for so many of its characters – the beauty of the sunset or the beauty of family, friends, life itself is more intense and more beautiful than ever. Such a sense evokes compassion towards literally all – not only towards the victors – but victims and victors alike as she sees in her beloved *Iliad* or in Aeschylus' *The Persians*. This tragic reality comprises for Weil aspects of our greatness and not only our wretchedness: justice, compassion and intelligence as well as sin (ours and the consequences of others' sin –

our fate, our curse). She affirms, I repeat, the reality of sin. She also affirms sin, both as personal and as consequence of the actions of others, as there for all Christians to attend to by attending to the kenotic incarnation-cross of Christ, (including in its social structural form), the only purely innocent, sinless human and the one and only God at one and the same time.

This reading on the centrality of the cross and the reality of the tragic (as something like a paradoxical medium *metaxu*, between our greatness and our tragic wretchedness) frees Simone Weil's Christian vision from the sin-pessimism of the later Augustine or Calvin or Pascal (we are 'lumps of sin' for Augustine) just as the cross and the tragic free her as well from the vulgar optimism on humanity of too much Christian humanism. Weil arrived, in my judgement, at a deeper Christian vision of God as hidden, of Christ as incarnate and crucified, of ourselves as wretched (i.e. as great, tragic and sinful all at once); and even of creation as sparks of the Good let loose in the world. Hers is an exceptional and powerful Christian vision – and one that can be understood partly as a revised, i.e. tragic, form of a Christian Platonism. Her Platonism, transformed by a tragic sensibility and her insistence on work, is perhaps her deepest philosophical formulation of her Christian vision. But Platonism is not Weil's only option for an useable past. Witness her love for the Stoics, her deep respect for the logical, rigorous and meditative power of Descartes, her reverence for Kant's thoughts on reason, acknowledging its powers and, through that very acknowledgment, the limits of reason. Indeed she called the greatest use of reason an acknowledgement, like Kant's, of its limits. Recall as well, Weil's sometime sympathy even for the Manicheans. Did any other twentieth-century Christian thinker share these diverse sympathies? Outside Christianity recall Weil's love of certain texts of the Buddhists, the Hindus (especially the *Bhagavad-Gita*) and the Taoists (especially the understanding of religion as a 'way' of non-active action). If Christianity had travelled East rather than West, Simone Weil, in spite of her love of the Greeks, would not have been deeply disturbed: Buddhist thought would have strengthened her kenotic christology; the *Gita* would have become her new *Iliad;* and Taoism would have shown her a way to understand Christ as way, truth and life.

But that historical possibility, like Pascal on Cleopatra's nose, is merely a great 'what if': Christianity did not move East. It entered the Hellenistic world. For Weil that meant that Christianity entered the luminous world of pre-classical Greece (note her love for pre-classical Greek folklore and myth) and classical Greece. Recall, above all, her love for both tragedy and philosophy, both Homer and Aeschylus, Sophocles and the Hippolytus (little more) of Euripides and, of course, all of Plato.

In sum, Simone Weil was a Platonist but one with a difference. The difference again comes about through her joining Plato, unlike the Plato of other Christian Platonists, not only to philosophy (Socrates and, for her, the so-called pre-Socratics, especially Heraclitus and Parmenides) but also to tragedy. A remarkable achievement for the interpretation of the Greeks.

Since the Romantic rediscovery of the Greeks and the seemingly endless debates, especially in German thought, on *which* Greeks (Aristotle and neo-Platonism for Hegel; tragedy for Nietzsche; the pre-Socratics for Heidegger), the interpretation of the Greeks by Simone Weil is a singular one. For her the greatness of Greece (which, like many before and after her, she partly romanticised) included not one singular choice but practically all the great forms and expressions of the ancient Greeks. The folklore, the myths (especially the Christ-like myth of Prometheus), the poems of Pindar, the epics – above all the *Iliad*, the poem of force; the pre-Socratics, especially Heraclitus; the tragedies, especially Aeschylus, Sophocles and the Hippolytus of Euripides; Plato and his Socrates; and the later Stoics. The almost sole exceptions to her praise of the Greeks were, for distinctly Weilian reasons, the *Odyssey* and Aristotle. Even here, however, for Weil, the *Odyssey* is partly good, i.e. the part like the *Iliad*; and Aristotle is acceptable when he is like Plato. On the later Platonists she is more reticent but, especially on Plotinus, approving.

She did not look for which part of Greek culture can serve as *the* clue to Greece's greatness. Greek tragedy or philosophy; Heraclitus or Plato; folklore-myth: she embraced almost all. And therein, lay her genius as a kind of Christian Platonist with a difference. For she consistently reads Plato as related not only to the Pythagoreans and their religious and ritualistic desire for the world of intelligibility in mathematics and music (proportion and harmony), but also the excessive and transgressive, not harmonious, religious ritualistic (for her mystical) Eleusinian mysteries. Both these sources, mathematics and the mysteries, influenced her reading of the rational and mystical Plato. Moreover, she reads Plato, as not simply against 'the poets', as he famously called Homer and the tragedians, but as himself possessing a tragic sensibility. Witness her reading of the speech of Agathon in the *Symposium*, her reading the tragic theme of the *Republic* and the *Timaeus* long before other scholars argued for the harmony of the tragic-hopeful sensibility between Aeschylus, Oresteia and the *Timaeus*. For as in the *Timaeus*, intelligence persuades (*peitho*) but never compels necessity (*ananke*).

With all their extraordinary achievements, the early Christian Platonists reflected too little on the tragedies and the tragic sensibility in either the Greeks or Christianity. They did see clearly the rational texts and mystical character of Plato in the texts that we possess – the *Dialogues* (which Weil dared to name Plato's popularisations of his discoveries). At any rate, Simone Weil's singularity as a Christian Platonist is, I believe, partly occasioned by her use of tragedy to rethink Christianity (especially the gospel of Mark as contrasted with the gospel of John) just as she rethinks the relationship of Homer and the tragedians (Mark-like) to Plato (John-like). I do not know why the early Christian Platonists were so right on the Christian theological relevance of Greek philosophy – especially Plato whom they cherished, developed and when necessary challenged (e.g. through the Christian notions of creation and incarnation) and at the same time so reticent, even wrong, on the Christian theological relevance of the tragedies. A partial exception is Augustine. His Platonism is clear and never abandoned (as the *De Trinitate* shows and the *Retractions* make ever clearer). His later tragic sensibility gave rise to his late-in-life profound anti-Pelagian reflections on the effects – consequences of 'original sin'. But so convinced was Augustine that the ancient tragic concept of fate denied God's omnipotence that he never developed what he could have for his own Christian Platonic anthropology: a Christian Platonist tragic sensibility on our weird human combination of essential goodness and both sinful and tragic actuality.

Simone Weil did what Augustine might have done but never did. She restored tragedy to a prominent place in both the reading of Plato and the reading of Christianity. She accomplished this remarkable feat without exaggerating the claims for the range and power of tragedy over philosophy (as Nietzsche did) and without denying our drive to justice as natural to us (indeed she finds a sense of justice *as* equilibrium in the *Iliad* itself). Weil strongly affirmed the power and goodness of our intelligence (as in the worlds of intelligibility opened by mathematics and philosophy). She affirmed the power and essential goodness of our rare experiences of love not as ego-love but as love of the *other* (the neighbour) especially the oppressed other in the order of *caritas*. She never flinched from a vision of the all-pervasive reality of sin – both personal sin, (the ego as she interprets its dilemma is Augustine's ego '*curvatus in se*') and the societal effects of sin. Here Augustinian concupiscence is not her category but fate – always, as she insists, with the sense of curse for past sins, our own and others – the family (Aeschylus and Sophocles), history (Thucydides), the entire race (Augustine).

That Weilian anthropology is consonant with, indeed analogous to, her christology. There incarnation and cross (always thought together) play such central roles that she is reticent on resurrection – although, as far as I can see, she need not, in principle, have denied it. A Weilian anthropology is consonant as well with her willingness to name God both Love and Hidden-as-Void. That anthropology is also consonant with her highly speculative understanding of a certain cleavage in God at creation where 'the sparks of the good are let loose in the world', and her even more speculative reflection on the incarnation as so kenotic that it suggests a cleavage in God, i.e. in the Trinity.

Even when one disagrees (as I basically do with her 'cleavage' metaphor as distinct from her 'kenotic' metaphor for creation and incarnation) one cannot but be stunned by the purity of her intelligence, the power and the courage of her christological speculations – at once Christian and Platonist and something more. That 'something more' in her odd christology occurs above all through her unique readings of both Plato and Christianity. Nor did she stay intellectually and spiritually with Platonism and Christianity alone. She found the same kind of Weilian vision of our situation in her readings of Taoism, the *Bhagavad-Gita*, and Buddhism. She allowed these traditions to be other and yet reconcilable with her Christian Platonism. She neither simply Christianises nor Platonises. Rather she shows how those other traditions too can aid, develop and challenge aspects of both Platonic and Christian self-understanding. She did this in the same spirit as she elsewhere insists that atheism – a real atheism not the relaxed intellectual hypothesis of moderns, for example, the atheism portrayed in Dostoevsky – may be a necessary ascetic purification for any authentic faith in God.

This Weilian vision sounds – even to many traditional Christian Platonist eyes – too radical, even excessive (as her critic Bataille sensed), indeed as impossible. In an exact sense, her vision is impossible. Like Kierkegaard, Simone Weil implicitly understood faith, in Kierkegaard's words, as a passion for the Impossible. Weil understood the Impossible to be a category for both the limits of our reason (Kant) and the *es gibt*, the sheer givenness and *gift* of the Impossible. For Weil, the Impossible is best – but not solely – discerned in the Kenotic incarnation and cross of Jesus Christ.

Implicitly, Weil understood God as the Impossible. Explicitly she named humankind not merely the Pascalian paradox of greatness and misery but Impossible. Above all, she clarified the Impossibility of Jesus Christ as not only the kenotic incarnation and not only the cross but, impossibly, as both together – each understood properly only through the other. Many contemporary thinkers now attempting to recover the category of the Impossible as a major initial category for genuine thinking on God and/or the Void (Levinas, Derrida, Meltzer, Caputo, Kearney, and my own recent work) can find Simone Weil a great ally as well as a radical intellectual and spiritual challenge. Like Kierkegaard, she was an early apostle of the Impossible. Moreover, unlike the rest of us, even Kierkegaard, Simone Weil was not only an 'apostle of the Impossible'. In her strange and unnerving thought, and her even stranger and most unnerving life, Simone Weil was Impossible.

Bibliography

Simone Weil

Attente de Dieu, Paris: La Colombe, 1950. Translated by Emma Craufurd as *Waiting for God,* New York: Harper and Row, 1951.

Intuitions prechretiennes, Paris: La Colombe, 1951. Translated by Emma Craufurd as *Intimations of Christianity among the Ancient Greeks,* London: Ark Paperbacks, 1987.

La condition ouvrière, Paris: Gallimard, 1951.

La Connaissance surnaturelle, Paris: Gallimard, 1950. Translated by

Richard Rees in *The First and Last Notebooks*, London: Oxford University Press, 1970.

La pesanteur et la grace, Paris: Plon, 1947. Translated by Emma Craufurd as *Gravity and Grace*, London: Ark Paperbacks, 1987.

La Source grecque, Paris: Gallimard, 1953. Translated by Emma Craufurd as *Intimations of Christianity among the Ancient Greeks*, London: Ark Paperbacks, 1987.

L'Enracinement: Prelude à une declaration des devoirs envers l'être humain, Paris: Gallimard, 1949. Translated by Arthur Wills as *The Need for Roots*, London: Ark Paperbacks, 1987.

Oppression et liberté, Paris: Gallimard, 1955. Translated by Arthur Wills and John Petrie as *Oppression and Liberty*, Amherst: University of Massachusetts Press, 1973.

Selected Essays, Translated by Richard Rees, London: Oxford University Press, 1962.

Simone Weil: An Anthology, Translated by Sian Miles, New York: Weidenfeld and Nicholson, 1986.

The Simone Weil Reader, Edited by George Panichas, New York: Moyer Bell, 1977.

Allen, Allen, and Eric O. Springstead, *Spirit, Nature, and Community Issues in the Thought of Simone Weil*, Albany: State University of New York Press, 1994.

Fiori, Gabriella, *Simone Weil: An Intellectual Biography*. Translated by Joseph Berrigan. Athens: University of Georgia Press, 1989.

Springsted, Eric, *Christus Mediator: Platonic Mediation in the Thought of Simone Weil*, Chico, Calif.: Scholars Press, 1983.

CHAPTER 14

Can We Love God?

Werner G. Jeanrond

Many of us have learnt since our childhood, either from the bible or our catechism, in Sunday School or in countless sermons and homilies, that the greatest commandment for Christians is to love God. The Matthean Jesus is reported to have told a Pharisee, when asked about the greatest commandment in the Torah,

> 'Love the Lord your God with all your heart and with all your soul and with all your mind. This is the first and greatest commandment. And the second is like it: Love your neighbour as yourself.' All the Torah and the Prophets hang on these two commandments. (Mt 22:37-9)

The Matthean Jesus thus gives a very concise and concentrated summary of what he considers to be the central message of the entire Jewish religious tradition as manifested in the Torah and the Prophets.[1] That means here we find Jesus's interpretation of what the Law, i.e., the normative ordering of the divine-human relationship, and the prophets, i.e., the dynamic and contextual call to reorder the divine-human relationship in specific historical circumstances, entail. One could say that in this passage, which has parallels also in Mark (12:28-31) and in Luke (10:27-28), we reach the heart of Christian life and discipleship, but not only of Christian faith. Rather these utterances of Jesus are directly quoting Moses's relating of God's commandments in Deuteronomy 6:4-5: 'Hear O Israel: The Lord our God is one Lord; and you shall love the Lord your God with all your heart, and with all your soul, and with all your might'; and in Leviticus 19:18, where it says 'You shall love your neighbour as yourself.'

There can be no doubt that the call to love God, the neighbour and oneself is at the centre of the Jewish and the Christian

1. Birger Gerhardsson speaks here of an overarching hermeneutical programme. See his *Hör Israel! Om Jesus och den gamla bekännelsen*, Lund: Liber Läromedel, 1979, 147-70.

experience of God. Therefore theology, as the second order reflection upon first order religious experience, must deal with this central message of faith. But that is easier said than done. The difficulties are many. First of all, it is very difficult to speak about love today. There is certainly no other word which is used in so many and so many conflicting ways as 'love'.

Love is portrayed as something which miraculously happens to people so that they fall in love, but it is also described as something which one can make (i.e., 'to make love'). Love is described as a happening, as a virtue, as a feeling. The only common denominator that I can see among all the different descriptions and definitions of love is its relational nature. 'To love' is a transitive verb and thus it is impossible to state simply 'I love'; instead I must say whom I love, or with whom I am in love, or because of whom I feel that I am falling in love.

Second, to make matters even more complex, the biblical texts talk about loving with one's heart, mind and soul. Thus, it seems not enough to say that I love or you love etc. But there seem to be different agencies within one single subject that are capable of loving, namely heart, mind, and soul. Third, the biblical texts seem to suggest that love of God, love of neighbour and love of self are, though related, nevertheless not identical. But is not love one? Is not any loving attention to the poor and oppressed in this world automatically also love of God? Or are there different experiences of love? What difference is there then between loving God and loving other human beings?

Fourth, how can we as theologians critically and self-critically talk about loving God, and thus about establishing a right relationship with God, when we do not even know what loving other human beings or loving my own self really mean. Should we not first clarify the meaning of love on earth, so to speak, before we can venture to talk about love in heaven? When we say we love God, we use analogical language taken from our human realm and project it on God. But can we do this in a critical and self-critical manner, since we still debate the meaning, content and varieties of love and therefore have not reached any conclusive definition of love. In other words, does it make sense to talk about loving God as long as we do not know yet what love really means here and now?

And finally, how can we say anything meaningful about relating to God in love when we know so little about God. Is not our poor state of knowledge a powerful argument against any love-language in relation to God?

In view of these questions it seems rather daunting to enter into a discussion on what it means to say that we ought to love God. Yet we have seen that this love is at the heart of the Christian message, and thus the future of Christian faith will depend on the proper attention by Christian believers to this love. However, this realisation does not mean that the future of Christian faith depends on the successful conclusion of this theological reflection. Rather my task in this reflection is only to discuss the theological implications of the question in what way it makes sense to state that we can love God.

In this regard it is important to appreciate the limits, but also the potential of theological reflection: Christian theology does not offer a foundation for Christian love. Rather it offers critical and self-critical reflections upon the significance, implications and potential of Christian love. As such it might be able to offer some clarification here or there, and – all being well – maybe also some critique and encouragement.

I propose to approach our topic in the following five steps: First, I shall discuss the starting-point of a Christian reflection upon how to love God. Second, I shall reflect upon love and otherness. Third, I shall analyse the unity of love. Fourth, I shall offer a few comments on the social context of love. And in my fifth and final section I shall consider some aspects of a spirituality of love.

I THE STARTING POINT FOR CHRISTIAN REFLECTION ON HOW TO LOVE GOD

Twenty years ago Christian theology was divided over the question of whether one should embark on christology from above or from below. Theologians such as Wolfhart Pannenberg and Hans Küng argued that we ought to begin with Jesus's human condition in order to grasp the significance of Jesus as Christ. Others such as Karl Barth and Karl Rahner argued that we ought to begin with a discussion of God's gracious plan of salvation in order to grasp the significance of Jesus as Christ. A third voice in this debate, that of the Cambridge theologian Nicholas Lash, argued that we had neither sufficient access to things divine nor indeed to things human so as to begin either here or there. Instead Lash recommended that we begin at the interface of things divine and human, i.e., where Christians believe they meet with God's gracious self-disclosure on earth, namely in the ministry, death and resurrection of Jesus of Nazareth.[2]

Similarly, when studying the possibilities of human love for God, we cannot start from one end of this mutual relationship. Rather any adequate discussion is bound to enter into the dynamics and the potential of this divine-human relationship as we encounter it in the history of Israel's relationship with her God, and in the tradition of those who confess that Jesus Christ has shown the way how to relate to Yahweh God, the God of Israel.

To contemplate the possibilities of loving God means for Jesus, and every fellow Jew, reflection on God's covenant with Israel. The parameters of proper divine-human relationship are defined both from within the ongoing experience of this covenant and from the expression in terms of proper order which this covenant received in the Torah. It seems to me to be of crucial importance that we appreciate again the ordering function of Israel's sacred law, and that we do not reduce this function to its legalistic caricatures as in Christian anti-Jewish polemics. Hence, contrary to much confessionalist Christian propaganda, it does make good sense to speak of the law of love, if by this expression one wants to highlight the particular character of Israel's understanding of the relationship between God and human beings, between human beings and God, and between human beings themselves – friend and enemy alike. Law understood first of all as an ordering agency is, as such, no contradiction to love. Moreover, love could well be understood as the fulfilment of law along the terms outlined by Jesus. But that means that the relationship offered to Israel by God contains the potential of fostering dynamic and free attitudes of mutual respect and care.

Jesus never abandoned these parameters of divine-human order and relationship. Rather he re-emphasised the love command from Deuteronomy as we have already seen. But there may be a somewhat different emphasis here. 'Deuteronomy speaks of Israel's love for God in the context of the covenant established at Sinai, using terminology familiar from the political

---

2 Nicholas Lash, 'Up and Down in Christology', in Stephen Sykes and Derek Homes, eds., *New Studies in Theology*, Vol 1, London: Duckworth, 1980, 30-46.

rhetoric of the culture. Here the love that God commands from Israel is not primarily a matter of intimate affection, but is to be expressed by obedience to God's commandments, serving God, showing reverence for God, and being loyal to God alone (10:12; 11:1, 22; 30:16).'[3] Quoting the commands of love to neighbour and enemy from Leviticus, Jesus stands firmly within his Jewish tradition, though he shifts the emphasis within love for God from loyalty to the covenant to the intimacy of a parent-child relationship (*abba*).

At times Christian scholars have been keen to drive a wedge between the Jewish and the Christian understandings of love, thus attempting to prove the superiority of Christian faith in God, and, if not explicitly stated, at least by implication the inferiority of the Jewish understanding of divine-human relationship.[4] This line of research was misguided on many fronts. First of all, Jesus was rarely concerned with theoretical or doctrinal clarifications. Rather than defining love as a principle, he aimed to live it and to demonstrate God's love and its healing effects on all human beings notwithstanding their particular legal or religious allegiance, confession and credentials.

Thus, the question arising for Christian believers is not whether Jesus's love command and praxis were unique in the Ancient Near East,[5] but whether his perspective on divine-human relationship offers a viable interpretative praxis of the Torah, now open for everybody who genuinely searches for God's creative and redeeming grace and presence in this world. According to Jesus, the result of God's love for us is that we can become children of God, which means that we can enter into a close relationship with God. This intimate relationship with God is perceived by Jews and Christians alike as God's gratuitous gift ('love comes from God', 1 Jn 4:7). God's loving presence cannot be 'made'; it can only be received – however at a cost, namely the cost of accepting God as God. Or said in a different way:

---

3. Katherine Doob Sakenfeld, 'Love (OT)' in *Anchor Bible Dictionary*, Vol 4, New York: Doubleday, 1992, 376.
4. See, for instance, Anders Nygren, *Agape and Eros: The Christian Idea of Love*, trs. Philip S Watson, Chicago: University of Chicago Press, 1982.
5. '[T]he consensus of recent research is that the association of the two Pentateuchal passages that give rise to the double commandment did not originate with Jesus himself.' William Klassen, 'Love (NT)', in *Anchor Bible Dictionary*, Vol 4, 385f.

one can enter into an authentic love relationship with God only if one accepts God's otherness. But how can one do this?

II LOVE AND OTHERNESS

When God's name is discussed in the third chapter of the Book of Exodus, the text stresses God's readiness to be known as the one who will be present with his people, especially at a time of suffering, terror and repression, but it stresses equally God's own godness. God will be present as the one who chooses to be present.[6] Thus, this crucial text about divine-human relationship emphasises God's self-disclosure in history, but also God's radical otherness. God wishes to be present with men, women and children, but not as one of them, but as God. God therefore disallows Moses to instrumentalise him for Moses' own liberationist purposes. Instead God promises presence with the suffering people, but as the one he is, or better: as the one he wishes to be known by his people. The respect for God's otherness is then a necessary dimension of any human relationship with God, an insight strongly affirmed by the mystical traditions within Islam, Judaism and Christianity.

But, we have to ask, can one love somebody who does not wish to disclose every aspect of his being to us? Is it not a contradiction to state with the Johannine community that 'God is love' (1 Jn 4:8), if that same God wishes to protect his godness against those who want to relate to him? Can one really love such a God?

Before we can attempt to answer this question, it seems necessary that we reflect more upon the connection between love and otherness.

We are encountering otherness every day of our lives: we experience that our children are not quite the same as we their parents are. We become aware of the fact that our students do not think in quite the same way as we their teachers do. Even within the same church we recognise that other believers worship differently. We meet people whom we cannot stand at all, people who bring out the worst in us. We are challenged politically, culturally, intellectually, morally and religiously by others who

6. That is how Martin Buber translated Exodus 3: 14. See Martin Buber with Franz Rosenzweig, *Die Fünf Bucher der Weisung*, Cologne and Olten: Jakob Hegner, 1954, 158: 'Ich werde dasein, als der ich dasein werde.'

destroy the old dream of a harmonious conformity of all people in one land. How are we to cope with this phenomenon of otherness outside of us? Shall we attempt to suppress or to destroy this constant challenge of otherness? Or shall we face otherness and thus accept that we are challenged in our very efforts of maintaining our identity?

Moreover, we may even discover otherness within ourselves. To my horror I begin to sense at times that I am not quite the person that I thought I was or that I would like to be. Hence otherness appears also at the centre of my personality and threatens to destabilise my relationship to my own self. How should I react to this threat? Shall I suppress it? Shall I accept the otherness within me? Shall I ignore it and keep on playing the role I am expected to perform? How shall I relate to my destabilised self? How will I be able to restore my battered identity again?

There seem to be two approaches toward developing individual and communal identity: either we define our identity against all those others whom we do not want to be and whom we do not want to face. Or we begin to develop our identity in a constructive *Auseinandersetzung* with all those others outside and inside of us. That means we either construct our identity against others or together with others. Either otherness is perceived to be a threat or it is accepted as a constructive challenge to self-transformation. In the first case there is no real interest in the otherness of the others as such; rather there is only the threat of the other, the fear of the other, and possibly the resulting fight against the other. In the second case, however, the other opens new possibilities of being in the world for us. The other is then not encountered through fear and violence, but through curiosity, interest, surprise and expectation.

This second kind of relationship with the other opens the possibility of a genuine meeting with the other as other. And again, two options emerge: either I try to own or possess the other and thus make him or her a victim of my egocentric projects; or I attempt to appreciate the other as other, consider him or her as a sacred mystery worth discovering through a dynamic and lasting relationship. This second option respects not only the otherness of the other, but it also respects the otherness of myself. And both selves can now develop in a genuinely dynamic and creative partnership.

Returning now to our struggle of how to relate to God's otherness, we can say that God's otherness does not make our love for God impossible. Rather the opposite is the case: God's otherness is the very condition of our love for God. As the German theologian Eberhard Jüngel insists, God is a mystery for us, but a mystery worth pursuing in our lives.[7] God is not secretive and thus mischievously withholding his true face from us. Rather, as a mystery God invites us into a love relationship with him, a relationship through which we might discover always new and different dimensions of God as we walk along with him. But at the same time we may also experience new dimensions and aspects of our own selves and of those selves whom we meet on our way.

For the Christian movement Jesus of Nazareth has become the paradigm of a successful divine-human relationship. According to the gospels, Jesus's relationship with God – whom he called the Father or Abba – was characterised by expectation, passion, despair, hope, pain and joy. It was not just a happy love affair involving only feeling like we see daily on TV. Rather Jesus's relationship to God was a life-long struggle with God involving heart, mind and soul. This complex relationship was inspired both by the Jewish law and the prophetic expectation. According to both it was possible to enter into a right relationship with Jahweh God, a relationship marked by respect for God's otherness. It was this same respect for God's otherness that impressed later Christian thinkers so deeply that they maintained it even in their own subsequent speculation about the nature of the Godhead itself: the Trinity is the ultimate Christian attempt to safeguard the mysterious otherness of God.[8]

If God is love, then God respects freedom and otherness, especially our otherness as his creatures. Through the process of creation God shares his being, that means his love, with us. Therefore God's creative presence will never swallow us up, but remains concerned with the creative development of our own relational selves. Thus, we can say that God creatively and redeemingly defends our freedom to love and to relate, to love and to develop. This continuing and respectful love of God for us makes our love for God first of all possible. Moreover, only

7. Eberhard Jüngel, *God as the Mystery of the World*, trans. Darrell Guder, Edinburgh: T & T Clark, 1983.

8. See James M Byrne, ed., *The Christian Understanding of God Today*, Dublin: Columba, 1993.

through the praxis of love do we gain adequate knowledge about God. The First Letter of John considers love as the only access to God: 'God is love. Whoever lives in love lives in God, and God in him.' (1 Jn 4:16b).

But how does our love for God relate to our love for other human beings, for nature, and for our own selves? Are there different loves or is there a unity of love?

III THE UNITY OF LOVE

We have seen already that there is a close connection between love and the search for identity. And we have also become aware that there are threats to any love relationship. The philosopher Paul Ricoeur has repeatedly stressed the temptation to confuse self with ego.[9] 'Ego' denotes an attitude which reduces each and every thing to the insatiable demands of a person's selfish clinging and totalising tendencies. An ego can neither tolerate nor enjoy otherness. 'Self' denotes a searching person who wishes to develop in relation with others. A self is fragile and longs for the other. The problem, however, is that self and ego often appear together in one and the same person. And this mixture leads to many distortions of love.

The biblical texts both document and challenge this mixture at the same time. The gospel of Mark, for instance, can be read as the story of Jesus the Christ, but also as the story of Jesus's friends' failure to grasp the difference between ego and self. Peter especially – the main protagonist among the disciples – has a hard time appreciating the possibilities of proper relationship to God's emerging kingdom. Instead of entering more deeply into God's loving presence by taking up his own cross in discipleship to Jesus, Peter wishes to maintain the *status quo*, he prefers a discipleship which preserves his egocentric projects and interests intact, and he therefore dissociates himself three times from the suffering Jesus. Mark portrays Peter as the man of big words and fashionable doctrinal statements who collapses, however, as soon as the demands of a real love relationship to Jesus and to God become clear. Mark paints a very sombre picture indeed of early Christian love for God and Jesus.

John's gospel, to cite another example, which is so rich in

---

9. Cf more recently Paul Ricoeur, *Oneself as Another*, trans. Kathleen Blamey, Chicago and London: University of Chicago Press, 1992.

statements about divine-human relationship, displays a tragic dimension of Christian-Jewish polemics. It takes part in the long list of Christian documents and attitudes which build a corporate Christian identity partly at the expense of others. Christians are those who are not Jews. Here Christian identity is established at least to some extent against the vilified others, i.e., the Jews.

The Hebrew Scriptures, too, display the tension between, on the one hand, a striving for the development of creative religious identities and, on the other, an establishing of identity against others. Within the same Holiness Code in Leviticus 17-26, we read, for example, how Israelites are admonished to love their neighbours as they love themselves, including the foreigner in their midst (19:33-4), but that they are nevertheless entitled to purchase slaves from surrounding peoples. Love, it seems, is often in tension with the exigencies of the particular contextual projects. That is why such a broad gap exists between the command of love and the reality of identity projects which conflict with the creative dynamics of love.

This all too brief look at some of our biblical texts demonstrates the fragility of love as a means of constructing creative and mutually respectful relationships. But there is no alternative to love, if we look for real human growth and development. Of course, we can respect the other as other without entering into a close relationship with her or him. We can respect God as radical other without longing to experience God's presence and otherness more intimately. We can even respect our own otherness without pursuing a closer relationship with our mysterious selves. But without involving ourselves in closer relationships we cannot grow.

The thesis of the unity of love in John's Letter means ultimately that it does not really matter in which direction we begin our exploration of loving relationships: we may begin to explore love first of all by relating to other human beings, we may begin to love God, we may begin to love God's creation, we may begin to love our mysterious selves. Any authentic love will eventually point to new possibilities of loving relationships with all the others. The crucial decision is thus whether or not one wishes to embark on a search for one's true vocation in love or in fear. According to the Johannine reflection, love and fear are opposites.

In Paul Tillich's language, we may want to say that the creative exploration of otherness is the opposite of the threat of total separateness. The individualisation of the person includes the possibility of reunification with the power of being which often comes to passionate expressions of love. That is why Tillich refuses to separate *eros* from *agape*. Moreover, he warns against any self-destructive tendencies in the name of love, since such a love would not promote the creative unification of selves, but their dissolution. A 'love' which is not just, even just to the lover, cannot be creative and therefore is ultimately not love.[10]

When I decide to search for my own inner self through an exploration of otherness with whom I may be able to reunite, I will unavoidably press forward to find out more about the ultimate mystery of our lives and our universe.

The Christian religion is only one among the many religious movements today that describe ways of successful relationships between all persons and things. The Christian way favours forms of dynamic love relationships as the way toward the fulfilment of God's creative project with this universe. However, does the Christian potential of describing, explaining and assessing promising ways of loving God, God's creation, the other and my own self, really depend on the prior definition of the uniqueness of Christian faith, or on any agreement on the superiority of the Christian way to love over against any other way? In view of our reflection so far, it appears that love needs freedom to explore the other as other without prior indictments and prejudices.

In this regard it is significant that Jesus never challenged the legitimacy and usefulness of the major religious and cultural institutions of his own Jewish religious tradition, such as Torah, Temple, family and land. All he questioned was their overestimation as guarantors of a successful love relationship to the human or divine other.[11] Any human institution must be measured according to its ability to enable us to develop free and loving relationships to the divine and human other. The point is therefore not whether my love displays the right ecclesial, patriotic, confessional or national colours. Rather the point is that

10. Paul Tillich, *Love, Power, and Justice*, New York and London: Oxford University Press, 1954.

11. See also Werner G Jeanrond, *Call and Response: The Challenge of Christian Life*, Dublin: Gill and Macmillan, 1995, 12-15.

whatever my context may be, it will need to be transformed in such a way that love in all its aspects becomes possible again. The identity which genuine love promotes is always inclusive. That means genuine love searches for the other as other and transcends any artificial boundary set up between self and other. If, however, a human identity is constructed exclusively – that means at the expense of others – it is not built on a genuine desire to love.

The awareness of the dangers of exclusive identity projects brings us back to the social context of love.

IV THE SOCIAL CONTEXT OF LOVE

The close connection between love of God, love of neighbour and enemy, and love of self is clearly emphasised in the biblical love command, as we have seen. Moreover, we have tried to appreciate that one cannot love God or neighbour or self without loving the respective other. Love is always embraced in a social context and it therefore finds expression in time, space and language. At the same time, love helps to transform this social context. To be sure, love does not move the loving person outside of time, space and language, that means outside of the limits which Christians confess as their created matrix. But love explores new dimensions of divine-human and human-human relationships here and now, and hence love becomes the power of disclosing more of God's mysterious presence in our world. As such, love becomes an occasion of God's self-disclosure and concealment within the parameters of history, in other words love becomes the occasion of revelation. I say 'it becomes' the occasion of revelation, because this revelation cannot be manufactured, rather it can emerge only under the conditions of love.

Love cannot be made, but we can cultivate a context in which it may prosper. The first aspect of such a context must be freedom. Without freedom there can be no love. The second aspect of a context for love is the distinction between an inclusive and exclusive search for identity. Does my search for selfhood seek the other or does it reduce the other somehow to a mere function of my own ego? The third aspect is the desire for otherness. This desire may lead to the letting go of all preconceived images and ideas about the other and directs all of its attention to developing respect and then love for the other as other.

The fourth aspect is the desire for radical otherness. This desire looks for the ultimate other, God. The Moses story about the meeting with God at the burning bush reminded us that a genuine encounter with God can take place only on the basis of respect for God's godness. And that means God can be encountered only on God's terms. God is an other who resists all of our attempts at instrumentalising or rationalising him in order to suit our cherished images. A true meeting with God will resist any images, pictures and prejudices on our part. The Buddhist discipline of letting go of every image and desire may well be one of the most adequate ways of preparing for any genuine divine-human relationship. Great Christian mystics, such as Meister Eckhart or John of the Cross, have witnessed to similar preparations. Yet, since we are limited by space, time and language, any knowledge of God emerging from such a mystical love-encounter with God can only be fragmentary, and therefore may, at best, lead to an even deeper desire for more insight into the mystery of God.

We must ask now whether or not the social conditions within the Christian movement today are enabling the development of loving relationships between human beings and between human beings and God. The test-case is, of course, how the churches deal with otherness. Do they encourage the exploration of otherness and radical otherness? Do they offer pastoral help to the individual who wishes to confront the otherness in himself or herself? Do the churches provide a social network of mutual encouragement for Christian believers to develop an inclusive praxis of love? Or do they concentrate on the exclusive demarcation of their own identity against other churches or religious movements? Do the churches work for a climate in which children and young people learn to trust in their vocation as explorers of God, of other human beings, of God's created universe and of themselves? Do the churches work for the awakening of each believer's longing to find out more about otherness and radical otherness? Or are the churches afraid of the challenge to their institutional identity which may arise from a new culture of inclusive love? Are the churches, i.e., the organised communities of Christians, willing to promote a new spirituality of creative and redeeming love in a world marked by hatred, by fear of otherness and by broken relationships?

V TOWARD A SPIRITUALITY OF LOVE

For the Apostle Paul there was no doubt what was the most important aspect of Christian discipleship. The greatest among the divine gifts of faith, hope and love is love. For Paul, love provided the deepest experience of a new outlook on reality. In his famous reflection on love in 1 Corinthians 13 he states:

> Love is patient, love is kind. It does not envy, it does not boast, it is not proud. It is not rude, it is not self-seeking, it is not easily angered, it keeps no record of wrongs. Love does not delight in evil but rejoices with the truth. It always protects, always trusts, always hopes, always perseveres. Love never fails. (1 Cor l3:4-8a)

It is interesting to note Paul's awareness that love stands in a situation of moral struggle. However, he does not moralise here. Instead he goes beyond moral considerations and praises love as the ultimate quality of human existence, 'if I give all I possess to the poor and surrender my body to the flames, but have not love, I gain nothing.' (1 Cor 13:3) Thus, Paul rescues love from moral casuistry and opens the way towards a spirituality built on love. And, as we have seen, the Jewish tradition has provided Jesus and Paul with all the essentials for such a spiritual exploration.

Love is God's gift of himself and not a human product. The Christian way of exploring this gift of love in its diverse forms, which all point to its intrinsic unity, receives ultimate encouragement from the experience of God's lasting love for his creation even at moments of total rejection, such as when God reconfirms his solidarity with the violently murdered Jesus of Nazareth in the mysterious event of the resurrection.

VI CONCLUSION

The Christian theologian asked to consider whether one can love God comes here to the end of his task and his resources. He can clarify the starting-point for such a reflection, he can contemplate the relationship between love and otherness, he can analyse the unity of love, he can discuss the social context of love, and he can point to the development of a spirituality of love. Thus, he can reflect upon possibilities and ambiguities of attempting to love God in our postmodern context, and he can destroy a few unloving prejudices against other religious explorations of what it means to love God.

But whether the individual child, woman and man today can embark on the life-long experiment of loving the other, the self and ultimately also God, and how that love may eventually transform the individual person, her family, her religious community, her country and her world, the theologian cannot know. His intellectual analysis does not give him a privileged insight into the future dynamics of love, however much he personally may desire it.

Afterword

Dear Gabriel,
I can't tell you how overjoyed your brother Augustinians are on seeing your exceptional career being recognised by a *Festschrift* of essays contributed by your peers.

I was of the generation of students in the 1960s, what are known as the heady days following on the Second Vatican Council. We and our mentors were straining to emerge, like chickens out of eggshells, from old structures and patterns of thinking, into the light of new ways. After the Province Chapter of 1966 you landed in our midst with a mandate to guide us through the changes. Your arrival announced: the straining is over, *tempus appropinquavit*, the new times are here.

Everything that had gone before would seem to have been a preparation for the task. The excitement of personal discovery in your beloved Oxford enkindled an enthusiasm for a method of study which you have kept aflame ever since. This constituted an alternative to the old thesis way of doing theology, in which you had been exercised at the Gregorian, and anticipated many of the new ideas which found expression in the new theology of the Council.

Back in Austin Friars School, Carlisle, after Oxford you divided your energies between housemastering, rugby coaching, history teaching, music and developing your new method of theological thinking, working out of your field of history. In Carlisle you played a major role in a team of dedicated Augustinians who built up Carlisle to recognition as a major Catholic presence in the north of England. To all pursuits you brought your characteristic enthusiasm, a quality which, thankfully, still shines brightly.

Then, your time of preparation over, you came back to your native Dublin and began what you have become best known for, your contribution to church and academic life.

A number of statements remain in my mind from the middle sixties. (You may not be totally responsible for the exact wording, but they do capture some of what you and those times stood for.) 'If literacy is no disadvantage to the historian, neither is it to the theologian.' 'Some people have difficulty with the realisation that Aristotle was not one of the twelve apostles.' 'Logic is not the only path to truth.'

A number of words characterise your career, in teaching posts in Ballyboden, Milltown Park, The School of Ecumenics and Trinity College, as well as in your many contributions to public debate. Courage. Colour. Integrity. Ecumenism. Courtesy. Style.

I would like to think that your Augustinian community supported you in what was at times a lonely place. You have upheld the Augustinian tradition of commitment to the intellectual apostolate, and have a place of your own in the affections of the friars, to whom you have always been loyal. Together with your sister Paula and brother John, the Augustinians are very happy to be associated with this occasion of recognition, in thanking you for what has been and wishing you *ad multos annos*.

Desmond Foley OSA

Select Bibliography

BOOKS

Transcendence and Immanence: A Study in Catholic Modernism and Integralism, Oxford: Clarendon Press, 1980.

Asking the Father: A Study of the Prayer of Petition, Dublin and Wilmington: Michael Glazier, 1982.

Creation and Redemption, Dublin: Gill and Macmillan, 1988.

MONOGRAPH

One Church: Two Indispensable Values: Protestant Principle and Catholic Substance, Irish School of Ecumenics Occasional Paper 4; Dublin: ISE, 1988.

CHAPTERS IN BOOKS

'Church Renewal: 1869-1977,' in Michael Hurley, SJ, Ed., *Irish Anglicanism 1869-1969,* Essays on the role of Anglicanism in Irish life presented to the Church of Ireland on the occasion of its Disestablishment by a group of Methodist, Presbyterian, Quaker and Roman Catholic scholars, Dublin: Allen Figgis, 1970, 23-38.

'Theology of Redemption in the Fathers' and 'Contemporary Perspectives on Redemption Theology,' in Wilfred Harrington OP, Ed., *Witness to the Spirit: Essays on Revelation, Spirit, Redemption,* Proceedings of the IBA 3; Manchester: Koinonia Press, 1979, 133-148, 149-166.

'Church, State and the Ideal of Freedom,' in Alan D Falconer, Ed., *Understanding Human Rights: An Interdisciplinary and Interfaith Study:* The Proceedings of the International Consultation held in Dublin 1978, Dublin: Irish School of Ecumenics, 1980, 165-181.

'Newman and Modernism: A Theological Reflection,' in Mary Jo Weaver, Ed., *Newman and the Modernists,* London and Lanham: University Press of America, 1985, 185-207.

'Towards an Irish Theology: Some Questions of Method,' in Enda McDonagh, Ed., *Irish Challenges to Theology: Papers of the Irish Theological Association Conference 1984,* Dublin: Dominican Publications, 1986, 88-101.

'Defining Modernism,' in R. Burke, G Lease and G Gilmore, Eds., *Modernism: Origins, Parameters, Prospects,* American Academy of Religion, Working Group on Roman Catholic Modernism, nd, 3-13.

'Weighing the Arguments,' in *Divorce: Facts: Catholic Viewpoints,* Dublin: Dominican Publications, 1986, 20-26.

'Catholicism and Modernity,' in R. L. Hart, Ed., *Trajectories in the Study of Religion,* Atlanta: Scholars Press, 1987, 229-252.

'Forgiveness and Community,' in Alan D Falconer, Ed., *Reconciling Memories,* Dublin: Columba, 1988, 99-115. Second Edn., Alan D Falconer and Joseph Liechty, Eds., *Reconciling Memories,* Dublin: Columba, 1998, 195-215.

'Laberthonnière and Newman,' in Arthur Hilary Jenkins, Ed., *John Henry Newman and Modernism,* Internationale Cardinal-Newman-Studien 14, Sigmaringendorf: Glock und Lutz, 1990, 41-55.

'Conscience, Guilt and Sin,' in Seán Freyne, Ed., *Ethics and the Christian,* Trinity College Dublin: Studies in Theology, Dublin: Columba, 1991, 58-74.

'Some Implications of Cosmology for our Understanding of God as Creator,' in James M Byrne, Ed., *The Christian Understanding of God Today: Theological Colloquium on the Occasion of the 400th Anniversary of the Foundation of Trinity College, Dublin,* Trinity College, Dublin: Studies in Theology, Dublin: Columba, 1993, 81-87.

'Justice, Ecology and the Quest for Christian Unity,' in Oliver Rafferty, SJ, Ed., *Reconciliation: Essays in Honour of Michael Hurley,* Dublin: Columba, 1993, 112-129.

'Creation and Original Sin,' in Michael J Walsh, Ed., *Commentary on the Catechism of the Catholic Church,* London: Chapman, 1994, 82-111.

'Foundations in Systematics for Ecological Theology,' in K. W. Irwin and E. D. Pelegrino, Eds., *Preserving the Creation: Environmental Theology and Ethics,* Georgetown, 1994, 35-59.

'Foreword,' George Tyrrell, *Medievalism: A Reply to Cardinal Mercier,* London: Burns & Oates, 1994, 7-19.

'Hope in the Church,' in Maureen Junker-Kenny, Ed., *Christian Resources of Hope,* Trinity College, Dublin: Studies in Theology, Dublin: Columba, 1995.

'Theological Analysis and Public Policy Debate in a Pluralist Society,' in Bernard Treacy, OP and Gerry Whyte, Eds, *Religion, Morality and Public Policy: A Doctrine and Life Special,* Dublin: Dominican Publications, 1995, 75-91.

'Irish Catholicism: A Monolith?' in Terence Brown, Ed., *Cultural Identity and Tolerance,* Dublin: Cultures of Ireland, 1996, 41-54.

'Liberal Democracy, Crisis and the Christian Vision,' in Denis Carroll, Ed., *Religion in Ireland: Past, Present and Future,* Dublin: Columba, 1999, 140-154.

'Theological and Philosophical Modernism,' in Darrell Jodock, Ed., *Catholicism Contending with Modernity: Roman Catholic Modernism and Anti-Modernism in Historical Context,* Cambridge, Cambridge University Press, 2000, 88-112.

'Newman, Divine Revelation, and the Catholic Modernists', in T. Merrigan and I. Ker, Eds., *Newman and the Word,* Louvain, 2000, 49-68.

'Mysticism and Modernism,' in Linda Hogan and Barbara Fitzgerald, Eds., *Between Poetry and Politics: Essays in Honour of Enda McDonagh,* Dublin: Columba, 2003, 16-31.

REFERENCE ARTICLES

'Modernism,' in Alan Richardson and John Bowden, Eds., *A New Dictionary of Christian Theology*, London: SCM, 1983, 376-378.

'Traditionalism,' in Alan Richardson and John Bowden, Eds., *A New Dictionary of Christian Theology*, London: SCM, 576.

'Modernism,' in Joseph Komonchak, Mary Collins and Dermot A Lane, Eds., *The New Dictionary of Theology*, Dublin: Gill and Macmillan, 1987, 668-67

'Original Sin,' in Joseph Komonchak, Mary Collins and Dermot A Lane, Eds., *The New Dictionary of Theology*, Dublin: Gill and Macmillan, 1987, 727-731.

'George Tyrrell,' in *Dictionaire de Spiritualité*, Vol 15, Paris: Beauchesne, 1991, cols 1372-1383.

ARTICLES

'A Prophet of Gloom?' *The Clergy Review* 51 (1966) 604-612.

Review Article, 'Rosemary Haughton The Transformation of Man,' *Irish Theological Quarterly* 36/ 2 (1969) 123-128.

'Some Reflections on the Character of George Tyrrell,' *The Heythrop Journal* 10 (1969) 256-274.

'Tyrrell's "Medievalism,"' *The Month* July-August (1969) 15-22.

'Prayer and Asceticism,' *The Furrow* 22 (1971) 671-685.

'Theological Models in the Doctrine of Original Sin,' *The Heythrop Journal* 13 (1972) 121-142.

'The Problem of Original Sin,' *The Furrow* 24 (1973) 13-26.

'John Robinson's Christology,' *Studies* (Winter 1974) 367-378.

'When You Pray: Heart in Pilgrimage,' *The Way* (July 1974) 231-242.

'Contemporary Perspectives on Redemption Theology,' *Milltown Studies* 1 (Summer 1977) 39-53.

'Christian Response to Religious Pluralism,' *Studies*, Spring/Summer 1978 66-76.

'Knowing God,' *The Furrow*, 30 (1979) 436-449.

'History, Truth and Method,' *The Irish Theological Quarterly* 47 (1980: 1) 43-55.

'Prayer of Petition,' *Doctrine & Life* 30 (1980) 137-149.

'Some Classical and Romantic Trends in Theology,' *Milltown Studies* 6 (Autumn 1980) 36-61.

'Theology's Next Decade,' *The Tablet* (15 March 1980) 264-265.

'Thoughts on the Sunday Liturgy,' *The Furrow* 32 (1981) 11-23.

'Faith and Theology: 1. Conflicting Mentalities,' *The Tablet* (11 April 1981) 361-362.

'Faith and Theology: 2. The Ultramontane Influence,' *The Tablet* (18 April 1981) 391-392.

'Faith and Theology: 3. The Pluriform Church,' *The Tablet* (9 May 1981) 446-447.

'Edward Schillebeeckx and the Renewal of Catholic Theology,' *Doctrine & Life* 31 (1981) 90-101.

'Jesus at Table,' *The Furrow* 32 (1981) 555-563.
'J.K.L.: Ecumenical Pioneer,' *The Carlovian* (1982) 14-19.
'Faith and Imagination,' *Doctrine & Life* 32 (1982) 72-80.
'The Final Report: A Challenge to the Churches,' *Doctrine & Life* 32 (1982) 360-371.
'The Challenge of Martin Luther: A Sermon,' in *Martin Luther 1483-1983: Three Commemorative Sermons,* Dublin: Lutherhaus, 1983, 14-20.
'The Church: Community of Faith,' *The Furrow* 34 (1983) 403-415.
'Northern Ireland – Test for Ecumenism,' *Studies* (Winter 1983) 283-290.
'Athens and Jerusalem,' *Hermathena* (1984) 9-12.
'Catholic Theology during the Last Two Decades,' *Doctrine & Life* 34 (1984) 52-62.
'The Synod and the Universal Church,' *Doctrine & Life* 34 (1985) 494-502.
'Catholicism and Modernity,' *Journal of the American Academy of Religion* 53/3, 773-796.
'Apologetics in the Modernist Period,' *The Chesterton Review* 15 (1989) 79-93.
'A Response to Walter Kasper,' *The Irish Theological Quarterly* 55 (1989) 114-124.
'How Well Was Vatican II Received?' *Doctrine & Life* 39 (1989) 412-420.
'Table d'Hôte Catholicism,' *The Furrow* 42 (1991) 407-414.
'Focus on Veritatis Splendor: Ecclesial Implications,' *Doctrine and Life* 43 (1993) 532-537.
'An Ecofeminist Contention Examined,' *The Irish Theological Quarterly,* 60/3 (1994) 216-224.
'Ecology and the Theology of Creation,' *Search* 18 (1995) 106-115.
'Interpreting Original Sin,' *Priests and People* (March 1996) 87-91.
'Art and Religion,' *Doctrine & Life,* 46 (1996) 586-591.
'Science Religion and Scientism,' *The Irish Review* 27 (2001) 48-54.
'A Thinking Church? For Garret Fitzgerald on his 75th Birthday,' *Doctrine & Life* 53 (2003), 451-468.

UNPUBLISHED PAPERS

'Religion and Science: A Response to Professor David McConnell,' Presidential Meeting, College Theological Society, Trinity College, Dublin.
'George Tyrrell: An Irish Gentleman in Search of a Religion,' Travis Smith Lecture, St Bartholomew's Church, Clyde Road, Dublin.
'Faith and Culture,' Public Lecture, Trinity College Dublin, 1996.
'Religious Life: Making Sense of Where we Are,' CORI AGM, 1997.
'Religion on the Defensive' Irish Association.
'The Quest for Jesus and the Search for God Today,' Public Lecture, Trinity College Dublin.
'St Augustine's Drogheda: 700th Anniversary: A Homily.'
'Nature, Art and Christian Theology,' Presidential Address, College Theological Society, Trinity College, Dublin.

'Resisting Fideism' A Response to Dr Lewis Ayres, College Theological Society, Presidential Meeting.
'Christianity a Missionary Faith,' Christ Church Cathedral, Dublin, 1998
'Fundamentalism and the Roman Catholic Church' Glenstal Ecumenical Conference, 1994.
'Faith and the Necessity of Theology,' Centenary Address, Mary Immaculate College, University of Limerick, 1998.
'Modern Ireland,' Unitarian Church, Dublin 2002.

The Contributors

DENIS CARROLL retired recently as lecturer in historical and systematic theology at Trinity College, Dublin. His publications include a biography of Thomas Russell, *The Man from God Knows Where*, Dublin: Columba, 1995.

DESMOND FOLEY OSA is Provincial of the Irish province of the Augustinian Order.

SEAN V FREYNE retired recently from the Chair of Theology in Trinity College, Dublin and is currently Director of the Mediterranean and Near Eastern Studies Programme there. An authority on Galilee, Early Christianity and Judaism, his most recent publication is *Texts, Contexts and Cultures: Studies on Biblical Topics*, Dublin: Veritas, 2002.

MICHAEL PAUL GALLAGHER SJ is Professor of Theology at the Gregorian University, Rome and a former student of Gabriel Daly. His many books include *Clashing Symbols: An Introduction to Faith and Culture*, London: Darton, Longman and Todd, 1997.

WERNER G JEANROND is Professor of Systematic Theology at the University of Lund, and a former colleague of Gabriel Daly at Trinity College, Dublin. Currently writing a study of the love of God, his publications on theological hermeneutics include *Text and Interpretation as Categories of Theological Thinking*, Dublin: Gill and Macmillan, 1988 and *Theological Hermeneutics: Development and Significance*, Basingstoke: Macmillan, 1991.

MAUREEN JUNKER-KENNY is Associate Professor of Theology at Trinity College Dublin, specialising in Christian ethics. She has recently edited *Memory, Narrativity, Self, and the Challenge to Think God: The Reception within Theology of the Recent Work of Paul Ricoeur*, Münster: LIT-Verlag, 2003.

DERMOT A LANE is a parish priest in south Dublin, and is President of Mater Dei Institute, a college of Dublin City University. His publications include *Foundations for a Social Theology: Praxis, Process and Salvation,* Dublin: Gill and Macmillan, 1984, and *Keeping Hope Alive: Stirrings in Christian Theology,* Dublin: Gill and Macmillan, 1996.

TERENCE P MCCAUGHEY retired recently as Senior Lecturer in the School of Irish and Celtic Languages, Trinity College, Dublin. He has also taught in the School of Hebrew, Biblical and Theological Studies at TCD, and currently lectures at the Irish Scool of Ecumenics. An ordained Presbyterian minister, he is the author of *Memory and Redemption: Church, Politics and Prophetic Theology,* Dublin: Gill and Macmillan, 1993.

ENDA MCDONAGH is Emeritus Professor of Moral Theology at St Patrick's College, Maynooth. His many publications include *Doing the Truth,* Dublin: Gill and Macmillan, 1979 and *Faith in Fragments,* Dublin: Columba, 1996.

JOHN D'ARCY MAY is Associate Professor of Interfaith Dialogue at the Irish School of Ecumenics, Trinity College, Dublin. His most recent publication is *Transcendence and Violence: The Encounter of Buddhist, Christian and Primal Traditions,* New York and London: Continuum, 2003.

A. D. H. MAYES is Erasmus Smith's Professor of Hebrew at Trinity College, Dublin. His publications include *The Old Testament in Sociological Perspective,* London: Marshall, Morgan and Scott, 1989.

JOHANN BAPTIST METZ is a former professor of fundamental theology at the University of Münster, and the author of a number of important studies in political theology, including *Faith in History and Society: Toward a Practical Fundamental Theology,* London: Burns & Oates, 1980.

ANDREW PIERCE is Lecturer in Ecumenical Studies and co-ordinator of the Ecumenical Studies Programme at the Irish School of Ecumenics, Trinity College, Dublin. His study of the modernist crisis will be published shortly by the university press in Leuven.

GERALDINE SMYTH OP is Senior Lecturer in Ecumenical Studies at the Irish School of Ecumenics, Trinity College, Dublin and is currently Prioress of her Dominican congregation. Her publications include *A Way of Transformation*, Berne: Peter Lang, 1995.

DAVID TRACY is Andrew Thomas Greeley and Grace Mc Nichols Greeley Distinguished Service Professor of Roman Catholic Studies at the University of Chicago Divinity School. His publications include *The Analogical Imagination: Christian Theology and the Culture of Pluralism*, London: SCM, 1981, and *Plurality and Ambiguity: Hermeneutics, Religion, Hope*, 1987; London: SCM, 1988.